D1283015

A PRACTICAL GUIDE TO

RABBINIC
COUNSELING

Other Professional Resources by Jewish Lights

Jewish Pastoral Care, 2nd Ed.:
A Practical Handbook from Traditional and Contemporary Sources

Jewish Visions for Aging:
A Professional Guide for Fostering Wholeness

Jewish Spiritual Direction:
An Innovative Guide fromTraditional and Contemporary Sources

Professional Pastoral and Spiritual Care:
A Practical Clergy and Chaplain's Handbook
(A SkyLight Paths book)

How to Be a Perfect Stranger:
The Essential Religious Etiquette Handbook
(A SkyLight Paths book)

Other Jewish Lights Books by Abraham J. Twerski

A Formula for Proper Living:
Practical Lessons from Life and Torah

Happiness and the Human Spirit:
The Spirituality of Becoming the Best You Can Be

—— A PRACTICAL GUIDE TO ——

RABBINIC COUNSELING

YISRAEL N. LEVITZ, PhD
ABRAHAM J. TWERSKI, MD

JEWISH LIGHTS Publishing

Woodstock, Vermont

www.jewishlights.com

A Practical Guide to Rabbinic Counseling
2012 Classic Reprint, Hardcover Edition, First Printing
© 2012 by Yisrael N. Levitz and Abraham J. Twerski

A classic reprint from Jewish Lights. *A Practical Guide to Rabbinic Counseling* was originally published by Feldheim Publishing.

Library of Congress Cataloging-in-Publication Data
Available upon request.

10 9 8 7 6 5 4 3 2 1
Manufactured in the United States of America
Cover design: Heather Pelham

Published by Jewish Lights Publishing
A Division of Longhill Partners, Inc.
Sunset Farm Offices, Route 4, P.O. Box 237
Woodstock, VT 05091
Tel: (802) 457-4000   Fax: (802) 457-4004
www.jewishlights.com

DEDICATION

THIS BOOK WAS encouraged and supported by the Legacy Heritage Fund Limited, whose purpose is to honor and perpetuate the legacy of scholarship, Torah values, and learning that were the hallmarks of my parents' lives, Bella and Harry Wexner z"ll. Committed Jews and committed Zionists, my parents held true to their beliefs throughout their lives of hard work and struggle, achieving only late in life their dream of creating one of the major retail conglomerates in the world. This book is meant to honor their devotion to Jewish values and their respect for Jewish scholarship and research.

The vision and values of Bella and Harry Wexner permeated both their private and business lives. Devoted wife and husband as well as business partners, they believed that Torah values ought to be brought to all parts of one's life and not be reserved for the Sabbath and holidays. The Torah, they believed, acts as a moral compass, always pointing the way to ethical living. The rabbi's role is a vital one, because it falls to the rabbis to bring their congregations not just Torah learning, but the application of its values to all aspects of daily life.

Historically, rabbis have always been the consummate scholars and teachers of the Talmud and Torah law. Upon the rabbis' ascension to community leadership, however, there has always been an implicit expectation that they serve in many more capacities than that of learned teacher. A rabbi is expected to be more than a scholar. He is expected to be an inspired and inspiring spiritual leader to whom one turns in times of distress. Throughout Jewish history, the rabbi, in addition to his role as Torah scholar, has also assumed the roles of many helping professions. He has often acted, in effect, as a marriage counselor, psychotherapist, personal coach, bereavement counselor, social worker, and mediator in community disputes.

Until now rabbis were not trained for these additional roles. They simply worked intuitively. In more recent times, however, it has become evident that rabbis need to be better trained for their ever more challenging and complex roles as community leaders. With this in mind, the Legacy Heritage Fund Limited established the Bella and Harry Wexner Kollel Elyon and Semikha Honors Program at Yeshiva University under the auspices of the Rabbi Isaac Elchanan Theological Seminary (RIETS).

Dr. Yisrael Levitz, the program's first director, designed and facilitated an intensive skills training program whose aim was to give rabbis the requisite skills that would enable them to function competently in a wide range of rabbinic responsibilities, particularly pastoral counseling, dispute resolution, crisis intervention, and communication skills. Presenting an innovative and creative approach to the training of rabbis, the program honors the innovation and creativity that marked the accomplishments of my parents, Bella and Harry Wexner.

This book captures the heart and soul of the program in order to disseminate it widely and thereby assist rabbis worldwide in their vital roles. This book is meant to equip rabbis for the real-world challenges of modern day realities by providing them with a broad knowledge base and practical insights into the kinds of issues in which they will need to engage as rabbinic counselors. We hope that the many pragmatic therapeutic strategies discussed in these pages will provide a broad base of knowledge and support for rabbis, enhancing their ability to provide comfort and solace where it is needed most by those struggling with life's problems.

Susan Wexner

CONTENTS

Acknowledgments

AT THE CORE OF THIS book is my (Levitz) experience with the hundreds of rabbinic students whom I have been privileged to teach over the past twenty years. These are the students of the Rabbi Isaac Elchanan Theological Seminary, the Bella and Harry Wexner *Kollel Elyon*, and the Gruss *Kollel* in Jerusalem. The pure motivation of these rabbinic students to serve the Jewish community, their dedication to personal and spiritual growth, and their eagerness to become both skilled and dedicated rabbinic leaders is a continuing source of inspiration.

This book would not have been possible without the invaluable support, vision and encouragement of Ms. Susan Wexner and the Legacy Heritage Fund Limited. Susan Wexner, a pioneer and visionary has been in the forefront of the current movement to raise the level of rabbinic preparedness for service to the Jewish community. Her courageous initiatives and the mission of her work over the past several years has honored and perpetuated the memory and legacy of her parents Bella and Harry Wexner z"l. They were indeed individuals of great personal integrity, who were committed to sustaining scholarship, perpetuating torah values, and supporting many great and worthy causes. It is a distinct honor to dedicate this book to their blessed memory.

We would also like to thank our reviewers Leslie Newman and Bracha Steinberg for their many helpful suggestions, in-depth comments, and technical advice, in reviewing the multiple drafts of this book. We are indebted as well to Rabbi Zevulun Charlop and Rabbi Chaim Bronstein for having facilitated the publication of this book in so many ways, and to Rabbi Dovid Refson, Dr. Pinchus Kahn, Dr. David Pelcovitz, Rabbi Dovid Miller, and the rabbinic students of the Gruss Kollel in Jerusalem, who read early drafts of the manuscript and provided candid feedback, critical insights, and valuable comments.

For the both of us (Levitz and Twerski) the publication of this book has been a most gratifying experience both personally and professionally. As colleagues and friends, our collaboration has provided us with the unbeatable combination of intellectual and spiritual stimulation, along with a warm and supportive comradeship. For this too we are grateful.

With gratitude to the Almighty, we hope this book is as rewarding to read as it was to publish.

Yisrael N. Levitz
Abraham J. Twerski

PREFACE

THE DISCIPLINE OF medicine, with its knowledge of human physiology and pathology growing by leaps and bounds, has evolved into a multiplicity of medical specializations. In contrast to the general practitioner of yore, most physicians now develop expertise in a rather limited area of medicine.

The rabbi of today resembles the general practitioner of yore. In addition to being the spiritual leader of his congregation, conveying the wisdom of Torah, rendering decisions on issues of Jewish law, and conducting certain rituals for the congregation, the rabbi is also widely sought as a counselor to his congregants. He is often the first person to whom they turn for help.

Counseling requires an understanding of the human thought process, both normal and abnormal. The increased complexity of modern life has given rise to a variety of problems — intrapersonal, interpersonal, individual, and communal. Many of these, in turn, involve psychological and emotional factors that defy the rules of logic. People accustomed to logical behavior may not be able to understand how a person who appears to be rational can believe that his sometimes grossly inappropriate behavior is perfectly acceptable. Traditional rabbinic training, while providing the rabbi with a wealth of knowledge from the rich heritage of Judaism, does not address many of the concepts that are essential for proper counseling.

It may be asked, Do people have more problems these days, or are we just more aware of them? The answer is: both. Some of the factors responsible for an increase of problems found in contemporary society include:

▶ Exposure of young people today to more explicit immorality and violence in the media.

▶ Financial pressure on both parents to be wage earners, often affecting the quality of parent-child relationships.

▶ Greater mobility in our post-industrial society, rocking stability and requiring families to adjust to their new environments.

▶ The current culture, which has little tolerance for discomfort.

Increased awareness of problems is in itself a cause for increased incidence of counseling needs. The popularization of mental health concepts has resulted in people defining as problems mood variations and behaviors that had heretofore been considered a normal part of life. Because of the greater availability of mental health services, the tolerance for accepting emotional discomfort as a variant of normal living has significantly decreased.

A rabbi may be consulted for a myriad of reasons:

▶ A person's deviant behavior

▶ A couple's faltering marriage

▶ A single man or woman's frustration caused by a series of unsuccessful relationships

▶ A person's emotional problems

▶ A "sandwich generation" couple's feeling overwhelmed by caring for elderly parents as well as their young children

▶ A family at wits' end because one of them is alcoholic/drug addicted/a compulsive gambler/or addicted to the internet

▶ The abuse of a husband, wife, or child

Providing counseling in these instances is in addition to his traditional role of comforting the bereaved and ministering to the sick.

Given the many responsibilities that the modern rabbi must

bear, he is personally subject to demands and stresses that did not burden his predecessors. While there is a rabbinic tradition of addressing problems of a religious nature, there is no such tradition to help the rabbi cope with these new responsibilities.

A rabbi who has not formally learned the requisite skills of counseling comes to depend upon his personal attributes alone (intuition, empathy, sensitivity, life experience, and native intelligence). These are certainly important components of good counseling and need to be part of the rabbi's repertoire, but they alone are not sufficient. Basic counseling skills must be acquired.

In this volume, Yisrael N. Levitz and Rona Michelson draw from their vast experience as mental health practitioners to offer a wide range of basic counseling skills that can be applied to the various counseling situations a rabbi is likely to confront. These rabbinic counseling skills, competently employed, can enormously enhance the helping process.

Yisrael Levitz also addresses the ramifications of the modern rabbi also acting as a mental health practitioner. In contrast to mental health therapists who only interact with patients in their office at scheduled times and have no other relationship with them, rabbis often see and interact with those they counsel in a variety of situations (for instance in shul or at a social function). Their dual relationships with congregants often complicate the rabbi's role as counselor, encroaching on his objectivity, which is so vital for performing this function. Levitz cites examples of possible conflicts that may arise due to this unique relationship.

The patient who consults a mental health therapist generally verbalizes his problem. The troubled congregant, however, may present the rabbi with a quasi-religious question and the rabbi is expected to ferret out the psychological problem concealed underneath. Or, the troubled congregant may not even consult the rabbi, who must be alert to signs of distress and may have to initiate contact with that congregant.

In addition, multiple demands on the rabbi, even if he juggles them well, may result in his acting distracted at home. (My mother used to say, "You cannot be equally considerate of the whole world and your family at the same time.") In addition to deprivation of their rabbinic father's attention, his children may be expected to behave like "the rabbi's children," rather than like who they are in their own right. Also, the rabbi's wife, so often and even unexpectedly deprived of her husband's presence and attention, may be expected to assume the role of *Rebbetzin*, with responsibilities she may not have anticipated. Levitz notes that "the rabbinate is a family business, open seven days a week, twenty-four hours a day" and points out the incursions the role of rabbi makes on his family life.

We have no record of rabbis of yore being sued for breach of confidentiality. Today, this is a real concern. In conjunction with acting as a mental health therapist, who is almost exclusively occupied with what is in the patient's best interest, the rabbi also has religious principles to consider. For example, if a woman confides to her rabbi that she had an extramarital relationship, which according to Torah law may prohibit her from remaining in the marriage, is the rabbi required or even permitted to alert the husband in order to prevent his continuing in a forbidden relationship? Or, if a rabbi encourages a child from a secular family to become Torah-observant and that the child refuses to eat at home or join the family in its activities on Shabbat, is he liable for estranging the child from his parents? If the rabbi discourages a *kohen* from marrying a divorcee, can the woman sue the rabbi? Issues such as these necessitate the rabbi becoming knowledgeable about legal pitfalls. Sylvan J. Schaffer discusses the thorny issue of rabbinic confidentiality.

As the one who officiates at marriages, the rabbi is consulted by the couple before their marriage and has the opportunity to provide premarital counseling. Lisa Aiken discusses how the rabbi can help prevent problems from arising in the relationship and, when it is necessary, he can recommend therapy for one or both partners. Neal Levy cites the principles of marital counseling, identifying the more common causes of disharmony and how the rabbi can help resolve these.

The debunking of the myth that spousal abuse and domestic violence do not occur in Jewish families has resulted in spouses often seeking the rabbi's advice and help in coping with an abusive relationship. In an article by myself and Lisa Twerski, we discuss this problem, correcting prevailing misconceptions and providing guidelines for such counseling.

Another myth that has a tenacious hold on Jews is that "*shikker is a goy*," which results in a dangerous denial of alcohol problems in the Jewish community. Also, to our sorrow, the drug epidemic has not spared Jews, and compulsive gambling has destroyed families. In another article, I point out that all addictions are "equal opportunity destroyers," describing some characteristics of addiction and what the rabbi's role is in providing help.

The number of people who have been unsuccessful in achieving marriage has grown to crisis proportions. Rosie Einhorn and Sherry Zimmerman combine their experience in counseling and family law to advise the rabbi on how he can help both the individual and communal aspects of the problem.

Unfortunately, Jewish history has been riddled with disasters that have befallen us. However, in our times there has never been anything of the magnitude of the Holocaust, whose effects are still felt by children and grandchildren of its survivors. Also, living under the threat of terrorism in America was brought to the fore by 9/11. Many children have been exposed to terrible highway accidents and tragedies that have befallen their families or friends. David Pelcovitz describes both children's and adults' reactions to disaster and Post-Traumatic Stress and offers practical guidelines for the counseling rabbi.

Conflicts in the community and within the family are not infrequent, and the rabbi is often called upon to resolve them. Robert A. Baruch Bush introduces the concept of "transformative mediation," explaining how the rabbi can be more effective in this function.

Visiting and comforting the sick has been a traditional rabbinical function. Daniel and Susan Jackson give us a deeper understanding of the complexities of the rabbi's visit to the hospitalized patient and the importance of rabbinic sensitivity to the needs of both the patient's family and the hospital staff.

Phyllis Dvora Corn and Benjamin W. Corn offer us a rich perspective on the rabbi's function and the support a rabbi can provide to both patient and family when there is little hope for recovery. From their extensive experience counseling dying patients they help us better understand how a rabbi can provide optimum support and comfort in those dire circumstances.

The rabbi plays a crucial role in helping bereaved family members and friends adjust to a loss. Maurice and Dodi Lee Lamm analyze the grieving process in both its healthy and unhealthy manifestations.

Optimum intervention for mental disorders — to provide support, reassurance, and proper referral — requires familiarity with the more commonly encountered psychiatric illnesses. Rael Strous provides concise and lucid guidelines for the rabbi and also discusses the most dreaded psychiatric denouement, suicide: its prevention, management, and support for the survivors.

Whereas the rabbi can be of help with mental disorders, there are many cases where the expertise of mental health professionals is necessary. Norman Blumenthal describes the various mental health professionals that may be consulted, the more common treatment modalities, the more popular schools of psychotherapy, and explains the referral process. He also addresses the role of the rabbi when issues of religion are involved in the therapy.

*   *   *

It is conceivable that enumerating the various psychological problems that a rabbi might encounter will frighten away someone who has chosen a rabbinic career.

A young man came to my grandfather for certification of his qualifications to be a *shochet*. My grandfather spent some time alerting him to the awesome responsibility borne by a *shochet*, whose error would result in countless people eating *treif*. At first, the young man said that he was aware of this. As my grandfather began writing the certification, however, the young man cried out, "Rabbi, please, I don't want the certification. I am afraid of the responsibility." My grandfather smiled, continued writing the certification, and said, "So, who then should become a *shochet*? Someone who is not afraid?"

If the rabbi is concerned about the responsibilities he will bear as a counselor, that is in his favor. Sincerity and responsibility are essential in counseling. Of course, a rabbi must work on his counseling skills. Hopefully, this carefully compiled collection of essays will provide some concrete assistance.

Abraham J. Twerski, M.D.

Personal Reflections

Yisrael N. Levitz, Ph.D.

AT THE AGE OF twenty-three, I assumed the pulpit of a 400-member congregation that had already seen three rabbis come and go during its five-year history. Despite the warm welcome I received, there were some decidedly strong reservations about my youth and more than a modicum of skepticism about my ability to survive the challenges of a fractious and polarized synagogue. The frequency with which rabbis were dismissed from their post had not only divided the congregation, but had also given it the reputation of a school of barracudas.

Most of the synagogue's members were significantly older than I, and more than a few people voiced concern about my ability to counsel congregants who were more than twice my age. I don't know what my defenders argued, but with John Kennedy leading the nation at the time, youthful leadership seemed to be the spirit of the day. Despite skepticism about my survivability, reservations about my ability to heal and shepherd an unruly flock, and concern about my counseling skills, I was, nevertheless, elected to serve as the synagogue's rabbi. Within the first five years of my tenure, I was offered a lifetime contract. I might still be at the same pulpit had I not enjoyed the counseling challenges so much that I decided to become a clinical psychologist.

As a matter of fact, my age presented no barrier to those who needed a rabbi in moments of crisis. At critical times, rabbis are ageless. Over the years, I became a familiar figure at the local hospital, an all too frequent presence at the funeral home, and found myself drawn into the most intimate moments of people's lives. Like most rabbis, there was hardly a day when I was not involved, one way or another, in my congregants' personal dramas.

I was always somewhat uncomfortable, however, with the many assumptions congregants made about my expertise in human relations. By virtue of being a rabbi, it was assumed that I was knowledgeable about the psychology of human behavior, capable of resolving interpersonal conflicts, and that I had a special understanding of the problems, conflicts, and struggles of daily life. It was assumed that I was adept at counseling individuals of all ages, as well as couples and families exhibiting all kinds of problems.

Yet I had no formal training in rabbinic counseling, and like most congregational rabbis, worked intuitively. I cared deeply and empathetically for those who turned to me for help and found the role of community sage fulfilling. I believed myself to be a credible counselor, yet always had a discomforting feeling that there was more to good counseling than what I practiced.

My rabbinic training came from the world of the *beit midrash*, where the focus was primarily on the study of Talmud and Jewish law. I spent years immersed in the study of complex Talmudic and halachic texts, analyzing abstract issues, and struggling to internalize the problem-solving styles of my great teachers and their predecessors. Like most rabbis, I was trained for teaching and preaching. Counseling was something I was simply expected to know intuitively.

The years spent in yeshiva grappling with the complexities of Talmudic disputes had little prepared me for the complexities of community disputes. I was trained to resolve differences between the seemingly intractable positions of rabbinic sages, but it was insufficient training for resolving differences between husbands/wives, parents/children, let alone the innumerable disagreements among synagogue members.

I was prepared to counsel on halachic matters and answer

questions about *kashrut*, Shabbat and Yom Tov. I was not prepared to counsel the parents of a drug-addicted teenager, the family of a dying child, or a depressed woman contemplating suicide. Nor was I taught what to say to a family whose father had just been imprisoned for a serious crime.

I had learned how to make halachic judgments based on principles that differentiated right from wrong, kosher from *treif*, guilt from innocence. Halachic reasoning requires the development of a cognitive style called "linear thinking." Linear thinking is important in a legal system where guilt, damages, or responsibility needs to be determined. It is not helpful, however, in a counseling context. Finding the culprit in a marriage or determining the guilty party in a synagogue feud is not what a rabbi should be doing if he wants to be helpful.

Yet, I modeled myself after my teachers and other rabbinic figures. When students would turn to them for help, they would listen to the problem and invariably give advice. I believed this to be what rabbinic counseling was all about. A good rabbi only needs to analyze a situation fairly, form an opinion, make a prudent judgment, and then give his best advice. I didn't know that advice is not always helpful, no matter how sage. It often goes unheeded no matter how persuasively delivered, is sometimes hurtful, and is certainly not the most effective counseling approach.

This point was driven home to me one day, when a fifth-grade teacher brought me an essay written by a student in her class. The topic was "Socrates" and it read as follows: *"Socrates was a great man. Socrates was a wise man. He gave advice to people. They killed him!"*

I know that I tended to dispense large amounts of "sage" advice to people who came to me. I may have had better luck than Socrates, but that did not mean that my wisdom was helpful, especially to people struggling with personal conflict or complex interpersonal issues such as: whom to marry, where to move, which career to choose, or whether to divorce or remain unhappily married. Advice has limited value when it is merely a subjective opinion masquerading as divine wisdom.

Helping people by validating their struggle, exploring their alternatives, prioritizing their issues, clarifying their thinking, and examining the implications of their conclusions, are skills that are often outside the repertoire of too many rabbis. They were not part of my repertoire either.

In retrospect and with the acuity of hindsight, I look back on my rabbinic years with a modicum of regret. I know now that I missed many opportunities to be a more effective counselor. I can no longer bring back my bedside chats with the young man, diagnosed with an inoperable malignant tumor, who wanted so much to speak with me about his inevitable death. He needed to say things to his rabbi that he could not say to his family. In my vain attempt to give him hope, coupled with my own difficulty in coming to grips with the reality of his hopeless situation, I diverted discussions about his death with good cheer and prayer. I was denying his situation as well as denying him the opportunity to talk about something critical. He was undoubtedly far more prepared to deal with his death than I was.

On the surface, counseling looks deceptively simple and straightforward. To the untrained eye, it appears to be no more than good judgment, empathy, and intuition. Good counseling however, is a complex process. It requires a foundation of knowledge, a conceptual framework, skillful practice, and years of good training, supervision, and experience in order to reach a level of competence. Few rabbis have been adequately trained, and despite their good character, empathic inclinations, and intellectual acumen, they lack the most basic skills of effective counseling. Over the years I have rarely met a rabbi who did not feel the need for additional training in pastoral counseling.

When I think back upon my rabbinic years I realize that despite my varied successes in counseling, in essence what I didn't know could fill a book. So here it is — a guidebook for rabbis who aspire to be good shepherds, as well as good teachers.

A PRACTICAL GUIDE TO
RABBINIC
COUNSELING

The Rabbi as Mental Health Practitioner

Yisrael N. Levitz, Ph.D.

THE SKILLED RABBINIC counselor is not only a source of support for distressed congregants in times of personal crisis, but is also in a position to foster insight, generate awareness, and promote attitudinal and behavioral changes in those who turn to him for help. In this vein, the rabbi shares with other mental health professionals the common function of supporting and helping others find their strength to cope effectively and even grow in times of crisis, vulnerability, and distress.

In other respects, however, the rabbi's helping function is far more complex than that of most mental health professionals. There are dynamics intrinsic to the rabbinate with regard to the helping function that are unique in the field of mental health. Counseling issues or personal problems, for example, will often be presented differently to rabbis than they normally are for mental health practitioners. Unlike other professionals, rabbis are often entangled in the vortex of community life, play multiple roles in the lives of those whom they counsel, and may be the subject of exaggerated projections by congregants. All of these of course, play a role in the community rabbi's function as a rabbinic counselor.

A rabbi is expected to be available to all synagogue members who turn to him for help. Mental health practitioners, on the other hand, can generally screen their clients, deciding even before their first session whom they wish to see and who would not be an appropriate client. Since there are no mental health screening procedures for synagogue members, the rabbi is left to work with a full spectrum of individuals who range from the normal to the pathological. They are his flock and he is expected to shepherd them all.

PROBLEM PRESENTATION

The way in which a rabbi becomes aware of a problem is important to the extent that it will often determine his response. Where an individual, for example, comes to his/her rabbi and directly presents a problem in a forthright and candid manner, the rabbi, in effect, has clearly been invited to enter the world of the congregant as a helping person. In most instances a rabbi's counsel is sought in just this overt way. "We are having difficulty in our marriage." "Our son is going out with a non-Jewish girl, what should we do rabbi?" Or, "It is a year since my father died and I am still feeling depressed." The rabbi, in these instances, can engage the congregant concerning his issues as skillfully and sensitively as he knows how and be as helpful and supportive as the situation calls for. In this instance, the presentation of the problem is most similar to how it is done with mental health professionals.

Unlike mental health professionals, however, there are many instances when a rabbi cannot wait for an invitation to help. Should a tragedy occur involving one of his congregants, as soon as he is made aware of the situation, he is expected, as part of his calling, to either appear at the home of the suddenly bereaved or at the hospital bed of his stricken congregant. He need only be informed. Unlike mental health professionals who work by appointment only, he does not require a special request for service. He can assume that, as the rabbi, his support and counsel will generally be welcomed, even expected.

OUTWARD SIGNS OF HIDDEN PAIN

There are other instances when a congregant's request for help is more covert, elusive, and surreptitious. One rabbi recently shared with me an incident where a congregant had approached him with what appeared to be a straightforward halachic question. He simply wanted to know "if someone who commits suicide could be buried in a Jewish cemetery." The rabbi, wondering about the motivation behind the question, astutely suspected that this might be more than a halachic query. He invited the man to his office and told him that he would be happy to discuss the matter with him, but was simply curious as to what it was that prompted the question. After a few moments of discussion, the man admitted to being very depressed and that he was actually contemplating suicide. With the rabbi's counsel the man was able to seek professional psychiatric help and was able to get beyond his crisis. This was not only a case of sensitive pastoral intervention that saved a man's life, but an example of a person indirectly signaling a deeper problem.

It is not at all uncommon for rabbis to be asked questions of enormous personal import, couched as requests for religious information. "What is the Jewish view on homosexuality, rabbi?" asked a congregant who needed the rabbi's help with regard to her son, who had just informed her that he was gay. She was too embarrassed to openly reveal her son's homosexuality to the rabbi, so she discussed her feelings and concerns more generally before ascertaining that she would feel comfortable revealing things to him.

Rabbis, trained to be expert in religious, halachic, and philosophical matters, tend to respond candidly and forthrightly to questions that seem appropriately within the bailiwick of a religious authority. Yet, many an anguished cry for help is couched in an innocent religious query, and it requires a developed sixth sense to detect possible hidden meaning behind deceptively unpretentious questions. Simply asking the congregant, "What prompts your question?" often suffices as a way of determining if the question is indeed innocent or a veiled attempt to ask for assistance.

Many congregants who suffer from religious obsessions and compulsions, for example, will regularly ask about religious minutiae. Similarly, many anxious, guilt-ridden, or depressed individuals will engage their rabbi in religious or philosophical discussions that are directly related to assuaging their psychic pain, all under the guise of a quest for rabbinic expertise. As a general premise, if an issue or rabbinic question persists in similar or various forms, the rabbi should consider exploring the motivation that prompts them.

CONSEQUENTIAL SYMPTOMS

Yet another way in which problems present themselves to a rabbi is the most covert and elusive of all. They are problems seen only by their consequences. The individuals in distress do not even come to the rabbi for help. These are instances where a congregant either cannot ask for help out of a sense of shame or hopelessness, or conversely, is convinced that the problem will resolve itself in time.

Convinced that others cannot detect their anxieties, concerns, depression, marital difficulties, or health problems, the signs of their distress are nevertheless signaled in their behavior. A congregant may distance himself/herself from the synagogue, coming less frequently to services or no longer participating in the usual array of community activities. Once vital, he may appear depressed, listless, and pallid. These are often the types of problems brought to the rabbi by concerned others who feel helpless to intervene, but hope that by calling the rabbi's attention to the problem, he will step in. The limitations of social propriety often preclude individuals from reaching out to one another. They feel it would be inappropriate for them to probe too much, lest they be perceived as meddlesome. It is not uncommon for rabbis to be approached, for example, by concerned neighbors who believe that a particular child is being sexually or physically abused, yet are reluctant to take action themselves.

In these instances, the pastoral function becomes manifest in skillful and sensitive pastoral outreach. If a rabbi is able to clearly communicate a sincere sense of concern, then even individuals who are not at the moment prepared to discuss their problems tend to appreciate the rabbi's caring gesture. Those who do welcome the extended hand tend to be grateful for the rabbi's effort. I have often wondered if this pastoral gesture, as difficult and venturesome as it often is, might not be the noblest and most caring gesture of all for a community rabbi.

TIME AND PLACE

Another evident difference between rabbinic counseling and that of professional mental health practitioners relates to the rabbi's use of time and place. There is a widely held perception among congregants that the rabbi is (or at least should be) available at all times to respond to those who need help. It is assumed that the rabbi, available as he is at synagogue services, community functions, and social gatherings, can be approached at any time by congregants with serious matters on their minds.

Congregants in distress might commonly engage their rabbi at a wedding reception, in the street or supermarket, by phone late at night or immediately following a lengthy synagogue service, and expect him to be fully engaged and empathic. The rabbi, however, might be preoccupied with other pressing matters, personal or professional, but nevertheless might feel compelled to be responsive whenever and wherever approached. It seems, at times, as if every call is urgent, every need compelling, every circumstance an emergency.

The role and function of a community rabbi often does not allow for the luxury of a buffer zone. Unlike mental health practitioners, the rabbi often engages with his congregants in the real world, not in the cloistered privacy of a professional office. The rabbi meets his congregants in a world where life and death dramas are played out in real time, not in the analytic arena where memories and role playing bring meaning to past events. The rabbi's counseling environment cannot always be the safe sanctum of his office or study. Frequently, he finds himself riding in a funeral procession with a grieving family that has suddenly suffered a tragic loss. They need his comfort at that moment and not at some later time in his office. He will find himself at the bedside of a sick congregant who has just been diagnosed with a life-threatening illness or in a hospital waiting room with an anxious family immediately after one of their loved ones was in a serious accident. There are no appointments with crises and the rabbi's consultation room is wherever he is needed to assuage pain.

Rabbis function on the front lines of life. The boundary between personal and professional space is often unclear. It is neither uncommon nor inappropriate for a rabbi to counsel outside the parameters of a scheduled time and designated place. A rabbi who meets a congregant on a bus, train, or plane, for example, might find himself engaged in counseling if the congregant asks for it at that moment. In contrast, should a psychologist meet a patient on a bus, it is unlikely that he would engage him in a discussion of issues normally raised in a counseling session. The boundaries between personal and professional space that guide mental health practitioners are simply not appropriate for rabbis, who are expected to be available whenever and wherever approached.

By virtue of the boundaries that are necessary for the professional mental health practitioner (answering services, office hours, sessions by appointment, etc.), a psychologist is able to determine whether a request for help is truly urgent or of a more banal nature. It is not that mental health practitioners do not have emergencies, it is that they are generally not expected to react to them outside the context of their offices or scheduled office hours. Most mental health clinicians would certainly not consider conducting a therapy session on a train or in the middle of the annual synagogue dinner.

For psychotherapists, the ability to determine when and where they are able to see a client is a critical factor that affects the counseling experience for both client and professional. It allows the professional to structure a time and place most suitable for helping by providing the client with an environment that is conducive to privacy, undivided attention, a sense of safety, and confidentiality. In addition, it also allows the professional to maintain personal boundaries, so as not to feel resentful of the demands made upon his/her time.

In this sense, the role of the community rabbi is more complex than that of other mental health professionals because his relationship with congregants has both formal and informal components. He must combine the formal role of teacher, *posek* (deciding issues of Jewish law), and preacher with the informal function of a shepherd tending his flock. Congregational expectations that the rabbi is always available when called upon for help tend to make it impractical for the rabbi to buffer himself in the same way as do other mental health practitioners.

Yet, rabbis also need boundaries that can provide some degree of psychic space. It is therefore important for a rabbi also to differentiate a crisis from a more banal matter. Not every situation is urgent and not every call for help is an emergency. A congregant struggling with the decision of where to send his child to school is not presenting a situation of the same level of urgency as the sudden death of a family member. Certainly, there are counseling situations that can wait for scheduling within a more structured context. Without real boundaries to protect even a modicum of his personal space, a rabbi is always on call—lending new meaning to the rabbinate as a "calling" and confirming the adage that a rabbi can have an "off day," but never a "day off."

It can become overwhelming for a rabbi if he begins to feel a loss of control over his time. This also tends to add stress to his family and personal life, which is no small matter for his wife and children.

There are many rabbis who deal with this by establishing a specific time and place for pastoral counseling sessions. Telephone answering services and secretaries serve as an initial screen for a rabbi's incoming calls. If properly trained to be both sensitive to the caller as well as able to differentiate an urgent from a less pressing matter, a competent secretary can be an invaluable aide to the busy rabbi.

Since it is not uncommon for rabbis to be approached at inopportune times or under inappropriate circumstances with complex counseling issues, where the rabbi is unable to give the matter the kind of attention it requires, it would be in the congregant's best interest for the rabbi to suggest that the matter be discussed at another time and in a more appropriate place. A mutually convenient appointment time could be agreed upon right then and there or the rabbi could ask when would be a good time to call the congregant in order to make an appointment. A special time and place (rabbi's office or congregant's home) allows for far greater counseling effectiveness than an inappropriate one—even if the latter allows for a more immediate response.

THE POWER DIFFERENTIAL

In any relationship where the balance of power favors one person over the other, there is potential for exploitation. In the extreme, there is even potential for abuse. Professionally trained therapists are generally keenly aware of the power differential between themselves and their clients. One of the most challenging tasks for therapists is often to level the field and empower the client to work collaboratively with him/her in the therapeutic process. It is, in fact, a common goal of therapy to help clients discover their own strengths and potential.

The possibility for a rabbi to exploit a congregant whom he is counseling also centers around the unequal rabbi/congregant relationship. Rabbis, despite the fact that they are chosen by their community for a leadership role and are designated as spiritual head of their congregation, do not always feel the power of their position. Many rabbis experience a sense of powerlessness in their often vain attempts to have an impact on their community and to influence their congregations. However, within the context of a helping relationship they do tend to sense a greater degree of power when they are approached for help. At that moment there is a sense of being valued for their good judgment, intelligence, and wisdom. A rabbi's counseling function is often one of his most gratifying. In front of him may be sitting one of his most powerful congregants. At that moment however, when that congregant turns to the rabbi for help, it is the rabbi who is in the position of power.

Therapists are taught in their professional training to focus primarily on the needs of the patient. One of the most self-evident principles of counseling is that the patient, who is the more vulnerable of the two of them, not only needs to be protected, but the therapist is there for the patient's needs alone. Any therapist who uses a therapeutic relationship for anything other than the welfare of the patient is violating professional ethics.

Rabbis who counsel are bound by these same principles. The rabbi is expected to act solely in the interest of his congregant. A counseling relationship that is not focused entirely on the needs of the congregant, even if the congregant is not harmed by the rabbi's counsel, is nevertheless ethically problematic. If a rabbi attempts to influence a congregant, either overtly or covertly, to do something that is essentially for the benefit of the rabbi or the rabbi's synagogue, school, or community project, it is exploitation. This is true even if the advice does not hurt the congregant, but simply benefits the community.

Take, for example, the case of a rabbi to whom a dying congregant has confided that he has amassed a large fortune and is reluctant to leave the money to one of his children who has married out of the faith. As a rabbi of a struggling congregation, he might be tempted to suggest that the man leave his inheritance to the congregation. The very nature of the dual role of congregational rabbi and rabbinic counselor presents a particular challenge for the rabbi in need of funds. In that sense, it is far easier for a therapist to explore the possibilities of what to do with the money than it might be for the rabbi. To suggest a solution to the dying man's dilemma of a substantial gift to the synagogue, however, could be interpreted as a form of exploitation.

Similarly, when the young daughter of one of the synagogue's most prominent families turns to the rabbi for help with a painful problem, the rabbi must consider all the affected parties. The daughter might be in love with a man of whom her parents disapprove. She would like to marry him and is asking the rabbi to speak to her parents, who she thinks are being unreasonable. The influence of powerful parents and their ability to help or harm the rabbi makes this counseling situation and the dual role of the rabbi less than neutral. The rabbi might feel tempted by the opportunity to endear himself to the disapproving parents by advising against the marriage. In such cases, it is far easier for a therapist to function impartially than it is for a rabbi.

In essence then, the degree to which a rabbi uses his position of influence in a self-serving manner, to that degree he may be practicing exploitation. Of course, should a rabbi exert undue influence or coercion that is harmful to the congregant, it surpasses exploitation and becomes abuse.

DUAL RELATIONSHIPS: THE SPECIAL COMPLEXITIES OF RABBINIC COUNSELING

As a widely held rule among mental health practitioners, relationships with clients outside of the counseling context are avoided as much as possible. If a therapist has any kind of social, communal, or work relationship with an individual, he would not generally agree to see that person in a professional context. This way a therapist avoids being involved in what is known as a "dual relationship". By being outside the client's social world, the therapist is better able to be both neutral and unbiased when entering the client's private world.

One of the reasons that therapists try to avoid treating individuals with whom they have a dual relationship is because of the potential for ethical complications. If a psychologist is the president of his congregation, can he ask one of his clients, another member of the congregation, for a large donation to the synagogue? If his client is politically powerful and the therapist needs help with a building variance for his new office, can he ask his client to help him get his variance? If a client owns a jewelry store, can a therapist buy his wife a new ring there, expecting to get a good deal? These are examples of dual relationships that present ethical problems that therapists try to avoid. As a therapist, I would even avoid asking a client to mail a letter for me at the corner mailbox. After all, what if the client forgot to do it? Or worse, what if he lost it?

For a rabbi, the pristine relationship of therapist and client is neither practical nor prudent. A community rabbi is an integral part of his congregant's world. His function is, in fact, to have ongoing and often intense relationships with the members of his congregation, and it is precisely because of the trust and closeness engendered that congregants feel comfortable turning to their rabbi in times of need.

As a result of his being involved in the machinations of synagogue committees, community boards, personal rivalries, competing interests, and communal conflicts, it is simply not possible for the rabbi to maintain the kind of untainted relationships that mental health practitioners enjoy. Dual relationships cannot be avoided.

This duality makes counseling congregants more complex. Consider, for example, the rabbi who is called upon to counsel a powerful board member, toward whom he has strong negative feelings because this congregant always opposes and aggressively challenges him at meetings. Or conversely, he might be called upon to counsel a congregant for whom he feels a sense of strong camaraderie. In either instance it would interfere with his ability to objectively assess the presenting problem.

Many a rabbi would understandably find it difficult to believe that one of his most prominent congregants, a mild mannered, soft-spoken member of his Talmud study group, is a tyrant at home and abusive to both his wife and children. A rabbi might similarly feel cowed by a congregant's power among the shul members and feel tempted or even obligated to satisfy his every expectation.

A rabbi might be personally affected by the decision a congregant needs to make. When one of his strongest supporters, for example, seeks his help in deciding whether or not to accept an out-of-town position that would entail his moving away from the community, the rabbi might understandably find it difficult to be an unbiased counselor. The rabbi's objectivity is no less challenged if the congregant is one of his most vociferous opponents on the synagogue board. It might be quite a challenge for the rabbi to resist suggesting that his congregant leave town as quickly as possible. The swirl of intense relationships that are part of the rabbinate can evoke many conflicts and ethical dilemmas for the counseling rabbi.

Since a community rabbi does not have the luxury of choosing his congregants or those who turn to him for counsel, it is all the more important that he become sensitive to the feelings, both positive and negative, that he holds towards them. Where objective counseling is deemed problematic because of the dual nature of the rabbi/congregant relationship, the ethical alternative would be to either seek supervision, consult with another professional, or refer the congregant elsewhere.

There is sufficient support in psychological literature to indicate that a dual relationship in and of itself need not always be problematic. Even for therapists the taboo against dual relationships has lessened over the years. In small communities, the probability of therapists knowing patients in settings outside their office is not uncommon. It does not necessarily preclude a therapist from working effectively and ethically with a client. If he felt that he would be unable to remain neutral or unbiased with a patient, he too would either seek supervision with a trusted mentor or refer the patient elsewhere.

ASSESSING YOUR COUNSELING SKILLS

I have often been asked by practicing rabbis if I felt it really necessary for rabbis who have been counseling congregants for many years to seek further training. After all, the reasoning goes, as an intelligent, sensitive, and caring person with years of experience counseling people with all kinds of problems, should not that be enough? Isn't life experience the best training?

For many years I directed a social work program for clergy at the Wurzweiler School of Social Work. When interviewing applicants for the program, I always asked if they had ever done counseling and how good they thought they were at it. Invariably, rabbis and other clergy would report a sense of confidence about their competence in counseling and felt that their skills were honed by years of experience. The reason they were seeking an advanced degree was to further develop their already acquired skills. As one rabbi put it to me, "I've been counseling people for years and have seen it all. I basically want the degree in order to legitimate what I already do." In a sense, I understood how these perceptions evolved. Counseling appears deceptively simple. People who seek a rabbi's help in times of need are grateful for his caring attention and thankful for his help. Why, then, should he not feel that he has done a competent job?

Since I was supervising these clergymen over a two-year period, at regular intervals I would ask them to reassess their skills. At the conclusion of the first year of intensive training, surprisingly, even the most seasoned rabbis felt significantly *less* certain about their counseling skills than they did before they began. With their work being supervised, they had come to realize how complex the counseling process was. By the end of their second year of school, these same rabbis felt more comfortable with their helping skills in general, but had also realized that there was still so much more to learn in this deceptively simple field. In fact, most were now eager to go on to post-graduate work, with new respect for the complexities of the counseling process.

Ironically, what I also found was that rabbinic candidates who came with the weakest skills often had the most inflated opinion of their abilities and the least awareness of their shortcomings. Psychological studies have consistently indicated a tendency among people across a wide spectrum of professions to overestimate their level of performance. The upshot is that without the watchful eye of a supervising professional, many of us tend to overestimate our abilities. The gratitude and praise a rabbi receives from a congregant may not be as honest as the feedback he receives from a supervisor. This is because a congregant usually finds it difficult to give negative feedback to his rabbi, whom he perceives as trying to be helpful — even if the rabbi was not particularly helpful at all.

THE ESSENTIAL ELEMENTS OF EFFECTIVE RABBINIC COUNSELING

Rabbis who are effective counselors utilize many skills that are important in all mental health professions. Foremost and often most challenging for the counseling rabbi is the ability to create a safe environment for those who seek his help. This is accomplished when the rabbi engages his congregant respectfully and non-judgmentally. This is not always as simple as it appears.

It can be challenging when a rabbi is confronted with an issue that conflicts with his own cherished beliefs or his most valued religious, moral, and ethical principles. Rabbis are generally highly-trained, critical thinkers, acutely sensitive to the dichotomies of right and wrong. They are trained to make judgments and to discern the nuances of good and evil. It is not that easy, therefore, for a rabbi to suspend his tendency to judge, and instead learn to connect to the distress, conflict, grief, shame, or pain that is being experienced by individuals who turn to him for help. If he is able to do just that, however, then he has the opportunity to create the very empathic environment that is the *sine qua non* of a safe counseling relationship. A congregant needs at all times to feel that he is respected, as well as understood.

When a rabbi is authentically non-judgmental and shows genuine interest and attentiveness, he is generally perceived as being compassionate and understanding. Rabbis who provide a safe interpersonal atmosphere create an environment where congregants feel comfortable taking a candid look at their life's problems, are able to explore options that they had not previously considered, and see the consequences of their decisions with greater clarity. By providing an empathetically supportive environment, a rabbi can often get a congregant's own thinking capabilities operating again.

By listening empathetically and non-judgmentally, a rabbi allows individuals to feel safe about sharing their innermost thoughts, feelings, and experiences. There is evidence to suggest that no matter what the style or orientation of the rabbinic counselor, his congregant will feel the impact of being listened to attentively as one of the most helpful aspects of the interchange.

The basic process of disclosing one's problems out loud to another human being and examining them from a distance has been found to be one of the most critical dynamics of the helping process. Doing this allows an individual to externalize his thoughts and gain perspective on them.

Lastly, a rabbi can provide a framework for considering alternative approaches to thinking about a problem and arriving at a workable solution. This is not simply a matter of advising or imposing an answer on an individual, but rather a skilled process of exploring alternatives and considering their ramifications. A different way of viewing one's problems is often the key to promoting relief and self-healing. These premises, as challenging as they may be at times, are the basic building blocks of effective rabbinic counseling.

What follows in the next chapter is a discussion of the requisite counseling skills which build upon the foundation of a safe, respectful, and non-judgmental rabbinic counseling environment. If a sensitive rabbi is able to develop these skills and practice them — especially in consultation with and under the supervision of a seasoned professional — then his counseling work can become a true source of help and support for the members of his community.

BASIC PRINCIPLES OF RABBINIC COUNSELING

Rona Michelson, D.S.W.
Yisrael N. Levitz, Ph.D.

BY VIRTUE OF HAVING been ordained, people assume that a rabbi is surrounded by an aura of luminous wisdom and inspired insight. So he is often the first one they turn to when going through any of life's myriad crises. When congregants are having problems with a spouse, child, parent, in-law, or boss, there is an intrinsic expectation that the rabbi will know how to make things better. He will tell them how to make the spouse more appreciative or the in-laws less intrusive, how to inspire a child to study harder and clean his room, and how to talk the boss into giving a raise or a promotion. These are not uncommon expectations. Congregants simply ignore the fact that the rabbi, despite his scholarly abilities, good character, and noble intentions, is neither god nor guru.

Given these expectations, many rabbis find themselves devoting an inordinate amount of time to counseling congregants. Their schedules begin to look like those of psychotherapists. Yet unlike therapists, most rabbis are too busy with their other responsibilities to be carrying a full caseload of therapy clients.

For most rabbis, therefore, the course of counseling needs to be time-limited and well-defined. Yet, what can a rabbi reasonably expect to accomplish in a short period of time and what skills does he require?

THE COUNSELING MINDSET

The most basic need of individuals seeking help is to feel that they have been heard and understood. If they feel in any way misunderstood, judged, blamed, chastised, or criticized, safety and trust are diminished and the counseling process is doomed to failure. It is therefore important that the counseling rabbi listen with a suspended sense of judgment so that he accurately hears and understands what the congregant is saying. He should not attempt to divine feelings, intentions, motivations, or even solutions. He must simply listen.

Listening without judging, however, is no easy task for a rabbi trained in a scholarly world that requires critical judgment (as discussed in the previous chapter). Yet, should a counselee sense that the rabbi is judging him in any way, the counseling arena becomes unsafe. When this happens, defensiveness goes up and the effectiveness of the counseling is diminished. Only in a non-judgmental, non-critical, and accepting interaction will a congregant feel respected, understood, and ready to openly share his feelings, thoughts, and dilemmas.

A SYSTEMIC APPROACH

Another important component of the counseling process is the rabbi's ability to understand a problem in its full context. How, for example, does the counselee's problem affect others — such as family members, friends, or co-workers. Although it is natural to believe the person who is sitting in the office — and be empathic to how he/she is suffering and how another family member is the source of the pain — seeing things only through one person's perspective can be misleading. It limits the rabbi to the congregant's idea of the problem and, hence, the possible solutions. Instead, the rabbi should try to find out how the situation is affecting other family members. Is the spouse also unhappy? Do the children show signs of distress? By focusing on the *effects* of the problem instead of looking for "the culprit", the counselor will be able to devise strategies to solve the problem not just for the person in the room, but for all others who are affected by it.

For example, a woman came to her rabbi upset and complaining that her husband doesn't come home in time for dinner, so that he can spend time with the family before the children go to sleep. She portrayed him as self-centered, inconsiderate of the needs of his wife and children, and unwilling to pitch in with baths, bedtimes, and other family responsibilities. However, with some gentle probing the rabbi then discovered that the husband is avoiding coming home then because his wife, who is exhausted by the end of the day, has no patience and is angry and irritable with everyone around her. The husband goes to visit his widowed mother instead, because he doesn't want to come home to his screaming wife and his crying children. The case is no longer about a selfish husband, but rather about a vicious cycle where the wife is overwrought and feeling abadoned while trying to take care of her tired children and the husband wants to avoid getting embroiled in the yelling and screaming because he, too, is exhausted and afraid of losing his temper. If the rabbi can uncover the cycle and not judge it, he will find a human situation with no villians and no culprits — just two human beings with an understandable dilemma. By looking at the broader context, the rabbi can uncover the real problem and work with the congregant to solve it in a creative and helpful way. This strategy is generally known as the "systemic" approach to counseling.

THE INITIAL INTERVIEW

The first task of the rabbi is to find out the nature of the problem. Ask "when, what, where, how, and who." It is not advisable to ask the question "why", because it is a question that tends to put others on the defensive. For example, "Why did you do that?" is not likely to be heard as a simple inquiry. Instead it will be heard as, "You did something wrong!"

If the rabbi already knows all the information he needs about the congregant's family, friends, and others who are relevant to the problem, then he need not ask for it. If, on the other hand, he does not have basic information about the significant people in the life of the counselee, he then needs to acquire it. He needs to learn who is affected by the congregant's problem, who would be affected by a resolution of the problem, and how they, in turn, affect the congregant. The counseling rabbi needs to be able to move about in the congregant's world, and get to know the full cast of characters.

The objective of the first interview is to arrive at a mutually acceptable understanding of what the problem is. The rabbi needs to learn the congregant's perception of the problem. Why, for example, is the problem manifesting itself now? How long has it been going on? When did it start becoming a problem? What exactly is happening? When does it happen? Where is it happening? Where is it not happening? How does it affect others? What is their reaction to the problem? What are the counselee's underlying concerns, feelings, fears, and anxieties etc.?

The rabbi also needs to know what attempts have been made to solve the problem. Has it been discussed, yet, with family members? Have there been arguments? Have children been threatened or punished? Has the individual or his family ever sought professional help? Is anyone currently in therapy? What has been the result of attempts to solve the problem? The answers to these questions help the rabbi not to repeat the same advice or strategy that has failed in the past.

Similarly, it is important to ask how the problem came about. Was it in reaction to something else? Did the teenage daughter start dressing inappropriately when her best friend moved away, when her grandmother died, when her sister got married? Events that happened around the time of the emergence of the symptom may be important factors in hypothesizing about its root cause.

Most people believe they know why others act as they do. It is important though that the rabbinic counselor not come to quick conclusions about what motivates those who affect the world of the counselee. A symptom may have a meaning that is very different to the person who is exhibiting it than it is to the person who is disturbed by it. A teenage daughter may not be rebelling or seeking to embarrass her parents. She may be showing loyalty to a friend. She may be struggling with her own self-image.

A man who comes in complaining about his wife's distant behavior may have decided that she is angry with him or no longer loves him. She could, of course, be suffering from depression, going through menopause, or feeling anxious about a myriad of other concerns that simply drain her of energy. She may be choosing not to burden her husband with her concerns in order to shield him from worry or she may feel that he, in fact, would not understand her anxieties and so she feels lonely and distant. It is only with extensive exploration that we can begin to hypothesize about the dynamics of any given problem.

SETTING REALISTIC GOALS

In order to help someone, there needs to be a stated, agreed-upon goal. The goal must be something that is achievable, for if goals are not achievable then expectations of the counseling process will be unrealistic and the results disappointing. Examples of unrealistic goals that are basically not achievable are: "I want everyone to like me"; "I want my boyfriend to propose"; "I want to be happy all the time"; "I don't want to have worries anymore."

Having a firm understanding of what can and cannot be accomplished in counseling is referred to as a "contract" by mental health professionals. One aspect of setting up a therapeutic contract is identifying and negotiating achievable goals. Instead of everyone liking the congregant, perhaps a goal could be that he learn to value himself more, or learn how to be a better friend, or learn better manners. Instead of not having any worries, a realistic goal would be to learn how to cope in a more effective manner or learn more effective ways of relieving stress.

Once the destination is set, then guideposts can be marked. What would be the first "reportable" indication that things are getting better? The rabbi may ask, "How will you know when things are better?" "What will you notice?" "Will it be that you will be able to strike up a conversation with someone new?" "Will it be that you will be able to invite someone over for a Shabbat meal?" "Will it be that, although there's a work deadline looming, you can enjoy your child's birthday party?" Guideposts are indications of progress.

The steadfastness of the rabbi to remain engaged and to "shepherd" a person's change process is part of what enables a person to grow and heal and emerge as a stronger human being.

THE COUNSELING PROCESS

Active Listening—Reflecting Back

Feeling understood is a core human need that becomes even more critical in times of pain or distress. In order for a congregant seeking help to feel fully understood, it is important for the rabbi, from time to time, to reflect back what he is hearing and what he understands about what the communicator is experiencing. This is accomplished by paraphrasing the essence of the communication and asking for confirmation about whether he understood correctly. This is called "active listening."

For example, when someone reports being upset or angry, one's normal response might be to empathize or share one's own personal feelings or experiences. In the context of a helping relationship, however, the rabbi should, instead, simply listen in a manner that allows him to grasp the importance of the matter for the congregant and then reflect back what he believes to be the essence of the message. This needs to be done without interpreting or placing value judgments on what was said. Reflecting back the content of what was said, as well as the emotional undercurrent, is a powerful way of letting people know that they have connected with another human being who understands them and knows how they feel.

It is important to resist the temptation to supply quick solutions to the problem. The counseling process is considerably more effective if the counselor simply listens reflectively and resists coming up with sage solutions. Often all that is needed in order to be helpful is someone who will listen and understand another's inner experience. Being understood dissipates some of the loneliness and isolation of living with the burden of a problem.

Reflecting Emotions

Letting the other person know that you not only heard what he said but also understood what he felt is a powerful way of joining him in his pain. This is one of the most helpful things a rabbi can do.

Problems brought to a rabbi are often presented in a very rational manner. Emotions are often hidden and held at bay. However, they often lie just beneath the surface. When a person in distress presents a problem in a manner that appears to be cool and detached, it does not mean that he is not feeling pain, despair, or depression. Since a rabbi is not a mind reader, he cannot know for sure what it is that the individual is feeling. He needs, therefore, to observe verbal and nonverbal cues that might reflect underlying feelings.

If a rabbi believes, that under the circumstances, an individual should be feeling sad, the rabbi should not impose this feeling on the counselee. An example of this would be a rabbi saying to a mourner, "You must be feeling very sad about your father's death." The rabbi, not knowing what the relationship was between the individual and his/her father, might be missing the mark entirely. The mourner's father may have been a gentle, loving *tzaddik* or a tyrannical abuser whose death is the fulfillment of the child's lifelong wish.

The rabbi who is able to listen not only to the content of the individual's narrative, but observe the counselee's tone of voice, facial expressions, and other nonverbal messages, can more readily reflect the emotions beneath the words. If an individual describes his father's death, which occured while he was only a child and there are no signs of sorrow, the rabbi should not assume what the emotional reaction was at the time or what it is currently. If the rabbi is unsure of the emotional undercurrent, he need simply inquire, "What was that like for you?"

If, on the other hand, an emotion is very evident from content, tone, and body language (tearfulness, angry expression, crying), it would be insensitive for the rabbi to ask, "How did that feel?" It would imply that the rabbinic counselor is simply not paying attention. When feelings are self-evident and openly displayed, it is safe for the rabbi to reflect his reading of the emotion with a simple confirmation like: "That must really hurt!" or "She seems to upset you quite a bit!" or "It sounds like you are embarrassed a lot by his behavior." When a rabbi attempts to reflect the unspoken emotional content back to the congregant by putting it into words, it helps the congregant to better identify his own emotions as well as to feel better understood.

The rabbi should attempt to reflect back the feelings to the same degree the congregant is experiencing them. For example, if someone is annoyed with his neighbor's early morning carpentry noises, then the rabbi should reflect that he seems annoyed. If he's furious, then the rabbi should reflect that he seems very upset and angry. Often other people's responses are not the same as ours. The thing that makes us want to scream may only be mildly annoying to someone else and vice versa. Rabbis need to be sure that they are picking up the level of annoyance, anger, frustration, sadness, or any other emotion the congregant is feeling, and not project onto him or her what the rabbi might feel in similar circumstances.

When the congregant has conflicting feelings, it is often very helpful to reflect the juxtaposition of the conflicting feelings. "On the one hand you sound angry; on the other hand you seem sad about this." "You say you hate him, but you also seem to respect him a lot." "You say you love him, but you seem afraid of him as well." "In a way it sounds like you would like to move, on the other hand it seems like you'd really like to stay where you are."

When reflecting feelings back to an individual being counseled, it is important to use tentative phrasing in order to avoid appearing to "mind read", or worse — misreading the counselee's internal state altogether. The rabbi is not a mind reader and therefore can only reflect what seems apparent to him. Therefore, it is not advisable for him to say with certainty, "You are really quite angry about this," unless he has been expressly told this. The rabbi can say, "You *seem* quite angry about this." "You seem" reflects the rabbi's perceptions as an observer, not the other's internal state. In this way the rabbi does not run the risk of reading the other person's emotional state inaccurately.

Validating Emotions

One very positive thing that a rabbi can do for a congregant is to validate his feelings. That means simply letting the person know that you understand why he feels as he does. Often people feel self-conscious or embarrassed about things they are feeling. They may feel hurt, angry, jealous, or left out, and may say in the same breath, "I know I shouldn't feel this way." As a counselor, it is appropriate to let the congregant know that feelings are simply feelings. Emotions are not categorized as right or wrong. Only actions and thoughts are subject to scrutiny. Emotions and what triggers them need to be understood, but not judged. Validation does not mean confirming for the congregant that his feelings are correct, rather it means listening in a compassionate manner to what he or she is experiencing.

Clarification

It is not uncommon for individuals in distress to be unclear about their problem. There are times when individuals might even use slang, jargon, or terms that are unfamiliar to the rabbi. Similarly, they may make references to things that are outside the rabbi's realm of experience. At these times, the counseling rabbi should not let vague references or unclear statements pass and assume that he understands what is being communicated. Even though he might need to interrupt the narrative flow, if he is in any way confused or unclear, the rabbi must ask the congregant to clarify what has just been said. A simple statement such as, "I'm not sure I understood what you meant by...," "I don't think I understood what you just said," or "What did you mean by...," not only helps the rabbi clarify what the congregant is saying, but it also helps the congregant gain a greater clarity himself. In addition, it confirms that the rabbi is really listening and wants to fully grasp what is being related.

Focusing

Congregants who come in feeling overwhelmed and confused often present their problem in an unfocused manner, flitting from subject to subject. It is the rabbi's task to keep the counselee on track so that the information can be understood in a meaningful way. Allowing an individual to simply spew is not helpful, because in the end, the rabbi won't have a clear picture of what the problem is. Simply asking the counselee "in what way is this related to..." can help get the interview back on track.

Partializing

People rarely come for help when they are feeling fine and happy. Instead, they come when they are stuck, confused, or overwhelmed. There are often many components to a problem, all seemingly swirling about in the counselee's head and building on themselves in a confusing and painful way. Complex problems are often difficult to describe. With a large cast of characters, layers of intertwined events, and a multitude of feelings and perceptions, the counselee's narrative often reflects this complexity and can overwhelm the rabbinic counselor, as well.

One way of bringing clarity to such complex situations is to "partialize". Partializing simply means breaking things down into small components and focusing on them one by one. For example, a family that is overwhelmed by a new living arrangement (grandma has moved into the house and requires more care than anticipated) needs to take one step at a time to cope with this very complicated situation. Members can be encouraged to make a list of what needs to be done, prioritize the list, and then accomplish the items on it one at a time. Partializing is reflected in Alcoholics Anonymous's "one day at a time" philosophy.

COGNITIVE RESTRUCTURING

People often come to the rabbi not only with a problem, but also with a fixed opinion as to the cause of the problem. The rabbi must realize that an individual's hypothesis about the cause may or may not be the real reason for the problem. It is not for the rabbi to challenge the counselee's hypothesis in a confrontational manner. The rabbi is usually more effective if he works collaboratively with the congregant to consider possible alternate explanations.

People, when engaged in a problem, tend to think in a very linear manner. Linear thinking implies that there is only one cause for a problem. It often implies, as well, that there is a victim and a villian. They see the problem in a limited way, act as if that is the objective reality, and then attempt to solve the problem based on that reasoning. The rabbinic counselor would do well to assist the person in considering alternate hypotheses that can allow the person to begin to generate new solutions other than those attempted in the past and found ineffective.

It is not uncommon for human beings to generate hypotheses about the meaning, intentions, and motivations of others. We need to make sense out of life's events. The problem often lies in our reacting to our hypotheses as if they were facts.

This, of course, precludes those instances when a congregant presents just the actual facts, and not hypotheses. When a man reports that his wife told him that she no longer loved him and wanted a divorce, that is factual. If he does not know why she wants the divorce and believes that she must be involved with another man, that is a hypothesis, unless he has proof.

Rabbis who offer new possible meanings for current behaviors may bring about a major change in attitude. A child's perceived oppositional behavior, when seen as a desire to get more attention and affection from his mother or father, can suddenly become understandable, detoxified. Change is then possible. A parent's perceived interfering, when seen as concern for the child's welfare, can be valued rather than resented.

Reframing

One way of assisting people to see their situation in a more positive, productive way is through the use of reframing. Simply put, reframing is a process through which the same facts or behaviors take on a different hue because of how they are portrayed. A good example of reframing is beginning with a medium blue sheet of paper. If we frame it with a matting that is a navy blue, the paper will look light colored. However, were we to frame it with a white matting, it would look darker. Its color, of course, remains the same, but its context changes how it is perceived.

Often, when parents talk about children who are stubborn, it is possible to reframe that stubbornness as a positive attribute. "He is the kind of person who will work very hard to get what he wants." "He's not a quitter."

A child seen as withdrawn because he spends his time in his room reading instead of playing outside with the other children may be portrayed as having a poetic soul, as thoughtful or philosophical, or as having a wonderful imagination. But for a reframe to be effective, it must be true. If it is not a different perspective on the reality, it is simply not believable. Should the bookworm child like to read about blood and guts, then we can't speak about his poetic soul. Certainly, if someone is involved in destructive or self-destructive behavior, it is not very believable or true to give it a positive reframe.

Reframes are used to provide positive connotations to behavior. Reframing can be a powerful tool and can change dysfunctional patterns quickly.

The Use of Metaphor

Another powerful tool in helping people is the metaphor. All rabbis use *midrashim* and *aggadot* from time to time, as well as tales of famous rabbis and scholars. These stories often contain important truths about how we conduct our lives. This is how we transmit much of our tradition and values. Stories of kindness and caring teach people about the ability to be gracious and kind.

When a rabbi is talking to a congregant, there are times when a specific story may be helpful. But first, the rabbi must decide if the point of the story will be properly understood and if the timing is right. It is inappropriate to interject a story or midrashic insight at a point when it will interfere with a congregant's narrative flow, concentration, or focus. It is certainly not a substitute for empathic listening.

Metaphors may also be used to help a congregant conceptualize his situation or a solution in a new way. A metaphor, for example, that might be helpful for parents who are having trouble with a difficult child is that of a building under construction. All of us know that construction takes a lot of time and hard work. However, we can make sure that the construction is of a high quality if we invest a lot of time in it, watch it, offer suggestions, and make sure that the proper tools are used. Until it is built, it will often look imperfect and unfinished. Progress is not always steady. Before the finishing process is complete, there might be disruptions. There are rainstorms and work stoppages along the way, but eventually, with the right supervision, it is finally finished.

This metaphor can be plumbed in depth. Then parents will begin to understand that a child is an adult under construction—that with enough care and supervision and nurturance he will become just what the Divine architect intended.

Metaphors about growing—the budding and leafing of a tree, the blossoming, and finally the appearance of a fruit encourage people who are feeling stuck. People can then be counseled to be patient, because change is often imperceptible.

Metaphors about drowning, treading water, or sinking in quicksand are helpful for people who are "in over their heads." They can be encouraged to ask for some help or to stop working so hard. One particularly rich metaphor is about a performer who keeps a number of plates spinning simultaneously atop of long sticks. Mothers of large families often can relate to that one!

Difficult problems that are hard to get hold of can be thought of as fish that slip from one's hand. While teaching people to modulate their responses, one can use the metaphor of driving a car—shifting gears, applying just enough, but not too much pressure on the gas pedal according to the road conditions, and similarly, applying the brakes smoothly and effectively.

Metaphors are extremely useful in all kinds of circumstances. They must, however, be used judiciously in order to be effective.

Counseling Families

When more than one family member seeks assistance, the rabbi's job becomes more complicated. A typical parent/child or husband/wife issue will have two people each trying to prove that he or she is right and that the other is mean, cruel, insensitive, controlling, or just plain wrong.

The rabbi's first task is to join with both family members. That means he must find a commonality with each of them. Each must feel that the rabbi will give him or her a fair hearing.

When seeing couples or multiple family members, the rabbi's task remains that of listening and reflecting. Reflecting what the person is saying in no way implies that the rabbi agrees or disagrees; it simply allows the person to say what is on his mind and to feel understood. When one person is talking, the rabbi should try to keep others from interrupting, explaining that it is important for each person to have the opportunity to express the way he sees things and that each person will get a fair chance to speak.

Often, just hearing the other person's point of view begins to shift the perception of the problem. Frequently, family members don't listen to each other. Instead, they unthinkingly react out of their own needs.

The rabbi should validate the feelings and perceptions of each person: "I can see how feeling ignored by your spouse would really hurt." "I can understand that an automatic negative response to your suggestions would make you feel angry." He is not there to determine what really happened. He is not a detective and he is certainly not there to be a judge. Remember, each person sees reality solely through his own perceptions and from his own perspective, and each perspective has validity. If she feels that he is too hard on the children and he feels she indulges them too much, what is the reality? The rabbi has no way of knowing. Each will bring examples that validate their point of view. The facts in this instance may not even be as important as the perceptions and what is generating them.

Normalizing

When individuals come to you, feeling as if they are alone in experiencing such a problem, it is important for you to normalize their situation.

"This is not as uncommon as you think," a rabbi might say. "It is not at all unusual in families for one parent to be more indulgent and one parent less so. Sometimes they are able to resolve their differences, but many times parents get stuck and seek help."

Once a behavior or problematic interaction has been normalized, then possible strategies for dealing with the situation can be explored. Parents may think that theirs are the only children who won't clean their rooms or wives may think that theirs is the only husband who sits and reads the paper while chaos surrounds him. Husbands, in turn, may think that everyone else's wife always has a wonderful dinner waiting for him on the table when he returns from work. The knowledge that their problem is not an unusual one helps make it less toxic.

COMMUNITY RESOURCES

Once a problem has been defined, the next task is to explore how it can best be resolved. Alternative solutions might be explored and then actions that were previously thought impossible might suddenly be seen as feasible.

Individuals, however, generally need support if they want to change their behavior. Their rabbi then can suggest a number of options to assist them. Books, tapes, and websites are known to influence people's lives. Reading books pertinent to the individual's situation has become such a popular adjunct to therapy that mental health professionals now refer to it as "bibliotherapy." A self-help book can teach an individual to understand himself or his family members better or inspire him to interact in a new or different way. A novel might have a theme that the rabbi feels is therapeutic.

People feel less threatened by books and tapes. These work on a metaphoric level, separating the problem from the person's own experience. Then he becomes more open to helpful suggestions or lessons to be learned, because he does not need to employ his usual defense mechanisms. Also, identifying with a character in a story can serve as a cathartic experience for individuals who otherwise are unwilling or unable to cry.

If the rabbi is aware of others who have survived, overcome, or successfully coped with the congregant's same problem, he might ask them if they would be comfortable sharing their experiences, as well as their coping strategies, with the congregant. Similarly, a rabbi could recommend that the congregant join a support group. Groups that have been helpful include Alcoholics Anonymous, Alanon, Narcotics Anonymous, and other 12–step programs. There are also support groups for people with specific disabilities or challenges, e.g. parents of dyslexic children, people whose relatives have cancer, caregivers of Alzheimers patients, people with specific phobias, women going through menopause, etc. Often the group experience offers a level of support that no therapist could ever duplicate. When appropriate, such a referral can be very helpful. In the case where a person seems to be extremely depressed or has symptoms that are physical in origin, the first referral should always be to a family physician.

If the family is already receiving services from other professionals, it is important to understand what their involvement is. Often, too many people working with a family will only keep it dysfunctional. At a minimum, efforts should be coordinated so that helpers are not working at cross purposes. Should it be necessary for the rabbi to contact a mental health practitioner who has either worked with or is currently working with the individual, the rabbi should ask the congregant for written permission to discuss his situation with the professional. Ethically, mental health professionals are not permitted to even acknowledge that they are treating someone, much less discuss a case without the express written permission of the patient.

It is important for rabbis and mental health practitioners to communicate respectfully and to work cooperatively. The exception to this, of course, is when there is a clear case of incompetence, malpractice, or negligence. It is best for the rabbi to verify with other trusted mental health professionals about whether or not this is in fact the case, or merely the rabbi's good intentions getting in the way.

FINAL CONSIDERATIONS:
TRANSFERENCE AND COUNTERTRANSFERENCE

Sometimes people will redirect their feelings, especially those unconsciously retained from childhood, to a rabbi and confuse him with someone else. This is called "transference". The rabbi might be seen as all-good, all-wonderful, all-knowing, and all-powerful. As much as that might make him feel good, because it is an unrealistic perception of the rabbi as a human being, it tends to lead to disillusionment, disappointment, and anger.

The congregant is simply redirecting his feelings from another person onto the rabbi and idealizing him. On the other hand, the congregant might similarly transfer negative feelings from significant people in his life (e.g., parents and spouse) and project in onto the rabbi.

In most cases of rabbinic counseling, these transferences work against the process. When a rabbi allows himself to feel either venerated or devalued, this limits his ability to help. One aspect of healing, according to some theorists, is fostering a healthy, authentic relationship between the helper and the client. It is not in the rabbi's or congregant's best interest, therefore, to confuse the image that others have of him with reality.

Often a counselee will transfer his admiration and love toward a helping professional who listens to him the way no one else will. From a congregant's perspective, a rabbi might represent God, his grandfather, father, brother, or even son. A rabbi needs to remain aware of the responsibility that comes with his position and be meticulously careful not to exploit it. Receiving gifts or services from the congregant could be problematic. If the rabbi expresses his caring, the congregant might misinterpret it. Therefore, the rabbi needs to be very, very careful.

The rabbi might even engage in "countertransference" toward his congregant. He comes to know the congregant as a vulnerable, hurt, and frightened human being. Most rabbis have tremendous sensitivity to such suffering, and often come to feel overly protective of the suffering counselee. Maintaining proper boundaries, therefore, is very important because in order to truly help, a rabbi has to step back and allow the counselee to strengthen his psychological muscles and learn to cope on his own. In the same way that parents love and protect their children when they are small, all the while preparing them for independence, the rabbi's goal with each congregant must be to encourage him to grow into a more fully functional person.

SAGE RABBINIC ADVICE

Giving advice comes naturally for most people, and for rabbis, who are generally expected to give advice, even more so. Despite this expectation, even when a rabbi gives the most sensible and reasonable advice, he is likely to find that his wisdom is ignored, resisted, or rejected. He might suggest that a congregant take more time to listen to his children, spend an evening out with his spouse, or eat dinner with his/her family, only to hear that, "It won't work." He will be told that the other person won't go along with what is being suggested, that it was already tried and didn't work, or that it is too late for such measures. The congregant dismisses his suggestions as illogical, unworkable, or undesirable.

Rejection and resistance to a rabbi's most sage advice can render him helpless and frustrated. After all, the advice was so clear, logical, and useful, he might think. Therefore, he needs to understand that advice coming from an authority figure like a rabbi is often not easily accepted, simply because it is coming from an outside source and has not yet been internalized. Advice is simply not effective where an issue has not been clearly processed. This is what is achieved in counseling sessions, where issues can be explored in an atmosphere of empathy and understanding.

Advice has one other drawback for the congregational rabbi. It makes him culpable if things do not work out right. "Go back to your husband and tell him that he needs to do something about his temper," for example, could backfire into a nasty case of domestic violence. This is why it is better for both the congregant and the rabbi to explore a problem together, as well as its possible solutions. When a congregant "owns" the solution, there is at least a possibility for positive change.

As a final word, it is important for every rabbi to keep in

mind that individuals generally have hidden resources and strengths that are not visible at first. A person may come in for help, appearing weak, distraught, and overwhelmed. Once you engage him, however, in the counseling process, you are likely to discover strengths and capabilities that were not at first apparent. People are often stronger, more competent, and resilient than even they themselves know. Help them discover their strong points and you will have fulfilled your function well.

∾ 3 ∾
MENTAL HEALTH AND MENTAL ILLNESS

Yisrael N. Levitz, Ph.D.

COMMUNITY RABBIS ARE not expected to be clinical diagnosticians capable of assessing mental illness. Yet knowledge concerning mental health and mental illness is often a crucial factor in determining the direction a counseling situation needs to take, which referral needs to be made, or the cause of an otherwise incomprehensible behavior. A basic knowledge of mental health and illness can also help the practicing rabbi better understand the many individuals in his congregation who make up the tapestry of synagogue life.

An exact definition of mental health is elusive. It differs according to the school of thought that any given professional advocates. There are, in fact, a myriad of psychological theories and models, each with its own diagnostic approaches and clinical perspectives concerning what constitutes mental health. However, it is less important for a rabbi to settle upon one definition of mental health than it is for him to understand its ramifications from a broad, cross-theoretical perspective.

There is a particularly useful approach to understanding mental health, known as the Tripartite model, first proposed by H. Strupp and S. Hadley (1977).[1] Strupp and Hadley suggest that in order to answer the question, "What is mental health?" we must first determine who is asking the question. There are, they point out, three distinct perspectives on what mental health is. They are: the perspective of society, that of each individual, and that of professionals. Each entity views mental health from a different vantage point. Each has its own definition and criteria for what is normal and what is not, and each measures mental health with its own yardstick.

Society, for example, is primarily concerned with maintaining its social norms so that it can function with a reasonable degree of predictability and orderliness on the part of its members. Without its ability to predict and control the behavior of its members, a society is unable to function as a communal entity. As a member of society, I need to be able to reasonably predict how my fellow members will behave in different situations. If I greet someone by extending my hand, I expect that he will extend his, in what we call a "handshake." If the response to my extended hand is a scream or a howl, I will think this person bizarre or mentally ill — assuming there are no other explanations for his response. Behaving in a manner outside the framework of prescribed norms is "deviant". The more outside the bounds of normative behavior, the more bizarre the behavior will be considered and the more likely it is to be labeled mental illness.

From the perspective of the individual, what is important with regard to mental health is a personal sense of contentment and well-being. Mental health is based on each individual's sense of how well he or she functions and on his or her level of life-satisfaction. If I feel sad and depressed for no apparent

---

1. Strupp, H., and S. Hadley, "A Tripartite Model of Mental Health and Therapeutic Outcomes," *American Psychologist*, 1977, 32(3), 187–196.

reason, anxious, panic stricken, overwhelmed, or obsessed with unwanted thoughts, I might seek help because my satisfaction with life is severely diminished. If I fear riding an elevator, walking along the street, flying in an airplane, or eating in a restaurant, then I might seek help because my functioning is impaired. From the perspective of the individual, mental illness is not defined by society, but by one's own sense of efficacy and well-being.

Finally, mental health professionals view mental health from their perspective of theoretical models and psychological constructs. Since there are many models, there are many perspectives. There are medical models, psychoanalytic models, learning theory models, existential models, systems models, and several hundred forms of psychotherapy. There are even rabbinic models. Rabbis, no less than other professionals, have principles and standards of behavior that guide their judgment of the normal and the deviant. For the Reform rabbi whose young congregant chooses to join a Chasidic sect, his behavior may be as deviant as the behavior of an Orthodox rabbi's young congregant who decides to smoke on Shabbat.

What mental health is, then, depends on who is asking the question. The Tripartite model enables us to understand mental health through different lenses. Of course, there are times when all perspectives are in agreement. In a case where an individual is distressed because he is hallucinating and sees flying elephants, a diagnosis of mental illness will be self-evident from all perspectives. The individual will find flying elephants quite disturbing. Society will conclude that seeing flying elephants is outside the norm, and professionals will say that this person is suffering from psychotic episodes.

However, there are also times when society or one's community feels one way about an individual's mental health while the individual or professional feels differently. Thus, an individual may adjust perfectly well to society's requirements, yet feel distressed and unhappy. There are also times when both society and the individual may not perceive anything dysfunctional, while the mental health professional will.

> Several years ago, while traveling, I joined a minyan for *Shacharit* services in a synagogue I had never been to before. A man, who appeared to be the synagogue sexton (*shamash*), approached me after services and began to talk about the *yetzer ha-ra* — the evil inclination. He warned me about its insidious strategies to ensnare people who were not vigilant. I was impressed with his level of piety until he told me how he had chased his *yetzer ha-ra* with an umbrella that morning after it had popped out from behind a lamppost.
>
> As a psychologist, I quickly diagnosed the man as a paranoid schizophrenic with visual and auditory hallucinations. As I was about to leave the synagogue, however, several congregants, having seen me speak with him, commented on how fortunate they were to have him around. He was always in shul, watching over things (and undoubtedly on guard against his *yetzer ha-ra*), and if not for him, the shul would not be able to function. So he was a valuable member of his society, and aside from the occasional appearance of his *yetzer ha-ra*, he may not have been an unhappy man. It seems that the only one who thought that the man was dysfunctional was me — the psychologist.

The three perspectives on mental health can help a rabbi understand many a mental health dynamic. In the case of a young man, for example, who has become a *ba'al teshuvah* (one who returns to his religious roots), his family and his society of friends might think he has "lost his mind." The rabbi might think he is perfectly normal and mentally healthy because he has chosen to grow personally and spiritually. And the young man, because of the changes he has made, is feeling happier because his life has taken on more meaning.

In the case of an individual who is in the middle of a frenzied, manic episode, he may report never having felt better. For the rabbi, however, and the rest of society, this person will appear out of control and mentally disturbed.

There will be times when a sensitive rabbi may detect a mental health problem that others do not. Then the rabbi will have to decide whether he should intervene or not. It is always important however, in the field of mental health, to clarify where the problem lies: with society, with the individual, or with the professional.

CLINICAL DIAGNOSIS FOR THE COUNSELING RABBI

There are several categories of mental disorders that are so common that they are likely, at some point, to present themselves to the rabbi. These categorizations are drawn from the American Psychiatric Association's *Diagnostic and Statistical Manual of Mental Disorders*,[2] which is considered the major sourcebook for making diagnostic decisions in the mental health community around the world. These categories are obviously defined according to the professional perspective of mental health.

In their pastoral role, rabbis, no less than other mental health professionals, need to be familiar with these categories of mental disorders. In the following chapter, we discuss a select group of mental disorders and highlight how they might manifest themselves in either the counseling situation or congregational life.

---

2. *Diagnostic and Statistical Manual of Mental Disorders (Fourth Edition)*, American Psychiatric Association, Washington, D.C., 1994.

Understanding Mental Disorders: Guidelines for the Rabbi

Rael Strous, M.D.

RABBIS PLAY A CRITICAL role in the life of their community, beyond their function as spiritual leaders. Thus a rabbi may be called upon to intervene in a broad range of psychological issues, including those related to mental illness and family instability. It is, therefore, necessary for every practicing rabbi to be aware of some of the more common categories of mental illness, so that he can deal with them appropriately.

The rabbi is not expected to clinically manage a psychiatric condition. He may, however, be called upon to get involved. This may entail reassuring, encouraging, and emotionally supporting the family, and if necessary, referring a congregant to a professional mental health caregiver for further management. The rabbi's role in helping the individual or family suffering from the effects of mental illness can be crucial and should not be underestimated. However, without a basic knowledge of mental disorders the rabbi might feel very overwhelmed and helpless, despite a sincere desire to help. The objective of this chapter is to provide the basics a rabbi needs to know in order to recognize the signs and symptoms of the more common mental disorders, to outline how he can be most helpful, and suggest how he can conduct an informed discussion with another mental health professional.

ANXIETY DISORDERS: WHAT ARE THEY?

Anxiety alone is not a disorder. If it is not excessive, it can be very useful in motivating us to accomplish what we are reluctant to do. If there is too little anxiety in any given situation, motivation tends to be low. A moderate amount of anxiety can make us more productive. When anxiety is excessive and irrational, however, it can be quite debilitating. An individual who suffers from severe anxiety may, for example, be unable to come to the synagogue. A person may tell the rabbi that he cannot lead the services on a *yahrzeit* or accept an *aliyah* because it makes him anxious. Parents may ask for help for their son who is dreading his bar mitzvah because he is overly fearful of reading the *haftarah* or delivering an address. A bridegroom might say that he cannot walk down the aisle to the *chuppah* because he feels anxious or claustrophobic from all the people watching.

This category of mental disorder includes conditions where excessive anxiety is experienced or where repetitious actions are employed in the attempt to neutralize anxiety. An example would be when a person with an obsessive fear of coming into contact with germs spends an inordinate amount of time washing his hands. He might do anything to avoid touching doorknobs or shaking hands with people. Or a person might turn the lights on and off a certain number of times when entering a dark room as her way of reducing her anxiety.

Panic Attacks

A rabbi might see a worshipper who always sits near the door, paces the aisles, or frequently walks in and out of the synagogue. He might be doing this because it helps him avoid feeling "closed in" or experiencing an anxiety attack.

A person with a Panic Disorder can suddenly be overcome with feelings of intense apprehension, fearfulness, or terror, often associated with feelings of impending doom. During these attacks, the person can also experience shortness of breath, palpitations, chest pain, a choking or smothering sensation, and fear of "going crazy" or losing control. For example, a person shopping in the supermarket who has a panic attack may leave her loaded shopping cart in the aisle and run from the store.

A panic attack usually lasts approximately ten or fifteen minutes, however the episode is so intense that the fear and anticipation of its reoccurrence ("anticipatory anxiety") is often as disabling and intense as the episode itself. A panic attack frequently deludes the sufferer into believing that he is having a heart attack, resulting in many false-call visits to the emergency room.

Phobias

A repeated, irrational anxiety response to the same specific conditions or situation is called a "phobia". People with a phobia avoid that which causes their anxiety. For example, a person with claustrophobia may avoid going to an office on the 11th floor of a building because he cannot tolerate being closed inside an elevator.

Although the person realizes that his response is unreasonable and excessive, he believes that he has no control over this response, and so he avoids the stimulus. This "avoidance behavior" may significantly impair the person's social and occupational performance.

With "claustrophobia", a fear of closed-in places where the individual feels he has no control or options, a congregant will avoid sitting in a middle pew where he might feel trapped and unable to leave. He might want to be an usher or a *gabbai* so that he can move around freely. He might also avoid crowded social functions.

"Agoraphobia" is the fear of open spaces. Most commonly, a person who suffers from this is afraid to leave her home. The sufferer tends to have an irrational fear that she will be stuck in a stressful situation away from the safety of home and faint or collapse with no one around her to help.

"Acrophobia" is a fear of high places. If your synagogue is on top of a hill, with windows or a balcony that overlooks a valley, an acrophobic will avoid coming. People can also suffer from phobias of animals, insects, water, flying, and storms.

Social Phobia

A person might feel severe anxiety when asked to engage in some type of performance, such as speaking before a group or leading services. He may not be able to accept an *aliyah* in synagogue, for fear that others are watching him and he might collapse.

Obsessive-Compulsive Disorder (OCD)

One who suffers from an Obsessive-Compulsive Disorder is repeatedly haunted by annoying or objectionable thoughts, which he is unable to dispel ("obsessions"), or feels compelled to perform certain acts or rituals to avoid anxiety ("compulsions"). Often, these take over the person even though he realizes they are illogical. Obsessions and compulsions are often linked, so that a person who has obsessive thoughts that he is germ ridden may repeatedly wash his hands until they bleed, or stand in the shower or *mikveh* for hours. An obsessive thought or any attempt to resist the compulsive act that the person believes will drive away that thought may cause severe anxiety.

A rabbi may be consulted about a case involving Obsessive Compulsive Disorder because it often manifests itself in abnormal religious practice. A young man may repeat a prayer over and over again for fear that he might not have said it with the proper concentration (*kavanah*). It may take him an excessive amount of time to finish his prayers, particularly the *Shemoneh Esrei*, because he continually worries that he may have skipped a word, and so he ends up repeating the prayers over and over. A housewife may be convinced that she contaminated all of her meat dishes because she touched one without washing her hands after having touched a dairy product. Even though the Halachah may not have placed such a restriction on her, she will still find it difficult to accept even the most authoritative rabbinic ruling. One woman threw out three sets of dishes in spite of her rabbi's ruling that her dishes were halachically fine. For this reason, OCD is also called "the doubting disease," because the person who suffers from it cannot accept reassurance that he has done something correctly. He is chronically plagued with self-doubt.

OCD can be particularly troublesome when it affects a woman going to *mikveh*. *Mikveh* supervisors have reported that some women spend eight hours doing their preparations. A woman tormented by self-doubt as to whether she did everything correctly may resist marital relations, feel plagued by guilt, or persistently ask the same halachic question and need to be consistently reassured each month.

A rabbi may find himself being repeatedly consulted about issues that clearly show the person's feelings of self-doubt and guilt. But unless this person receives proper psychiatric treatment, the problem will not go away in spite of the rabbi's best efforts.

Post-Traumatic Stress Disorder (PTSD)

Following the 9/11 World Trade Center terror attack, many individuals who were in the vicinity of the attack or who watched it on television suffered from a range of recurrent anxiety and depressive symptoms. This cluster of symptoms are typical of Post-Traumatic Stress Disorder (PTSD). PTSD is a condition in which a person may experience recurrent anxiety or a variety of psychological and/or physical symptoms as a result of having suffered or witnessed a traumatic event, such as a physical attack, sexual assault, accident, fire, or life-threatening illness. Common symptoms of this condition include the persistent re-experiencing of the event, persistent avoidance of stimuli associated with the event, and increased arousal, hypervigilance, and feelings of being "on edge." PTSD symptoms may begin soon after the trauma or even years later.

Generalized Anxiety Disorder

With this condition, a person experiences persistent, but excessive "low-grade" anxiety, rather than the intensity of a panic attack. The individual finds it difficult to control the anxiety and it may interfere with his daily functioning. It is generally characterized by inordinate worry, disturbed sleep, easy fatigue, irritability, muscle tension, and difficulty in concentrating.

How Can a Rabbi Help?

It is not the rabbi's role to treat anxiety disorders. The rabbi can, of course, be reassuring. He can reassure the person that he is not "going crazy", and that anxiety disorders generally respond well to treatment. It is unwise for the rabbi to probe for the causes of the anxiety. Instead, he should encourage the person to avail himself of professional help. Today, both psychotherapy and medication are safe and generally effective treatment options.

If a person with a social phobia is reluctant to lead services or have an *aliyah*, the rabbi should not pressure him or allow others to do so. "Desensitization", the treatment for such a phobia, is best left to the professionals, preferably behavior therapists. However, the rabbi could play an important role in being empathic to the suffering of his congregant, assuring him that he will not be embarrassed or coerced into getting an *aliyah*. The rabbi, of course, needs to follow up by asking the *gabbai* not to call the congregant up to the Torah, simply by saying, "Mr. Schwartz would rather not have an *aliyah* and I think we need to honor his wish." It could be a serious breach of confidentiality to actually tell the *gabbai* that Mr. Schwartz has a phobia.

If the congregant is reassured in this way, the social phobic can feel more comfortable coming to the synagogue without the fear of being humiliated. The rabbi can be helpful in encouraging the congregant, in a sensitive way, to seek professional help. He should have the name of a competent behavior therapist on hand, in order to facilitate the congregant in getting that help.

Inasmuch as OCD often manifests itself in symptoms of a religious nature, the rabbi's role can be very important. Obsessive thoughts are not the same as *machshavot zarot* (alien thoughts) that the *mussar* works discuss. For example, during prayer, a person might find himself distracted by sundry thoughts. These are not considered to be obsessions, but are more akin to the *machshavot zarot*, or alien thoughts. An obsessive thought is usually of an unpleasant nature and is recurrent. Attempts to free oneself from the obsessive thought are invariably futile and may even increase its force.

A person is not responsible for an obsessive thought any more than he is responsible for anxiety. Telling him to concentrate more when he prays or to try not to think about it places the responsibility for the OCD on the sufferer and is counterproductive. OCD does not respond to reason. The person knows that the obsessions or compulsions are irrational, but cannot free himself of them. Similarly, reassuring the person does not relieve his self-doubting or indecision. The rabbi should encourage the person to seek professional help, which often employs medication, a specialized course of psychotherapy, or most commonly both.

MOOD DISORDERS

Mood disorders are an entirely different category of mental dysfunctions that includes emotional states that fluctuate from stable to depressed to elation and euphoria. What follows is a description of some of the most common types of mood disorders.

Major Depressive Disorder

This condition is characterized by a depressed mood or loss of interest or pleasure in nearly all activities. Accompanying the depressed mood there may be feelings of guilt or worthlessness, sleep disturbance (usually middle-of-the night awakening and inability to return to sleep), psychomotor retardation (sluggish movement), changes in appetite, decreased sex drive, unprovoked crying, impaired concentration, inability to make decisions, and death wishes or suicidal thoughts. Depression is usually extremely uncomfortable and often accompanied by marked functional impairment.

A person with any degree of depression may turn to a

rabbi for help. In cases of severe depression, the person may not even have the energy to ask for help or may feel so hopeless as to believe that there is no point in even asking. It is not unusual for a family member or friend to present the problem to the rabbi. Alternatively, the rabbi himself may detect a change in the person. Without any cause to warrant grief, the person may appear sad. There may be unintentional weight loss. A previously socially active person may become withdrawn, or a regular attendee at services or congregational activities may sharply limit his participation. A person may appear to be preoccupied with death and may ask the rabbi about the religious consequences of suicide. Or, he may become preoccupied with philosophical questions such as "What is the meaning of life."

Depression may also be masked by substance abuse, sexual promiscuity, and gambling. The sensitive rabbi should be aware that this individual's behavior, despite being dysfunctional and a way of "acting out," may also be a cry for help from a desperate human being suffering from depression.

Many people suffer from a minor form of depression characterized by prolonged sadness, but without most of the symptoms or intensity of Major Depressive Disorder. This is known as "Dysthymic Disorder". In this case, the rabbi might notice that his congregant is simply a bit down for periods of time.

Bipolar Disorder

Once referred to as "manic-depressive disorder", this is a condition where the individual's mood fluctuates dramatically between depressive and manic episodes. While depressive episodes were discussed in the previous section, in a manic episode, the individual will manifest symptoms of grandiosity, hyperactivity, decreased need for sleep, accelerated speech, flight of ideas, psychomotor agitation (jumpiness), irritability, and distractability. He will probably also show a marked impairment in social and occupational functioning, may spend money in a grossly reckless fashion, and lose his normal inhibitions.

A manic person often makes bizarre judgments and decisions. For example, one manic patient bought several cars in one day. Another made repeated and foolish long-distance calls, including calls to the White House. Another picked up a strange woman, wrote a letter disowning his wife and children, and left all his assets to the woman. A respectable scholar alighted the stage at a convention, singing and dancing totally inappropriately. Manic episodes and depressive episodes occurring in the same person at different times accounts for the term "bipolar".

In a manic episode, the family is likely to ask the rabbi to help restrain the person who is acting hyperactive. The manic never thinks he needs help, because he feels "on top of the world." He may approach the rabbi with plans for unrealistic projects. A person who has generally made modest donations may uncharacteristically and with sudden generosity give the rabbi a large sum of money. He may tell the rabbi that he has made a decision to sell his business, sell his home, move to another city, or divorce his wife. All such decisions may, of course, be appropriate when well thought out. In the manic, they are abrupt and clearly impulsive.

There is also a mild form of bipolar disorder known as "Cyclothymic Disorder". It is characterized by elevated mood changes that are of lesser intensity than a manic episode. These less elevated mood tends to alternate with a lesser depressed mood (Dysthmia — as described earlier). It is, overall, a much less dramatic degree of mood fluctuation.

What Can a Rabbi Do to Be Helpful?

Not uncommonly, family members will tell a depressed person, "All your blood tests are normal. There is nothing wrong with you. You just have to pull yourself together." This is equivalent to telling a drowning person to just pull himself together. This could aggravate the depression by suggesting that the person is lazy or derelict. The rabbi should help the individual and family understand that the depression is a bona fide medical problem that needs professional help.

In the case of what the rabbi feels may be a "masked depression", the rabbi should encourage the individual to speak about his concerns and underlying feelings. Most importantly, if at any time the rabbi believes he may be dealing with a more severe form of underlying depression, he should encourage the person to go to a mental health professional for further evaluation.

In a manic episode, the person may, at least temporarily, respond to the rabbi by restraining himself. But usually tendency to hyperactivity overcomes him. In such cases, the rabbi should help the family take the necessary steps to prevent the person from being destructive to himself and/or the family. This may involve supporting the family in arranging involuntary hospitalization. The family may be very reluctant to do so. If the attendant mental health professional recommends this, the rabbi can be helpful by encouraging the family to overcome their reluctance.

Perhaps the most important help that a rabbi can give to the individual in times of crisis is to tell him how "the wheel always turns." This may be an isolated "turn" or it may be a transition to lesser depressive or manic states following the intervention of medication and/or psychotherapy. This latter choice is a management decision that should be made by a competent mental health caregiver (usually a psychiatrist).

PSYCHOTIC DISORDERS

What Are Psychotic Disorders?

The category of psychotic disorders includes conditions where there is a significant impairment of mental functioning, particularly the ability to distinguish reality from fantasy. There is generally a major disturbance in thought and behavior that usually results in serious impairment of social and occupational functioning. Psychosis is often characterized by social withdrawal. It may occur in all age groups and may be either short-lived or long-term.

Psychotic disorders may appear in a number of forms, some more common than others. Several common psychotic disorders are discussed below.

Schizophrenia

A rabbi in a yeshiva environment may be called upon to deal with a student who reports that he is hearing voices telling him that he is evil and deserves to die. In addition, the student may inform the rabbi that he feels unsafe and that others in the yeshiva are talking about him. He says that they can read his mind and control his thoughts. He also thinks that the radio is talking about him. With such a constellation of symptoms for a significant period of time, the student may be suffering from schizophrenia.

Schizophrenia is arguably the most serious of all mental disorders. It is fairly common (one in a hundred individuals) and is usually characterized by delusions (having a false belief that is inconsistent with the individual's intelligence and culture, that cannot be corrected by reasoning) and/or hallucinations (having false perceptions based on one of the five senses, often sound in the form of voices). For example, these impaired thoughts are often expressed in the form of irrational fears (paranoia) that people want to hurt or harm him. In addition, it often includes disorganized behavior (e.g., acting irritable or withdrawn) and disordered (e.g., confused, incoherent) speech.

In addition to more active and agitated behavior, one particularly difficult aspect of the disorder includes a lack of motivation, a feeling of emptiness, an inability to feel any enjoyment, and a desire to withdraw from all social activities (these are called "negative symptoms"). While this latter behavior is unrelated to feelings of depression, individuals with schizophrenia often get depressed. In fact, a significant number of individuals with this condition may attempt to hurt themselves, both when in a state of psychotic disorganization as well as when simply depressed.

Individuals with schizophrenia unfortunately tend to deteriorate in their functioning over time. They seldom achieve the level of functioning that was present prior to the onset of the illness. It is important to note that while the severe elements of the illness usually present themselves for the first time during the late teens or early twenties (often a bit later in females), symptoms such as social withdrawal may be noticed by family members and friends long before the initial onset of the illness.

A rabbi may be consulted by the family of an individual who is psychotic and experiencing delusions of a religious nature. He might be asked by the afflicted individual about a particular delusional religious belief. He might also be asked by the individual for help in implementing a religious delusion, e.g., "Rabbi, please help me announce to the world that I am the Messiah."

Since psychotic disorders, in particular schizophrenia, tend to emerge for the first time at an age when individuals are still in school, someone's disordered thoughts or behaviors are often first noted by the rabbinic educator. Rabbis then must decide how to inform and involve the family. They also might have to decide whether or not to keep the student in the school and how firmly to encourage or even insist on treatment. These are difficult decisions, often problematic for both administrators as well as teaching staff.

Delusional Disorder

Individuals with a Delusional Disorder hold steadfastly to one false belief or a set of false beliefs that cannot be dispelled by logical reasoning. Though these beliefs are false, they are not necessarily bizarre in nature — they sometimes do occur in real life (being followed, poisoned, cheated on, sick in some manner, or having a significant body defect etc.). Usually, no hallucinations are present and the individual's functioning and behavior are not very impaired. Individuals with this disorder may approach the rabbi and appear completely normal aside from a single "false belief" (delusion) which the rabbi will struggle to set right using logical arguments — with no success. These individuals require psychiatric help.

Substance-Induced Psychotic Disorder

A Substance-Induced Psychotic Disorder is a pathology comprised of delusions and hallucinations, usually resulting from the use of a drug (e.g., amphetamines, cocaine, LSD, phencyclidine etc). Interestingly, in rare situations this condition may even result from the use of prescribed medication, when used incorrectly, or even as a rare, unexpected adverse reaction. The individual with this condition usually experiences a full recovery once the drug wears off. The rabbi can recognize this disorder from the sudden onset of bizarre behavior shortly after using drugs or taking a medication.

Brief Psychotic Disorder

With a pathology known as Brief Psychotic Disorder, there is a fairly sudden onset of psychotic thought and behavior (delusions, hallucinations, disorganized speech and behavior), which lasts at least a day but less than a month. It can develop in response to a severely stressful event (such as a sudden traumatic death in the family) and then disappear once the stress is dealt with or alleviated. The vast majority of individuals who experience this sudden disturbance in functioning go on to lead perfectly normal lives with no further reoccurrences of this disorder.

What Can a Rabbi Do to Be Helpful?

A rabbi may be consulted about whether or not to seek psychiatric help for a family member suffering from psychosis. There is great discomfort and stigma associated with needing help and more for committing a relative to a psychiatric facility. Rabbis should learn what competent psychiatric help is available in their community, as well as the level of care provided at the mental hospitals in their area. When knowledgeable and informed, the rabbi can be of significant help to families in need of this kind of information. If he believes that his congregant can receive a high level of professional care from a particular psychiatrist, he can confidently make the referral and assuage some of the family's concerns.

When an individual suffering from psychosis comes to the rabbi for help, it is important that he make him feel supported and understood. Experiencing psychosis is very isolating. The person feels surrounded by people who negate what he is thinking and seeing, while his delusions and hallucinations are as real to him as this book is to you. Therefore, attempting to talk him out of his reality will be counterproductive and may result in a loss of rapport which is so vital in the process of accepting help. Once rapport is achieved, it is advisable to explain to the sufferer that while you completely believe that what he is experiencing is real and meaningful to him, you do not experience things in that manner, but you are available to help him.

If an individual is in a state of acute psychosis, it is important to initiate medical treatment as soon as possible. The longer the duration of the untreated psychosis, the longer it takes for the individual to recover. Rabbis can often be very helpful in encouraging the individual to take medication and comply with psychiatric treatment.

Rabbis can also be helpful to families with a psychotic member by being empathetic to their plight. They, too, are likely to be suffering. They are often upset, frightened about an uncertain future, and angry. Their family member is probably lying around and not functioning. The rabbi needs to ask the family members how this person's illness is affecting their lives. They need a place to vent and express the many feelings they are harboring.

Family members tend to feel frustrated, angry, and critical. They see the person uninterested in helping himself; meanwhile the flow of family life is severely disrupted. So they criticize the person, trying to get him moving. But often, criticism can trigger a relapse. The rabbi needs to be sympathetic to the family's frustration and pain, yet nevertheless help them understand that their criticism only makes things worse.

It would also be helpful if the rabbi could explore ways in which family members could move on and find some gratifying life experiences beyond their mentally ill parent, child, or relative. There are times when such a family needs to hear that it is permissible to enjoy things again and rejoin the community.

In the case of the agitated, manic, or severely depressed patient, the rabbi may be required to help the family take the necessary steps to prevent the person from being destructive to himself and/or the family. This may involve helping the family arrange involuntary hospitalization. If their mental health professional recommends this, the rabbi can be helpful in overcoming the patient's and family's resistance.

One should be on the lookout for signs of depression or suicidal behavior/thoughts in the schizophrenic. Approximately 50% of schizophrenics attempt suicide and 10% succeed. All thoughts or expressions of such nature should be taken seriously and the individual referred for psychiatric evaluation/management.

PERSONALITY DISORDERS

A personality disorder refers to an impairment at some level of the personality structure, which in turn leads to social and/or occupational dysfunction. Mental health professionals define it as an inflexible, maladaptive, longstanding dysfunction of inner experience and behavior (often extending from childhood), which markedly deviates from socially acceptable standards. This pattern of behavior almost inevitably leads to clinically significant distress in the individual, and perhaps even more importantly, distress in those close to the individual. In fact, most often those close to the individual encourage or coerce him to seek help, because people with personality disorders do not generally recognize that they have a problem. They believe that most of their problems are caused by others.

What follows is a description of several of the most prominent personality disorders.

- **Paranoid personality disorder**. This is typified by a pervasive distrust and suspiciousness of others. A rabbi might be accused by a congregant of plotting against him. Individuals with this disorder constantly feel that they are being exploited and deceived by others. They bear grudges, read hidden meanings into benign comments, hold onto long-standing feelings of resentment, and feel cheated and betrayed both in their personal as well as business relationships. Such a personality disorder can be devastating to family life, but no less problematic in synagogue life as well.

- **Schizoid personality disorder**. These individuals detach themselves from social interaction and neither enjoy nor desire close relationships. They are indifferent to praise from others, show emotional coldness, and lack close friends. In general, they tend to be loners. A rabbi might be asked to reach out to a member of a congregant's family and interest him in coming to the synagogue or to find him a mate. Knowing the diagnosis can be helpful to a rabbi. These individuals are often resistant to professional help, but might form a superficial relationship with a rabbi. Despite the challenge of reaching out and the poor prognosis, the rabbi can nevertheless attempt to prompt the individual or the family of a schizoid personality to seek help.

- **Schizotypal personality**. These individuals behave strangely and have bizarre beliefs, which do not quite reach a psychotic level of unreality, where one is totally out of touch. Schizotypal personalities are extremely eccentric and may inundate a rabbi with bizarre questions of a metaphysical nature, such as, "If all of God's creatures give Him praise then what kind of praise do clouds give?" or "Do angels ever die?" In addition, a rabbi might be called upon to deal with a situation where a schizotypal is engaged in some bizarre form of religious ritual. In those instances, a rabbi needs to know that he is dealing with a disordered personality. Though the rabbi might have some degree of success in influencing the individual from time to time, the long-term prognosis for change is poor.

► **Antisocial personality**. These individuals engage in repeated behavior exhibiting exploitation, harm, and disregard of others. Rabbis are likely targets for such exploitation. An individual with antisocial personality traits might try to involve the rabbi in a scheme, promising that the synagogue will profit from it. The rabbi needs to know about this type of personality, so that he won't be taken advantage of, exploited, or even tricked into an illegal or unethical situation. Exploitation is often subtle and covert. Individuals with this type of personality disorder lack empathy and remorse, and tend to be aggressive and irritable. They also have problems with authority. Because the rabbi is an authority figure, he is a likely target for this individual's aggression. It is certainly in the rabbi's best interest not to have such an individual as a member of his board.

► **Borderline personality**. These individuals exhibit a pattern of instability in social relationships, self-image, and identity. They are often impulsive and commonly have thoughts of harming themselves. They are also subject to feelings of abandonment and harbor chronic feelings of emptiness. An individual with a borderline personality may come to the attention of a rabbi in the course of managing relationship conflicts, divorce etc. The rabbi should be aware that a person with this disorder can be seductive and act in a sexually provocative manner, or interest him as a particularly "engaging and exciting" member of his community. He may even feel the need or desire to "save" and "rescue" the individual from a difficult situation. He needs to be aware, however, that one of the most common traits of an individual with a borderline personality is that he/she quickly idealizes a leadership figure — such as the rabbi — and just as quickly devaluates him. Many a rabbi has been seduced, baffled, and then hurt by this pattern of vacillation between idealization and devaluation, which can take place in the blink of an eye.

► **Histrionic personality.** These individuals have a tendency to exaggerate and express their feelings in an overly dramatic way. They have a constant need for attention. Histrionic people tend to dress provocatively and, if a woman, she might wear excessive makeup. These types frequently have "urgent" questions for the rabbi, demanding a great deal of time and attention — often as a result of their underlying insecurities.

► **Narcissistic personality.** A person with a narcissistic personality exhibits feelings of grandiosity, while at the same time needs excessive admiration from others. These individuals demonstrate a grandiose sense of self-importance along with a sense of entitlement. This can be especially problematic in synagogue life. Rabbis may have great difficulty in dealing with such individuals, because they believe that everything should be done to satisfy their needs — since they are more important than anyone else. At the core, these individuals are very fragile, hurt easily, and if things do not go their way, they become very upset. The narcissistic personality can be very challenging for both the rabbi as well as other members of the congregation.

▸ **Dependent personality**. This is an individual who needs to be cared for and nurtured by others. A rabbi may find such individuals to be very needy from the emotional perspective. He should be aware that if this individual suffers the loss of a relationship — either through death or rejection — it could engender a severe crisis well beyond what one would normally expect.

Individuals with personality disorders present a special challenge for rabbis. Not only are they vulnerable, but in a sense they can engender vulnerability in the rabbi as well. Many a rabbi has been hurt by individuals with disordered personalities. Nevertheless, it is the rabbi's responsibility as shepherd of the flock to engage each individual in a respectful and supportive manner. He must, however, be constantly aware of the impact his behavior will have when dealing with individuals who manifest such intense behavior patterns.

It is particularly critical for him to maintain limits and boundaries. Given the often profound psychological needs of disordered personalities, he could find himself feeling overwhelmed trying to meet those needs. This includes feeling drained, agitated, or manipulated by the congregant, leading to feelings of resentment and a desire to reject him. The rabbi therefore needs to be especially vigilant about maintaining his and his family's boundaries, both regarding space and time. Personality disordered individuals are indeed a challenge for any rabbi, but with a sense of awareness of how fragile most disordered personalities are, he can learn to be both compassionate and self-protective at the same time.

COUNSELING CONGREGANTS IN CRISIS

David Pelcovitz, Ph.D.

IN RECENT YEARS, THE mental health field has become increasingly sensitized to the profound impact traumatic events can have on an individual's life. Rabbis are often viewed as pivotal sources of emotional and spiritual comfort at a time when victims are often paralyzed by confusion and grief. Trauma is likely when a person faces life and death danger or serious physical injury. To prepare themselves to effectively shoulder such a major responsibility, rabbis need to learn more about the spectrum of "normal" and pathological post-traumatic reactions, the most effective short- and long-term interventions, and how to identify those who require referrals for more extensive counseling.

When working with families undergoing even the most traumatic events, it is important to keep in mind that the norm is resilience. Over time, even those who seem to disintegrate in the face of tragedy gradually return to their previous level of functioning. However, sometimes the recovery process does not go smoothly. The most common diagnosis that should be considered after a congregant experiences or witnesses a life-threatening event is post-traumatic stress disorder (PTSD). The symptoms, as described in the diagnostic manual used by mental health professionals (DSM-IV) and outlined below, must last for at least one month and significantly impair the person's functioning.

DSM-IV DIAGNOSTIC CRITERIA FOR
POST-TRAUMATIC STRESS DISORDER

A. The person has been exposed to a traumatic event in which both of the following were present:

1. The person experienced, witnessed, or was confronted with an event or events that involved actual or threatened death or serious injury, or a threat to the physical integrity of self or others.

2. The person's response involved intense fear, helplessness, or horror. Note: In children, this may be expressed instead by disorganized or agitated behavior.

B. The traumatic event is persistently reexperienced in one (or more) of the following ways:

1. Recurrent and intrusive distressing recollections of the event, including images, thoughts, or perceptions. Note: In young children, repetitive play may occur in which themes or aspects of the trauma are expressed.

2. Recurrent distressing dreams of the event. Note: In children, there may be frightening dreams without recognizable content.

3. Acting or feeling as if the traumatic event were recurring (includes a sense of reliving the experience, illusions, hallucinations, and dissociative flashback episodes, including those that occur upon awakening or when intoxicated). Note: In young children, trauma-specific reenactment may occur.

4. Intense psychological distress at exposure to internal or external cues that symbolize or resemble an aspect of the traumatic event

5. Physiological reactivity upon exposure to internal or external cues that symbolize or resemble an aspect of the traumatic event

C. Persistent avoidance of stimuli associated with the trauma and numbing of general responsiveness (not present before the trauma), as indicated by three (or more) of the following:

1. Efforts to avoid thoughts, feelings, or conversations associated with the trauma
2. Efforts to avoid activities, places, or people that arouse recollections of the trauma
3. Inability to recall an important aspect of the trauma
4. Markedly diminished interest or participation in significant activities
5. Feeling of detachment or estrangement from others
6. Restricted range of affect (e.g., unable to have loving feelings)
7. Sense of a foreshortened future (e.g., does not expect to have a career, marriage, children, or a normal life span)

D. Persistent symptoms of increased arousal (not present before the trauma), as indicated by two (or more) of the following:

1. Difficulty falling or staying asleep
2. Irritability or outbursts of anger
3. Difficulty concentrating
4. Hypervigilance
5. Exaggerated startle response

E. Duration of the disturbance (symptoms in criteria B, C, and D) is more than 1 month.

F. The disturbance causes clinically significant distress or impairment in social, occupational, or other important areas of functioning.

IDENTIFYING POSSIBLE LONG-TERM DIFFICULTIES

Neither absence of high degrees of distress nor intense levels of emotionalism in the immediate aftermath of a traumatic event are necessarily predictive of long-term difficulties. Rabbis should "red flag" the following characteristics that research has found can increase risk for long-term adjustment difficulties.

- ► **High anxiety level.** Fifteen percent of the population have anxious temperaments that make them particularly vulnerable to anything that jeopardizes their protective shield. They are at a far greater risk for developing PTSD.

- ► **Prior history of highly stressful life events**, including Holocaust or terrorist attack survivors and their families.

- ► **Concurrent life stresses**, such as financial hardship, marital or job difficulties, social isolation.

- ► **Unrelenting Distress.** Those who show either continuous distress — consistently turning their back on the support offered by family, friends, or community, or those who are unable to think about the trauma.

- ► **Dissociation.** Individuals who showed high levels of dissociation during the time of the traumatic event.

- ► If the traumatic event was characterized by a sudden life-threatening experience, or perceived to be one, or the survivor was exposed to grotesque images, or the act was deliberate.

COPING STYLES

Research on how patients deal with painful medical procedures or other stressful situations has found that coping styles are on a continuum from "attenders" to "distracters" — active information seekers to information avoiders. "Attenders" deal with stressful situations in an active manner. For example, if they are about to get an injection from their doctor, they want to understand why and they prefer to assist in preparing for the injection. In contrast, "distracters" prefer to distract themselves while getting the injection. They are not interested in why the shot is necessary — they prefer to look the other way while thinking about something else.

Research also shows that a person's ability to cope is compromised if you try to turn a distracter into an attender or vice versa. For example, if one tries to force the distracter to talk about his/her understanding of why the injection is necessary or if one tries to force the attender to think about something else while getting the injection, the patient's anxiety level will increase and he will cope much less successfully with the stress of the medical procedure.

It is important for rabbis to understand that, particularly in the early stages of responding to traumatic events, the type of coping mechanisms used are less predictive of long-term resilience than whether a particular style works for a particular person.

SUDDEN CRISES

Rabbis are called to help in crisis situations with little notice and no time for preparation. As a source of comfort, guidance, and spiritual solace, rabbis are often viewed as playing a crucial role in supporting congregants facing what is often the most trying period of their lives. A call in the middle of the night might inform the rabbi of a fatal car accident, a fire, or someone sustaining a serious injury.

A rabbi in America was called early one morning to come

to the home of the grandparents of a young woman who had just been killed in a suicide bombing in Israel. He felt particularly helpless because there was little he could do of a practical nature. The funeral had already taken place in Israel, and, to compound his sense of helplessness, he could think of no words of wisdom that might lessen the impact of the tragedy. The feedback that he received later from the family was that they were grateful for his visit. His being there and sharing in their sorrow helped them feel less alone. Also, the quiet sense of support and compassion that he lent to the family the morning they received the news made them feel they could deal with things.

STRATEGIES OF SHORT-TERM INTERVENTIONS

In the Immediate Aftermath of a Traumatic Incident

In the immediate aftermath of a traumatic event, there are a number of interventions that have been found to be helpful. Fifty internationally recognized experts on Post-Traumatic Stress Disorder were surveyed to reach a consensus regarding what they thought was most essential in helping an individual through the early stages of a crisis. They concluded that the following interventions are important:

➤ Providing information about acute stress reaction and PTSD

➤ Helping the survivor of the traumatic incident understand that it is normal to be upset

➤ Encouraging conversations among family and friends about the trauma and associated feelings

➤ Educating family members and friends about the importance of listening and being tolerant regarding the person's need to repeatedly retell her story about the event

➤ Relieving irrational guilt

➤ Referring the person to a peer support group or trauma counseling, if needed

Keeping the above general guidelines in mind, the following specific approaches should be considered by the rabbi when ministering to individuals in acute crisis.

Goals of Crisis Intervention

The rabbi should realize that in providing crisis intervention, the immediate goal is to help the congregant stabilize his cognitive and emotional processes. Now is not the time to provide psychotherapy or to help the congregant gain insight and perspective into the meaning behind the crisis. Rather, the rabbi needs to provide support while encouraging the use of effective coping techniques.

PSYCHOEDUCATION ABOUT THE PSYCHOLOGICAL IMPACT OF TRAUMA

The power of knowledge in helping individuals cope with stress has been illustrated by trauma specialists using the following example: Imagine two families who have a child with chicken pox. In the case of the first family, the child is their fourth and the parents have already experienced successfully nursing their older three children through this illness. In addition, their next door neighbor and best friend is a pediatrician. In the second case, the child is an only child and the parents have no idea what is wrong with him. Also, they live in a rural area where they have no access to medical care.

In the first example, the experience of helping their child through the illness, although unpleasant, is not likely to be a source of great stress or worry. The parents have been through this before and have easy access to expert advice on how to nurse their child back to health. In the second example, one can only imagine how intensely stressful the experience must be. They have no one to ask, "Will my child survive?", "Will his face be permanently disfigured?" Understandably, the parents are very anxious.

The difference between the first and second scenario is knowledge. Knowing how to treat the illness, as well as knowing that the prognosis for a complete recovery is excellent, make all the difference in how the same event will be handled. The rabbi can, therefore, offer an invaluable service by providing congregants with basic knowledge about the psychological impact of traumatic events, as well as the nature of recovery from even the most tragic incidents.

If congregants are told that days and weeks after a traumatic incident they may experience the following reactions, they will feel less anxious about them.

> ▶ **Physical.** The most common symptoms are: fatigue, headaches, nausea, teeth grinding, and dizziness.

> ▶ **Behavioral and emotional.** Intense feelings often emerge in the immediate aftermath of a traumatic incident. High levels of irritability, anxiety, and depression are common, as are rapid and sudden shifts in mood. Behavioral changes may include angry outbursts, withdrawal, change in appetite or sleep patterns, pacing the floor, and/or increased or decreased sexual desire. The rabbi should note that he may become the target of displaced anger — an unpleasant experience that he should do his best not to take personally.

> ▶ **Cognitive.** It is common for a person to blame himself or others for events that are clearly acts of God. Although a rabbi should offer reassurance, it typically takes time

before the survivor of a traumatic event can accept and absorb that the event was not his fault. Other short-term changes in the cognitive realm may include difficulty concentrating, memory loss, and difficulty thinking clearly and making decisions. The rabbi is probably thinking more clearly than anybody else who was at the scene of a traumatic event. He may, therefore, need to take an active role in assisting the family to make rational decisions.

UNDERSTANDING TRAUMA

In the weeks following a traumatic event, if the rabbi notices that the symptoms of post-traumatic stress disorder are emerging, he can give his congregants a sense of increased control and normalcy by briefly explaining to them the source of these symptoms. The following explanations have been used by R. Bryant in his psychoeducation of individuals who have experienced trauma.

Reexperiencing the trauma. After surviving a trauma, one learns that his surroundings can be harmful; this can lead to a tendency to be on the lookout for other things that might be dangerous. It is therefore common to have upsetting memories and dreams. Intrusive thoughts, in the form of flashbacks or dreams, can pop into awareness involuntarily. By playing memories and images of the traumatic incident over repeatedly, the mind is able to process and resolve the trauma.

Avoidance. Avoiding any reminders of the trauma is common because thinking about such an upsetting incident is so distressing. Although doing this makes the person feel better for the moment, ultimately this can prevent the person from getting over the experience.

Another way people try to avoid the distress associated with the trauma is to block out the feelings that they have about it. People then feel emotionally flat or detached from things. Sometimes they feel like everything is strange or dream-like. This is a protective mechanism that provides distance from what happened. It is a way of turning one's back on the whole experience. This reduces the distress in the short term, but eventually gets in the way of resolving this experience because it doesn't allow people to connect with and process what they have been through.

Arousal. After a traumatic experience, many people report problems with sleeping and concentration, as well as feelings of restlessness and irritability. This happens because the body responds to trauma by entering a state of heightened physical arousal. Even though the trauma is over, the body might stay in the "alert" mode, i.e., prepared to deal with a threat.

PRACTICAL SUGGESTIONS FOR SURVIVORS OF TRAUMATIC EVENTS

Although it might seem trite, encouraging the congregant to try to rest and eat, even when he doesn't feel like it, is impor-tant, since feeling tired or hungry can make it more difficult for a person to marshal the emotional strength needed for recovery. In the weeks following a traumatic event, individuals should be encouraged to maintain as normal a schedule as possible. Such structure is more likely to facilitate healing than avoiding one's daily activities.

In the month following a traumatic incident, recurring dreams or flashbacks are to be expected. Rather than fight these admittedly unpleasant experiences, the congregant should be encouraged to let these feelings wash over him. This is prefer-able to getting caught up in the belief that these experiences are abnormal or shouldn't be happening. In fact, telling the survivor of a trauma that such symptoms are the mind's way of processing intolerable events can help normalize this process. Most likely these flashbacks and dreams will become less painful and less frequent after the first month anyway.

Similarly, congregants should be encouraged to give themselves permission to feel terrible. Reaching out and sharing those feelings with others should be encouraged. Although there sometimes is a place for prescription medication, if the rabbi should notice anyone trying to numb his pain with alcohol or drugs, he should point out that this is a short-term solution that can lead to a long-term problem.

GUIDELINES FOR FAMILY AND FRIENDS

Family members should be encouraged to respect the coping styles being used by the other members of the family. Conflicts sometimes are engendered by the belief that one should always talk things through or not talk too much. Becoming overly judgmental about the way other family members are dealing with the aftermath of the traumatic event can push away sources of support at the time when that support is most crucial.

Friends and family should also be helped to understand that becoming the target for the traumatized individual's anger should not be taken personally. In fact, it may even be a sign of closeness, because people tend to lash out at those with whom they feel the most safe.

Friends and family may need help in finding the balance between just "being there" for the person and knowing when to offer more active levels of support through talking, helping with chores, or offering other types of practical assistance. This is a particularly difficult balance to achieve, and the rabbi can play an important role in advising about this. Also, the rabbi can play an important role by pointing out what is not seen as helpful in times of crisis. Well meaning comments such as,

"You're lucky it wasn't worse," or sharing horror stories about other tragedies can amplify the person's sense of loss rather than offer the intended consolation.

THE RABBI AS ANCHOR

Often, there is no "right thing" to say. Those going through a hard time may need the feeling of support that accompanies a person's physical presence, rather than his words. When Job's friends heard about the terrible tragedies he suffered, they traveled long distances to offer him consolation. Yet they didn't say anything, because they realized that their physical presence was more important than words. Just being there was the type of support Job needed. "They sat with him on the ground for a period of seven days and seven nights. No one said a word to him, for they saw that his pain was very great" (*Iyov* 2:13).

Rabbis often underestimate the value of sitting quietly with a person. Also, providing small physical comforts like food, a warm blanket, or tissues is a concrete manifestation of support, as is helping the person fill out forms or locating the community resources he needs.

A common dynamic in the period immediately following a trauma is that family members tire of hearing the person repeatedly retell what happened. His need to talk about the event can try the patience of family members and friends. Yet part of the healing process often includes using others as a sounding board. The general rule of thumb is that as long as the person feels better talking about what happened, the rabbi should do his best to offer a warm and sympathetic ear.

Remember, in reaching out to congregants in the immediate aftermath of a trauma, the goal is to offer them an opportunity for venting and sharing. This is not the time to help the person gain insight or to find deeper meaning. It is better to begin with open-ended questions about the event and the person's thoughts rather than his feelings, because this is less threatening. Anyway, expressions of feelings almost always emerge spontaneously when a person starts sharing the facts and his thoughts surrounding the traumatic event. When dealing with controlled individuals who aren't comfortable expressing their feelings, respect their right to remain silent.

Rabbis should also keep in mind the difference between offering support and assuming the role of a "Pollyanna" who gives false reassurance that everything will be all right. Although well-intentioned, this tends to come across as a failure in empathy.

THE RABBI AS AGENT FOR PROMOTING ACTIVE VS. PASSIVE COPING

Through a combination of prayer, ritual, and counseling, rabbis can play an important role in helping survivors of traumatic events deal with feelings of helplessness in a more active and adaptive manner. Rabbis can foster active problem solving by asking a series of questions that promote logical thinking in the face of strong emotions. Such questions include: "What are your most pressing needs right now?" and "What do you think you most need to get done?" Then the rabbi can assist the congregant in making a prioritized list of what needs doing.

Another powerful mechanism is writing about the upsetting event. Numerous well-designed research studies conducted over the last fifteen years have found that writing about one's thoughts and feelings regarding stressful events can reduce illness, enhance the functioning of one's immune system, improve grades, and even increase the likelihood of unemployed individuals getting a new job. Encouraging the congregant to keep such a journal may help him process his experience over the long term. It also may prove useful at a later date, when memories fade, yet it is deemed therapeutic to revisit those from the early days following the trauma.

SELF-SOOTHING AND PRAYER

The ability to cope with upsetting situations by soothing oneself is central to the process of successful coping. This component of coping includes: calming oneself by praying, taking a walk, listening to music, or trying to relax.

Turning to God to answer our prayers is, perhaps, the most powerful form of coping. In addition to the obvious spiritual benefits, the psychological benefits of prayer include the comforting knowledge that there is something that we can actively do in the face of events that are otherwise out of our control. A number of recent studies have found that prayer is associated with improved coping with painful medical conditions and positive emotional adjustment following major surgery. Some studies even raise the possibility that participating in organized prayer lessens one's chance of being diagnosed with life-threatening illness.

LONGER TERM INTERVENTIONS AFTER A CRISIS

In recent years, mental health researchers have gone beyond a focus on pathology to study what differentiates individuals who fall apart in the face of adversity from those who seem to thrive psychologically no matter what difficulties they face. Invariably, these studies find that a central ingredient in resilience is having at least one person who cares. Those facing even the worst kind of trauma and loss are buffered and protected by the knowledge that they have somebody in their corner. Such social support is a key predictor of who will emerge relatively unscathed from even the harshest difficulties.

The rabbi can play an invaluable role as gatekeeper, making sure the family receives the right amount of social support and the right amount of time alone in order to process the impact of the trauma. Group therapists treating family members who lost a relative in the 9/11 attacks found just that: Among the most salient needs of the group was negotiating the balance between accepting social support and finding time to grieve privately. Often, after an overwhelming show of social support in the months following a loss, the level of support, in many cases, drops to lower levels than what was available before. A woman who lost a family member in a tragic accident recently told me that she, at times, notices that people cross the street to avoid having to talk to her. The level of discomfort that others often feel when their friends or acquaintances suffer a tragedy may manifest itself in avoidance — because people worry that they don't know the "right" thing to say and/or because another's loss sharply reminds us of our own vulnerability.

The role of the rabbi is crucial here. He should continue regular contact with the traumatized congregant well after the initial period of community support. Not only should he be certain to continue checking in, but he can also monitor the level of social support and enlist more when it is needed.

THE ROLE OF THE RABBI
IN THE SEARCH FOR MEANING

While in the early stages of facing tragedy, the congregant might not be ready to actively engage in a search for meaning, as time goes on, this search can be an essential ingredient in recovery. The rabbi is often the person who can play a pivotal role in assisting the congregant in the process of making sense of what happened. This form of active response to suffering is not new.

As our rabbis teach us in the Talmud, an active response to dealing with suffering is: "If a man sees that painful suffering comes upon him, let him examine his conduct" (*Berachos* 5a).

The Talmud seems to be instructing us that individuals should think about their behavior if they want to find meaning in their tribulations. The rabbi's role might be to help guide his congregant in this process, but the model should be that of "consultant" rather than "manager". In contrast to managers who actively direct and control, a consultant is there to guide and provide counsel without taking over. A rabbi's job is not to tell the individual what the meaning of his tragedy or crisis is. Rather, his role is to serve as a sensitive facilitator in the process of self-examination.

An important ingredient in finding meaning is the shifting of one's perspective about how to view the tragedy. This includes a gradually emerging insight that ultimately some good can come from even the most tragic event.

In a particularly eloquent description of the growth-inducing potential of facing crises, we are taught that troubles are for the long-term benefit of the individual. As it says: "Rejoice not against me, my enemy; for when I fall, I will get up; when I sit in darkness, Hashem will be a light to me" (*Michah* 7:8). Our Rabbis, of blessed memory, taught us, "If I had not fallen, I would not have picked myself up. If I did not sit in darkness, I would not have seen the light" (*Orchos Tzaddikim: Sha'ar HaTeshuvah*, Gate 26).

In a similar vein, Rabbi Shimon Schwab points out that the term *nichum aveilim*, which is typically translated as "the comforting of mourners", actually means to make them reconsider things. For example, seeing how prevalent evil is in the Generation of the Flood, the word *vayinochem* is used to describe

God's "regret" at having created man: "And Hashem reconsidered having made man" (*Genesis* 6:6). The central component of *nechamah*, also from the same Hebrew root, is a shifting of perspective, a gradually emerging insight that ultimately good can come from even the most tragic event.

A study of 271 adolescent cancer survivors is typical of this. Of the 76% who viewed themselves as "different" from others because of their experience coping with a life-threatening illness, 69% saw those differences as positive. These young men and women viewed themselves as being more mature, more likely to "know" the purpose of life, and more likely to treat others well.

Although it is more difficult for young children to find meaning in the face of tragedy, the rabbi can facilitate this process by involving them in learning or *chesed* projects geared to their age. A team of mental health specialists in Pittsburgh ask children who have encountered traumatic loss the following list of questions to assist their search for meaning:

> ► If you met another child whose parent died like yours did, what would you want to tell him about what you have learned?
>
> ► What would you want him to know that might help him?
>
> ► What do you think about yourself now that you've gone through this?

PLANNING FOR ANNIVERSARY REACTIONS AND OTHER TRIGGERS

There are numerous reminders that can trigger strong emotional reactions in the months and years following a trauma. Every *simchah*, such as a wedding, bar mitzvah, or graduation can serve as a potent reminder of loss. Rabbis should be aware, however, that even less obvious reminders are everywhere. Places, sounds, and smells, can serve as powerful triggers of strong emotional reactions. For example, for many who were near the World Trade Center on September 11th, 2001, a beautiful fall day can bring back searing memories. In turn, many Holocaust survivors who live in the New York City metropolitan area reported that the smell of the burning of the Twin Towers in the days following the attacks triggered unbearably intense memories of the smell of concentration camps.

TIMING OF ONSET OF TRAUMA SYMPTOMS

Although, in most cases, absence of symptoms in the immediate aftermath of traumatic events suggests a positive adjustment over the long term, the rabbi should be aware that at times there can be a delayed reaction. An enlightening example of this process was when the German government sought to deny reparations for psychiatric treatment of concentration camp survivors who showed no need for mental health intervention until decades after their liberation. The Germans argued that, by definition, difficulties that developed so many years after the Holocaust must have nothing to do with those people's experiences in the camps. Research clearly proved the Germans wrong. Many survivors were asymptomatic in the years following their liberation. They threw themselves into learning a new language, new vocations, marrying, and raising their families. It was only after their last child married and they faced retirement that the full emotional impact of the horrible loss and trauma of those years caught up with them. Once this delayed reaction to trauma was clearly documented by trauma researchers, the German government agreed not to place any time limit on its payment for mental health treatment of survivors.

COUNSELING SKILLS

Basic communication techniques that are familiar to rabbis in other counseling settings are appropriate in the initial stages of crisis counseling as well. A combination of paraphrasing, reflection of feelings, and asking open-ended questions can help provide the individual going through a crisis with feelings of support and validation. As noted earlier, it is important that the rabbi know that he shouldn't confront or probe in a manner that jeopardizes the psychological defenses being employed by the traumatized individual. Now is *not* the time to search for hidden reasons, and it certainly is an inopportune time for moralizing or preaching.

COUNSELING STRATEGIES

A brief summary of counseling strategies that might prove helpful in various stages of intervention follows.

Intervention at the Site of the Trauma

The SAFE-R model has been set forth by Drs. Mitchell and Everly to provide a guide for use by emergency medical personnel in the immediate aftermath of a crisis, such as an accident or natural disaster. The steps of this approach as modified for rabbis are as follows:

> ► **Stimulation reduction.** If possible, the rabbi should attempt to remove the individual from the immediate situation by taking him for a walk, getting coffee, or any other diversion.

> ► **Acknowledgment of the crisis.** Although seemingly obvious, merely asking the question "What happened?" can serve to encourage ventilation and provide the individual

with an opportunity to begin the process of sharing his perception and feelings about the event. Ultimately, constructing a narrative about the traumatic situation can serve as an important vehicle for coming to terms with it. Although this is just the very beginning of the process, it can serve an important function even this early in the coping process. An additional advantage of asking "What happened?" is that this helps contain the person's escalating emotions by temporarily asking him to return to the cognitive thinking domain. Drs. Mitchell and Everly then suggest that the question "How are you doing now?" be posed. This allows for cathartic ventilation in a somewhat more structured, secure manner.

► **Facilitation of understanding and normalization.** In this transition back to the cognitive realm, the rabbi reassures the congregant that his response — no matter what it might be — is a normal reaction to an abnormal event. This process of normalization is essential in helping the individual understand that even intense feelings or memories in reaction to the trauma fall within the realm of "normal" and that he shouldn't hesitate to reach out to others in seeking support or reassurance.

► **Encouragement of effective coping techniques.** Short-term stress management techniques can be discussed, including the importance of rest and exercise. A plan for coping with an acute crisis situation, including identifying sources of family and community support, can be jointly developed.

► **Restoration of independent functioning.** The rabbi should, if necessary, refer the person to a mental health specialist who can provide longer-term counseling, or, if indicated, medication.

Helping Deal with Anniversary Reactions and Traumatic Reminders

Rabbis can play a helpful role by reviewing the "Three Ps" with congregants who might be facing a distressing anniversary or other reminders of traumatic loss:

> ▶ **Predict** that even happy occasions can trigger strong feelings of sadness, anger, or loss. Preparing people for what otherwise might catch them by surprise lends an element of control that is easier to deal with than the unexpected.

> ▶ **Permit**. Encourage the congregant to give himself or herself permission to have strong feelings in response to the traumatic reminder. Validating and normalizing this can be a very helpful component of the coping process.

> ▶ **Plan**. Develop a plan for coping with the strong feelings associated with the traumatic reminders. Depending on the coping style of the individual, a combination of strategies that rely on distraction, turning to others, use of relaxation techniques, and/or use of creative outlets can help insure that there is a framework in place that can help the person deal with his feelings in as constructive a manner as possible.

Counseling Limitations

Rabbis should periodically check in with their congregant to see how he is coping. A series of questions that can simplify this assessment includes: "How well are you coping?" "Who, if anyone, helps you cope?" "What would help you deal with things now?"

If the PTSD symptoms described earlier persist for longer than one month, serious consideration should be given to making a referral to a mental health specialist who has both expertise and experience working with trauma. This is because some of the techniques used in working with psychological trauma are highly specialized. Specifically, if any of the following symptoms persist for more than a month and are clearly impairing day-to-day functioning, a referral should be made:

- ► Avoiding all places and people that serve as reminders of the trauma
- ► Persistently turning one's back on support from others, including pervasive withdrawal from family and friends
- ► Drinking alcohol or taking drugs as a way of "self-medicating"
- ► Acting angry and aggressive or picking fights, particularly when this isn't typical of the person's pre-trauma behavior
- ► Anxiety that does not gradually abate, particularly separation anxiety
- ► Enduring somatic complaints, like headaches or stomachaches
- ► Persisting sleep disturbance, such as problems falling asleep, staying asleep, or nightmares
- ► Persisting change in eating patterns
- ► Persisting difficulty concentrating at work or school
- ► Persisting self-blame, guilt, or feelings of unworthiness
- ► Self-destructive behavior or the desire to die, regardless of the duration

There is a role for medication in treating any of the difficulties described above—particularly in the case of sleep disturbance or high levels of physiologic arousal and/or anxiety. The rabbi should enlist the help of his mental health consultant in determining which mental health discipline is most appropriate.

VICARIOUS TRAUMATIZATION: THE IMPACT OF
TRAUMA WORK ON RABBIS

Vicarious traumatization is the transformation that potentially occurs within the rabbi as a result of empathic engagement with his congregants' traumatic experiences. Listening to graphic descriptions of horrific events and bearing witness to people's cruelty to one another can impact on the rabbi's view of the world as a safe and benevolent place. Research on the process of vicarious traumatization in psychotherapists working with traumatized clients has resulted in a number of findings that have implications for the rabbi. The most relevant results of this research suggest that rabbis who are at particular risk for being impacted by work with traumatized congregants are relatively inexperienced or those with a personal trauma history. Rabbis who were abused as children or who survived traumatic experiences themselves are at greater risk. Exposure to children's trauma may also be difficult for them.

In general, rabbis who are required to do a great deal of work with traumatized individuals are at greater risk for being negatively affected. Interestingly, however, there is a positive component to this type of work. Conducting counseling with trauma survivors forces rabbis to confront their own sense of meaning and hope. Paradoxically, in a process that has been termed "vicarious growth", empirical research has found that therapists who treat a higher number of abuse survivors report a more existentially and spiritually satisfying life than those with less exposure to trauma clients. This is because they learn that the other side to suffering from trauma is the strength of the human spirit. In fact, what typically emerges is that resilience is the norm. As the rabbi encounters traumatized individuals responding to crisis by growing spiritually, reordering priorities, and increasing their appreciation of what is valuable, they grow along with them.

The same body of research that describes vicarious traumatization and vicarious growth suggests that rabbis consider the following antidotes to the taxing nature of this work:

- ► **Name the monster.** Self-awareness and an understanding that dealing with traumatic situations is particularly draining and demanding can help lessen the strain.
- ► **Practice what you preach.** Building in rest, relaxation, physical exercise, avocations, and vacations are essential for recharging one's batteries in the face of such demanding work.
- ► **Obtain peer support.** Therapists who use social support as a coping mechanism are less negatively impacted.

The role of the rabbi in assisting those who are going through a crisis is invaluable. Perhaps in no other area of life are there so many opportunities to perform such critical acts of *chesed*. By familiarizing himself with short- and long-term strategies for intervention, the rabbi can fill this most crucial role in a manner that promotes growth for his congregant and himself.

BIBLIOGRAPHY

Ai, A., Bolling S., Peterson, C. 2000. "The Use of Prayer by Coronary Artery Bypass Patients." *International Journal for the Psychology of Religion*, 10:205–220.

Bryant, R. & Harvey, A. 2000. "Acute Stress Disorder." Washington: American Psychological Association Press.

Cameron, L. & Nicholls, G. 1998. "Expression of Stressful Experience through Writing." *Health Psychology*, 17:84–92.

Cohen, J., Greenberg, T., Padlo, S. et al. 2001. *Cognitive Behavioral Therapy for Traumatic Grief in Children Treatment Manual*. Center for Traumatic Stress in Children and Adolescents, Department of Psychiatry, Allegheny General Hospital, Pittsburgh, PA.

Diagnostic Criteria from DSM-IV. 1994. American Psychiatric Association, Washington, DC.

"Expert Consensus Panel for Treatment of PTSD." 1999. *Journal of Clinical Psychiatry*, 60:Supplement 16.

Fox, S.A., Pitkin, K., Paul, C. 1998. "Breast Cancer Screening Adherence: Does Church Attendance Matter?" *Health, Education and Behavior*, 25:742–758.

Layne, C. & Saltzman, W. 2000. School-based Trauma / Grief Group Psychotherapy Program, UCLA Trauma Psychiatry Program, Department of Psychiatry, Los Angeles, CA.

Levine, A. 1994. *To Comfort the Bereaved*. Lanham: Jason Aronson.

Miller, S.M., Fang, C.Y., Diefenbach, M.A., Bales, C.B. 2001. "Tailoring Psychosocial Interventions to the Individual's Health Information-Processing Style." In Baum, A. and Andersen, B. (eds.) *Psychosocial Interventions for Cancer*. Washington: American Psychological Association Press, 343–362.

Mitchell, J. & Everly, G. *Critical Incident Stress Debriefing: An Operations Manual for the Prevention of Traumatic Stress Among Emergency Service and Disaster Workers*. Elicott City: Chevron Publishing.

Rapp, S., Rejeski, W., Miller, M. 2000. *Physical Function Among Older Adults with Knee Pain: The Role of Pain Coping Skills*. Arthritis Care & Research, 13:270–279.

Stuber, M.L. 1998. *Is PTSD a Viable Model for Understanding Responses to Childhood Cancer?* Child and Adolescent Psychiatric Clinics of North America, 7:169–182.

Werner, E. 1993. "Risk, Resilience and Recovery: Perspectives from the Kauaii Longitudinal Study." *Development and Psychopathology*, 54:503–515.

Visiting the Hospitalized Patient

Daniel H. Jackson, Ph.D.
Susan T. Jackson, Ph.D.

THE STRUCTURE OF PATIENT CARE

When the rabbi visits a patient in the hospital, he is really making several visits at once.[1] He is certainly there to see the patient. He has also come to support the patient's family and to work with the patient's health-care team. By way of orientation, it is helpful to consider the three different constituencies that form the structure of patient care (Donahue and McGuire, 1995): the patient — who is experiencing the illness, the patient's family — who is having a different experience of the patient's illness, and the health-care team — composed of medical professionals committed to treating and caring for the patient. The rabbi's visit will be productive and genuinely helpful to the extent that he is mindful of each of these constituencies.

The impact of illness on the patient can be formidable. The person's life, in all its detail, is now on hold. Everyday routines, aspirations, and priorities have become, for the time being, irrelevant. His accustomed world is gone, and in its place is a world of uncertainty, fear, and dread. The person, now hospitalized, is confined to bed, unable to control his environment or the hospital schedules and protocols with which he must

91

comply both day and night. Established relationships are disrupted (Fletcher, Fletcher, and Wagner, 1996); autonomy, mobility, and privacy are lost. As a result of this illness, the patient is no longer capable of activities that once came easily to him. Therefore, in addition to coping with the many inconveniences and indignities associated with the experience of hospitalization, the patient may face future life transitions of proportions he never before imagined (Mayer and Tuma, 1990).

What is happening to the patient as a person is as important to him or her as the medical aspects of diagnosis, etiology, and treatment (Frank, 2004). The disjuncture between ordinary experience and the new experience of becoming a "patient" may well precipitate an existential crisis of great magnitude (Morgan, Calnan, and Manning, 1985). The person's accustomed sense of self falls under siege in the face of a sudden and overwhelming new reality. Coming to grips with this crisis can be a considerable challenge (Frank, 2002).

The family and the health-care team are also central components of the social structure (Barth, 1966) in which the patient is one of many participants (Emerson, 1976). Relationships with family members and with the medical professionals involved have direct and indirect effects on the patient (Belmartino, 1994).[2] The rabbi, therefore, needs to learn how to navigate the connections between the members of this network (Deane, 1992) in order to address patient concerns and fears, and ultimately to improve the patient's experience in dealing with his or her illness (Scott, 1992).

Despite his best efforts, the rabbi may find that it is simply not possible to visit the patient privately. Family members may be present in the room, medical personnel may be conducting tests, or the patient may be heavily sedated. Under these circumstances, which are not the exception but the rule in visiting hospitalized patients, the rabbi will do well to focus on the other constituents involved in the patient's care who *are* available to be visited. By giving them attention and encouragement, the rabbi will be providing indirect assistance to the patient.

This chapter focuses on the rabbi's role with respect to all three constituencies in the structure of patient care. First, the rabbi's work with families and the medical health-care team is examined. Then, the rabbi's work directly with the patient is discussed.

HELPING THE PATIENT'S FAMILY

The family is the most important resource the patient has. Relationships with parents, spouses, and children are critical to the patient's well-being throughout his illness. Yet family members, too, are subject to varying amounts of distress, depending on the suddenness and severity of the family member's illness. Their lives, like the patient's, are severely disrupted. In attending to their loved one's needs, they may set aside their own. Sleep deprived, inadequately nourished and hydrated, burdened with new personal, financial, and family worries resulting from the patient's illness, they may feel helpless and deeply anxious. They may experience even more distress about the patient's condition than the patient does. This factor alone can cause the patient great concern, complicating his efforts to master and grow from his own experience.

As the situation unfolds, there may be periods when medical professionals are uncertain about the diagnosis, the extent of the disease, or the efficacy of a procedure. In times such as these, anxiety, a function of uncertainty, runs particularly high. It is at this time that the rabbi can provide many helpful interventions. His presence alone is, in itself, an act of caring that serves as a source of comfort and support for both patient and family. At critical moments in the course of an illness, as family members anxiously await the outcome of exploratory tests, surgery, or invasive procedures, the rabbi's prayers and spiritual support are especially helpful. If patients and their families focus on the most disastrous possibilities in a situation that is still uncertain, the rabbi can acknowledge the discomfort and tension that comes from waiting, and emphasize that the outcome is still unknown.

Throughout the patient's hospital stay, family members may turn to the rabbi as their liaison and intermediary in communicating with the health-care team. For instance, families who feel overwhelmed or intimidated may not be able to ask important questions to the doctors and nurses. The rabbi can encourage the family to make their questions known, inform the medical professionals that the family needs help, or—with the family's consent—ask questions on their behalf. Similarly, if tension arises between the family and the health-care team, the rabbi can serve as an intermediary, calming their anger, stress, and anxiety, which all interfere with effective collaboration. Without taking sides, he can help express each set of needs and perspectives to the other participants in the situation, thereby restoring the open flow of communication.

Educating the Family

When families are new to the health-care process, or don't know what to do, the rabbi can provide a great service by helping them understand what to expect and what will be required of them. For instance, many health-care settings require a patient to formally agree to his proscribed treatment and to authorize a person to make those decisions if he is no longer able to do so. This establishes the protocols used to treat the patient and to keep the family informed as treatment unfolds. In critical cases—such as a patient admitted for stroke, heart attack, or serious trauma—the patient is unable to speak. The medical staff will then turn to the family to make major life care choices, such as to perform Cardiopulmonary Resuscitation (CPR) or not (Do Not Resuscitate [DNR]), to intubate or not (Do Not Intubate [DNI], to withdraw life support or not, and to ask whether or not they are interested in making an organ donation.

Families, understandably, find this process overwhelming. The rabbi can help them understand the ramifications of the choices facing them and encourage them to think things through, if it is not an emergency. For example, an elderly couple came in for the wife's routine chest X-ray. She went into cardiac arrest in the waiting room and was taken into the ICU (Intensive Care Unit). A staff member from the X-ray department was concerned about the husband's well-being. She notified the rabbi, who came in to meet with the husband. During the course of their conversation, the rabbi told the husband that the medical staff would be asking him a series of questions about how to care for his wife. Had the couple ever discussed her treatment under such circumstances? Had they designated someone to be her health-care proxy? At the rabbi's suggestion, the husband called his children. By the time the medical staff approached him about his wife's declining condition, he and his daughters were prepared to answer the necessary questions in a clear and composed manner.

Families may not understand the nature of the medical interventions proposed or instituted by the health-care team. The rabbi should become familiar enough with common medical procedures so that he can provide basic, accurate information, and if necessary, help patients and family members ask further questions of the health-care team (Frank, 2002, McGrae et al., 2003). Furthermore, in their anxiety and uncertainty, families may resist treatment recommendations, downplaying the patient's need for medical assistance or worrying unrealistically about the outcome of a given medical procedure (Verbrugge and Patrick, 1995). The rabbi contributes significantly to patient care by explaining that the patient's medical needs are legitimate and encouraging the family to adopt a realistic attitude in considering recommended treatments or procedures. If he sees an objective basis for requesting additional consultation, he may suggest that the family contact the primary care physician for an opinion. In all other cases, he emphasizes that "it is permitted" to accept the treatments recommended by the healthcare team (Harris, 1995).

Surprisingly, families may need to be educated about how to react to their loved one's complaints of distress and pain. There is no virtue in suffering (Abraham, 2000; Bleich, 1981; Rosner and Tendler, 1997). Yet many people think they are being "good" patients by not complaining when they are in pain (Frank, 2002). They may harbor misconceptions about the effects of pain medication or feel that asking for relief means they are weak. Such attitudes are usually counterproductive. Patients in pain do not rest properly. They do not do their work properly in rehabilitation and they are reluctant to get moving after surgery. Family members may share these misconceptions, and as a result they may not ask for relief on the patient's behalf.

Aside from the patient's direct communications that he or she is in pain, there may be a number of indirect, nonverbal signs that give the same information. A patient may frown, wince, move unusually slowly and carefully, or speak in a strained manner. If the rabbi suspects, from these and other signs, that the patient is experiencing pain, he should speak with the patient and the family about the importance of taking all possible measures to control and relieve pain. He might ask if they have spoken to the nurse or the attending physician about it. He might even share his observations about the patient's pain with the health-care team. When families see that the rabbi takes their loved one's pain seriously, and that there could, in fact, be acceptable medical solutions to the problem, they will be more likely to respond appropriately in the future.[3]

Families in Crisis

It is not unusual for the rabbi to discover that the patient's illness has created a crisis for the entire family. The most immediate type of crisis has to do with pressing needs arising from the hospitalization itself. The rabbi, recognizing that everyone in the family is affected by the patient's situation, should make a point of asking about each and every family member present, encouraging them to call him when they need his support. "How are *you* doing? Is there anything I can do for *you*?" In addition, the rabbi will often have occasion to counsel family members about the importance of self-care, despite the overwhelming pressure of their concern for the patient's well-being. By pointing out that the patient needs for them to be strong and healthy so they can help with his care, the rabbi may be able to persuade family members to get a few hours of sleep, eat a hot meal, or take a few quiet moments to walk around the block.

Another level of crisis may arise in response to life transitions associated with the patient's illness. A serious accident or illness, especially when accompanied by a hospital stay, often signals the beginning of the need for major lifestyle changes. Older patients who fall may experience less distress over their broken leg or hip that has confined them to a hospital bed than the prospect that their days of driving or living at home may be at an end (Williams, 1990). The structure of the patient's family will have to change in order to accommodate this new reality.

Family members will have to formulate alternative living arrangements and agree on how best to provide medical care.

The rabbi should be attentive to how both patients and their families feel about these changes. Apart from the many practical details that confront them, family members will also have their individual reactions to changes in the family structure and dynamics. As the patient's lifestyle changes, so does that of his or her loved ones (Pardue, 1991). A spouse who formerly was dependent on the patient may now be called upon to take charge. A child whose parent must leave the hospital for a nursing home now faces his or her own mortality in a new way. By raising these issues with family members, the rabbi thereby opens a discussion concerning the patient's change in needs and the family's complex reactions.

There are times when the rabbi's intervention enables family members to discuss the full ramifications of a patient's illness and more clearly understand its implications. The following example illustrates this.

> A rabbi went to visit an older patient in Acute Care. On the way into the room, he noticed two young men standing uneasily in the hallway. They avoided his gaze and did not return his greeting. They were clearly uncomfortable about something. Going into the room, the rabbi asked the patient how he was doing. The patient told the rabbi that he was dying of cancer and wasn't sure how long he had to live. He told the rabbi that although he was not religiously observant, he wanted the rabbi to say some traditional prayers with him before he died. The rabbi asked if he would like to say the traditional prayer of confession, *Viduy*, in Hebrew or in English. He said yes, and stipulated that he wanted his sons to hear the prayer.
>
> The rabbi went to the door and called the sons in. The rabbi noticed that the sons were very uneasy about the rabbi's

presence. When they stood at the foot of the patient's bed, the rabbi read the *Viduy* in Hebrew. The patient asked to read the prayer himself, in English, and did so with fervor. When he got to the part, "and if I die, may my death be an atonement for my sins," his sons gasped in shock. They objected to the rabbi's choice of prayer, asking, "What kind of prayer is this to say for a man who is sick?" At that point, the rabbi understood that the father had not been able to tell his sons that he was about to die. When the patient finished the prayer, the rabbi was able to tell the sons about their father's condition. He then withdrew, allowing the family to continue the discussion alone.

Finally, the rabbi may discover unresolved family dynamics coming to the fore in response to a health crisis. Longstanding conflicts between siblings, children, spouses, and former spouses may become evident as each participant relates to changes in the patient's status. Family members may be too preoccupied with their own emotional reactions to take in the patient's situation and needs. Therefore, they might not "hear" what is really happening with the patient.

In these instances, the rabbi needs to make certain that all the diverse voices and needs come together and are given fair consideration. The rabbi is in a position to redirect the family's attention back to the patient, whose needs should have first priority in this situation. By listening to each voice, the rabbi is often able to calm the maelstrom. This, in turn, benefits the patient, whose distress may have been amplified by the unfolding "family drama".

WORKING WITH THE HEALTH-CARE TEAM

The rabbi provides a vital link between the patient and family, on the one hand, and the medical staff, on the other. In his dual role of rabbinic caregiver and interpreter of rabbinic law, the rabbi can inform all parties in the medical process about relevant Jewish ethical concerns (Bleich, 1981; Brett and Jersild, 2003; Schneiderman et al., 2003). Moreover, as an informed and knowledgeable witness to unfolding events, the rabbi provides a fresh perspective. It is important for the rabbi to develop an accurate picture of the patient's health status by eliciting a non-jargonized assessment of the patient's condition and prognosis from the medical professionals.

This is especially critical in cases where the patient is not doing well (Collins and Long, 2003; Eyer, 1991; VandeCreek, 1991; Wastell 2002). Physicians, especially residents, are often reluctant to speak comprehensively and clearly about the patient's prognosis (Nuland, 1994). They are used to discussing a clinical situation in technical language, since they are involved with diseases and cases rather than with illnesses and people (Frank, 2002). If the rabbi is able to cut through elaborate medical terminology, he is in a better position to enable open communication between the health-care team, the patient, and the family. All parties benefit from the rabbi's listening, asking questions, and prompting constructive discussion of complicated and difficult issues. He also must do so in order to render an ethical opinion based on religious law. Equally important is that patients, families, and members of the health-care team interpret the rabbi's involvement as a genuine sign of caring.

To enhance his knowledge of medical interventions, it would be beneficial for the rabbi to develop relationships with a variety of highly regarded health-care professionals, such as internists, cardiologists, oncologists, psychiatrists, and medical social workers, with whom he can consult as needed (Cohen, Kessler, and Gordon, 1995). Through such relationships, the rabbi can learn about treatments and community services available for a wide range of needs. One way in which many rabbis begin to develop these relationships is by taking part in the Ethics Committee at the local hospital, or by organizing a medical ethics discussion group, with an emphasis on application of rabbinic law to specific cases.

Medical Professionals as People

Open dialogue with the medical staff ultimately helps with patient care. Medical professionals work every day with trauma, mortality, the limitations of available treatments, as well as many other frustrations associated with their jobs (Collins and Long, 2003; Regehr, 2001; Regehr, 2002). For example, a medical staff can experience uncertainty as they work to clarify a diagnosis or assess the efficacy of a treatment. This uncertainty may give rise to a number of reactions, including anxiety, tension, and impatience on their part.

Other emotional responses may accompany assignments to units in the hospital such as the Emergency Room or the Intensive Care Unit. Many Emergency Room personnel (Warren, Lee, and Saunders, 2003), through their repeated exposure to trauma, are affected by varying degrees of vicarious traumatization (see Pelcovitz, this volume). Staff members assigned to the ICU, by definition, work solely with patients who are in grave condition or who have just come out of the operating room. The mortality rate for ICU patients who are on life support for more than 48 hours is quite high (Azoulay et al., 2003; Edwards and Taylor, 2003; Lobo et al., 2003; Osmon et al,. 2003). The prognosis gets worse the longer the patient is in the ICU (Combes et al., 2003). Although there is some degree of desensitization to their surroundings, staff members nevertheless feel a deep emotional response to the situations they encounter (Warren, Lees, and Saunders, 2003; Wastell, 2002).

In many respects, the patient, family, medical staff, and institutional setting are conducive to forming a new kind of temporary family. As mentioned in an earlier chapter (Michelson and Levitz, this volume), the rabbi needs to be able to listen to every individual in this group, keeping in mind that they are akin to multiple "family" members with divergent interests experiencing the same situation in different ways. In fact, there may be outright conflict between the interests and goals of the various participants from the health-care system (Donahue and McGuire, 1995; Luce and Rubenfeld 2002; Poullier and Wilson, 1993).

For the individual, regardless of the severity of the illness, the institutional reality of medical treatment can be confusing, degrading, and enervating. Patients and their families want immediate relief and treatment, yet hospitals, like all medical facilities, have institutionalized ways of doing business. In turn, physicians and nurses have conflicting demands on their time, given their patient loads and professional obligations.

Just as the rabbi needs to hear and validate the experiences of patients and their families, so too it is important for him to provide a listening ear to members of the health-care team, who carry tensions associated with their work. Staff members rarely have the opportunity to talk about their feelings concerning these matters with a clergyman. As the rabbi interacts with the health-care team in the course of visiting a hospitalized patient, he may want to address this often overlooked need within the medical profession. A simple statement such as, "This must be very hard for you, dealing with cases like these," addressed to a nurse in the ICU or a physician who must discuss end-of-life options with a family, can be a powerful validation and morale builder. Members of the health-care team will be in a better position to give their best on behalf of the patient's care when *their* feelings have been validated and affirmed.

Care vs. Cure

There is a season for everything, and there is a time to discuss the end of a person's life (Curtis and Rubenfeld, 2001). At a certain point, medical treatment becomes futile (Nolin and Anderson, 2003) or only increases the patient's pain in exchange for diminishing returns (Rubenfeld and Crawford, 1996). At this point, there is the option to step back and allow the disease to take its course, offering the patient palliative care (comfort measures) only. This is the decision to move from "cure" to "care".

The rabbi should bear in mind that such choices affect everyone — the patient, the family, and the staff alike (Ciccarello, 2003). For family members, this may be their first experience with the death of a close relative and they will need to make considerable adjustments (Ganzini et al., 2003). The staff may already have standard assumptions about what the family and patient need, and how this process will affect them — assumptions that may be on target or not. Although staff members may have their own feelings of sadness and defeat when this moment comes, extensive exposure to mortality may have desensitized them to the emotional reactions of others. Therefore, it is imperative for the rabbi to work effectively and compassionately with all parties involved in dealing with the issues that arise when moving a patient from medical therapy to palliative care.

The attending physician, who generally informs the family that the patient's medical therapy has failed or is not expected to succeed, may request the rabbi's help in conveying this difficult information. Family members, understandably saddened and frequently overwhelmed at this juncture, often need the rabbi's help to articulate their concerns and ask questions about the progression of the disease, the patient's care, and treatment options.

There are no simple answers to the questions raised by the move from cure to care. At such times, however, family, patients, nursing staff, physicians, and administrators greatly appreciate the rabbi's assistance and support.

WORKING WITH THE PATIENT

Assessing the Patient's World

Upon entering a patient's hospital room, the rabbi is stepping into the middle of a drama that is already in play. It is important, therefore, that he quickly synchronize his actions with the rhythm of what is going on and adapt to the context of the patient's world. Even if he visited the patient earlier in the week, or earlier in the day, each subsequent visit is unique. Things change quickly in a medical setting. Yesterday, a patient and his wife of 45 years were waiting for test results about a lingering respiratory infection and today they are reeling from results confirming end-stage asbestosis. Only with an astute assessment of the patient's current situation can the rabbi clarify the objectives of each particular visit.

Sometimes the patient is asleep or away from his room, undergoing a lengthy medical procedure. The rabbi might leave a note wishing the patient well and offering further contact as the situation requires. On the other hand, if the patient is available, the rabbi should start by orienting himself to the patient's circumstances. He might engage the patient by asking, "How are you doing?" "How are you feeling now?" or "How are things going?" He then can take note of what is being said and what is not being said, gathering non-verbal clues from the patient's body language, facial expression, and tone of voice.

On occasion, the rabbi will conclude that an extended visit is not called for. If a patient is not strong enough for a sustained interaction or appears uncomfortable with the rabbi's presence, the rabbi should wish the patient a speedy recovery and leave. In so doing, the rabbi implicitly maintains the value of what a rabbinic visit has to offer, without assuming that everyone wishes to receive it.

Validating and Witnessing

The rabbi's most basic task is to listen to the patient's story and validate it. This task is not about fixing; it is about compassionate and empathic listening. Although at times the patient may require the rabbi's help with specific needs, such as communicating with family or staff, in many cases the patient simply needs to be heard.

Patients have their own concerns, and it may take them some time to get around to discussing what's on their mind. Even when they are ready, they may not express themselves in a straightforward manner. It becomes important for the rabbi to pay attention and listen carefully to what is being communicated. Those in distress are keenly aware of other people's hesitancy or their maintaining a distance. They need to feel that they are the sole focus of the rabbi's attention before they will invite the rabbi closer and impart something of their experience. No matter how busy the rabbi's schedule, it is of the utmost importance to take all the time necessary to focus on a patient's concerns. To the degree that the rabbi can keep the person-to-person connection dedicated exclusively to this patient at this moment will the patient feel comfortable enough to bare his soul.

The rabbi may find it difficult to listen without offering a solution to the patient's dilemmas. Nowhere is this more poignant than when the patient asks, "Why me?" "Why did God do this to me?" "Why must I endure this hospitalization and these painful medical procedures?" Generally, these questions are asked without the expectation of an answer. The rabbi must overcome his impulse to provide an answer, to act like he "knows". He must be willing to hear the question and affirm its validity as an important question for the patient, without offering a definitive answer.

Sometimes "Why me?" reflects a feeling of awe. A patient in the Cardiac Intensive Care Unit, a day after bypass surgery, was seen staring dazedly at the lit up vital signs monitors, with tears in his eyes. When the rabbi came by and asked, "How are you doing?" the patient responded, "Rabbi, I don't understand. Why me?" The rabbi correctly understood this to be not a complaint, but rather a question asked in awe — "Why did God do this for me?" It was a powerful existential statement expressing the patient's experience of having his life renewed. In response, the rabbi simply acknowledged and affirmed the patient's experience, giving neither a philosophical nor a perfunctory explanation. Through this process of "witnessing", the patient took comfort knowing that another individual had shared his experience of awe.

Gaining Access to the Patient

Gaining access to a patient and having the opportunity to spend a substantive period of time alone with him is not always an easy or straightforward task. Patients are usually embedded in a series of relationships with people who act as gatekeepers, controlling access to the patient's time and attention. In many cases, patients cannot speak their mind or express their feelings in the presence of family members or staff.

Sensitive family members will ask if the rabbi would like them to leave while he visits with the patient. Staff members, especially nurses, will either come back later or quickly complete their chores in order to provide privacy. In these situations, the gatekeepers are clearly being cooperative in allowing the rabbi to spend time alone with the patient.

Sometimes, however, gatekeepers seek to dominate the rabbi's meeting with the patient, asserting their own needs and interests. Family members may finish a patient's statement or speak for him as though he were not present. They may give full expression to what they have been going through, without giving the patient priority to express himself. When family members dominate the visit, they are letting the rabbi know that he has important work to do with them. Perhaps a spouse is having extreme difficulty with the rapid onset of mortality or the adult child of a woman who just suffered a massive stroke sees that she will no longer have the mother she remembers.

It may be possible for the rabbi to orchestrate events so that he is able to meet individually with the patient and attend to the needs of family members at a later time. On the other hand, the gatekeepers may prevent the rabbi from having any extended interaction with the patient at all. In such situations, the rabbi can do his best to offer sensitive care to those who lay claim to his attention. He can thus make every effort to help the patient indirectly, by attending to the needs of the people close to him.

Visiting Patients in Critical Condition

Visiting patients in the Intensive Care Unit (ICU) can be daunting and awkward. Many patients in the ICU are connected to respirators, heart monitors, tubes, and wires. They may have difficulty communicating because they are sedated or overcome by the symptoms of their illness. It is particularly at times like these that the *Shulchan Aruch* enjoins people to pray with a patient at his bedside in a language that he or she understands. For patients in ICU, simple phrases, clearly and audibly said, are the most effective. Many times, it might appear that the patient is not hearing or responding to the rabbi's visits. Yet, when patients begin to recover and once again become responsive, they may report vivid memories of the rabbi's visit and his encouraging words.

It is important not to speak in platitudes or to give false hope when talking to patients in critical care. A stroke patient, for instance, may never recover his speech or return to his previous way of life; for him this is a catastrophe. He will not derive any comfort from hearing the rabbi say, "Everything will be all right." Rather, the person fears that his life will never be the same and needs to express the devastation he feels. For the time being, as the patient experiences the pain of loss, the rabbi's role is to listen, to witness, and to validate the experience as it is presented to him.

It is, of course, helpful for the rabbi to encourage the patient to participate fully in any rehabilitation program recommended by the health-care team. The patient has reason to hope that these activities may provide some degree of gain. Yet the process of rehabilitation takes time and is fraught with uncertainty. Here the rabbi honors the patient's feelings and gives voice to his deepest wishes. He might say, for instance, "I hope and pray that God will lessen your pain, give you comfort, and help you have patience during this difficult time." Such a prayer has meaning to the patient because it resonates with his experience and with his hopes.

THE RABBI'S EXPERIENCE

It is up to the rabbi to provide spiritual support during the patient's hospitalization. The rabbi listens as a fellow human being cries out in pain or laughs with joy. He elicits each person's stories and feelings, and expresses their hopes and fears in prayer.

He calms them when they are agitated. Through the rabbi's actions, patients and their families can experience a greater sense of peace.

Yet, it is emotionally difficult for a rabbi to be around people who are experiencing anxiety, distress, and pain. The patient's plight brings the rabbi face to face with his own mortality and vulnerability, and perhaps with images of his own loved ones who suffered a crisis or illness. He feels a sincere wish to help, yet there are realistic limitations to the help he can offer. This can lead the rabbi to feel powerless and at a loss. Finally, for rabbis trained to answer spiritual questions with logical explanations, it is especially difficult to accept the fact that there are no answers to many existential entreaties.

To be sure, there are forms of assistance that a rabbi can render. Helping the patient, the family, and the health-care team to work well together is a significant contribution. Informing the health-care team about the patient's needs or helping family members to extend themselves effectively on the patient's behalf are other examples of how a rabbi can help. However, a rabbi is not in a position to "fix" the problems that the patient is facing. He cannot bring about outcomes that depend on the professional skill of others, on the primary facts of the patient's condition and prognosis, and ultimately on the will of God. What he can do is listen to the patient's lament, bear witness, convey that the patient is not alone, and understand as best he can. Over time, the rabbi may come to accept that in doing this, he is providing something that is, indeed, valuable and comforting to the patient.[4]

Every rabbi develops a style of spiritual care that draws from Jewish custom and practice, according to his personal preferences. Over the course of time, many situations become familiar to him and he develops a good sense of how to navigate them.[5] Other situations, though, can strike at the rabbi's core beliefs and he then has to make a choice about how to respond. For example, a family may want to withdraw respiratory support from a patient, when it is likely that the result will be the patient's imminent death. This outcome may be contrary to the rabbi's beliefs about how end-of-life issues should be handled. Similarly, the rabbi may be called upon to talk to a family about organ donation, a procedure that violates his personal halachic stance.

Reading and researching in the health-care field, as well as reviewing contemporary Responsa on medical issues, will help the rabbi gain knowledge and perspective on such situations. It is equally important for the rabbi to review and reflect, with a respected teacher or colleague on problematic situations he has encountered, and how he has handled them. He may need to explore issues that have emerged from working with particular kinds of patients, families, situational conflicts, or health-care personnel.

The rabbi is engaged in holy work, so his personal development is of central importance. Just as he may refer congregants to seek professional help, so should the rabbi seek consultation with senior colleagues as his experience increases, so that he may continue to learn.

The Rabbi's Prayer

Prayer is an appropriate closing to a session of listening, validating, and responding to need. When the rabbi offers a prayer, it should sum up the visit. The intent of this prayer is to repair a damaged but not necessarily broken link in a chain — the patient's sense of belonging to the larger community and of his connection to God.

Prayer should reflect the needs of the patient.[6] At times, the patient will spontaneously request a prayer. In other situations, when the rabbi is not sure what the patient wants, he might ask, "Would you like me to offer a prayer?" In both cases, it is appropriate for the rabbi to ask, "What would you like to pray for?" Since not every patient is comfortable with prayer, the process should not be forced. If the rabbi has the clear impression that a patient would refuse to hear or say a prayer, it would be appropriate instead to offer a parting blessing, such as "God should take away your pain, give you comfort, and a speedy recovery. God bless you." Even the least spiritually-oriented person will accept good wishes such as these.

The best prayers are short and to the point. They should be said with power and conviction, directly to the patient. The rabbi's prayer should be heartfelt, authentic, and not formulaic, whether read from a prayer book or said spontaneously. More importantly, as experience shows, the most effective prayer the rabbi can say is the final "benediction" offered on the way out the door. "May God give you strength and courage, take away your pain and anxiety, and give you peace."

ENDNOTES

1. We have focused on hospital visits for two reasons. First and foremost, in today's age, a seriously sick person belongs in the hospital. Anytime a rabbi is asked to visit someone at home who is seriously ill, the second question should be, "Why is he not in the hospital (or the emergency room)?"

A conversation could go as follows:

> *"Rabbi, could you visit my Uncle Chaim; he's not feeling well."*
> *"Oh, what's wrong?"*
> *"Well, he had chest pains during davening this morning and could use a prayer or two."*
> *"Which hospital did he go to?"*

This is an acceptable variation of the why question.

Second, for the ill patient, the hospital is a place "outside the camp," where he feels the most isolated and most in need of a sense of connection to his community.

2. It is important to remember that the rabbi-patient relationship is embedded in a larger structure of relationships within the health-care system. In effect, the rabbi visits the entire system, not just the patient. In a formal setting, the rabbi's visit does not go unnoticed. If staff members are impressed by the quality of the rabbi's visit, they may seek him out for other purposes. This engagement between staff and rabbi, in turn, can have a positive impact on the care the patient receives. Similarly, in informal settings, family and caregivers may anticipate the rabbi's visit, to the patient's benefit. For instance, the patient's surroundings might get an extra cleaning in order to make a good impression on the rabbi. The Gemara tells us that when Rabbi Akiva came to visit one of his students, "they" cleaned and swept the room to make ready for the distinguished guest. "This," the student told his *rebbe*, "saved my life."

3. This is equally true for ultra-observant denominations in secular hospital settings. The rabbi's presence reassures the patient of his "safety", as well as authorizes the patient to permit the staff to administer treatment.

4. As an analogy, consider the patient's room as a nightclub, with the patient as a blues singer and the rabbi as the audience. When hearing someone sing the sad and lonely blues, the audience does not jump up and say, "We can fix that!" Yet this is exactly what clergy are prone to do upon hearing the patient's complaint.

5. In broader terms, the rabbi needs to consider who is being served and how best to serve them. Such considerations are further complicated when patients and families wish to go against Jewish custom and practice. Rabbis need to determine how to weigh these voices with respect to their own comfort levels in order to best serve the patient. In some cases, a rabbi should consider consulting with rabbinic experts in the field for guidance and direction.

6. Unfortunately, sometimes a rabbi may use prayer to isolate himself

from the patient — for instance, if the rabbi feels uncomfortable visiting a patient who is in pain or suffering from a condition that is too "close to home." In such cases, it is difficult to ascertain for whom the prayer is really being said. Some rabbis step across the threshold, say a prayer, wish the patient a speedy recovery, and then leave. This accomplishes little beyond working through a list of names he might have. The patient gains nothing if the rabbi's prayer does not reflect a connection with the patient's concerns. This will only happen if the rabbi actually enters the room and engages with the patient.

BIBLIOGRAPHY

Abraham, Abraham S. 2000. *Nishmat Avraham — Medical Halachah for Doctors, Nurses, Healthcare Personnel, and Patients. Volume I: Orach Chaim.* Brooklyn: Mesorah Publications, Ltd.

Abraham, Abraham S. 2003. *Nishmat Avraham — Medical Halachah for Doctors, Nurses, Healthcare Personnel, and Patients. Volume II: Yoreh Deah.* Brooklyn: Mesorah Publications, Ltd.

Azoulay, Elie, et al. 2003. "Determinants of Post-Intensive Care Unit Mortality: A Prospective Multi-Center Study." *Critical Care Medicine* 31:428–432.

Barth, Fredrik. 1966. *Models of Social Organization.* London: Royal Anthropological Institute.

Belmartino, Susana. 1994. "The Role of the State in Health Systems." *Social Science and Medicine* 39:1315–1321.

Bleich, J. David. 1981. *Judaism and Healing: Halachic Perspectives.* Jersey City: KTAV Publishing House.

Brett, Allan S., and Jersild, Paul. 2003. "'Inappropriate' Treatment Near the End of Life: Conflict between Religious Convictions and Clinical Judgment." *Archives of Internal Medicine* 163:1645–1649.

Ciccarello, Gail P. 2003. "Strategies to Improve End of Life Care in the Intensive Care Unit." *Dimensions of Critical Care Nursing* 22:216–222.

Cohen, Sheldon, Kessler, Ronald C. and Underwood Gordon, Lynn (eds.). 1995. *Measuring Stress: A Guide for Health and Social Scientists.* New York: Oxford University Press.

Collins, S., and A. Long. 2003. "Too Tired to Care? The Psychological Effects of Working with Trauma." *Journal of Psychiatric and Mental Health Nursing* 10:17–27.

Combes, Alain, et al. 2003. "Morbidity, Mortality, and Quality-of-Life Outcomes of Patients Requiring >14 Days of Mechanical Ventilation." *Critical Care Medicine* 31:1373–1381.

Curtis, J. Randall, and Rubenfeld, Gordan D. (eds.). 2001. *Managing Death in the ICU: The Transition from Cure to Care.* New York: Oxford University Press.

Deane, Barbara. 1992. "The Spiritual Crisis of Caregiving." *Aging and Spirituality* iv: 1.

Donahue, John M., and Meredith B. McGuire. 1995. "The Political Economy of Responsibility in Health and Illness." *Social Science and Medicine* 40:47–53.

Edwards, Maria-Benedicta, and Kenneth M. Taylor. 2003. "Is 30–Day Mortality an Adequate Outcome Statistic for Patients Considering Heart Valve Replacement?" *Annals of Thoracic Surgery* 76:482–485.

Emerson, Richard M. 1976. "Social Exchange Theory." *Annual Review of Sociology* 2:335–362.

Eyer, Richard. 1991. "Building Mutual Trust and Respect within the Chaplain/Physician Relationship." Pp. 19–31. Binghampton: Haworth Press.

Fletcher, Robert H., Suzanne W. Fletcher, and Edward H. Wagner. 1996. *Clinical Epidemiology: The Essentials.* Baltimore: Williams and Wilkins.

Frank, Arthur W. 2002. *At the Will of the Body: Reflections on Illness.* Boston: Houghton Mifflin Company.

Frank, Arthur W. 2004. *The Renewal of Generosity: Illness, Medicine, and How to Live.* Chicago: University of Chicago Press.

Ganzini, Linda, et al. 2003. "Nurses' Experiences with Hospice Patients Who Refuse Food and Fluids to Hasten Death." *The New England Journal of Medicine* 349:359–365.

Harris, Jeffrey E. 1995. *Deadly Choices: Coping with Health Risks in Everyday Life*. New York: Basic Books.

Heimer, Carol A. 1992. "Your Baby's Fine, Just Fine: Certification Procedures, Meetings, and the Supply of Information in Neonatal Intensive Care Units." Pp. 161–188 in *Organizations, Uncertainties, and Risk*, edited by James F. Short, Jr. and Lee Clarke. Boulder: Westview Press.

Kalbfleisch, John D., and Ross L. Prentice. 1980. *The Statistical Analysis of Failure Time Data*. New York: John Wiley & Sons.

Lobo, Suzana, et al. 2003. "C-Reactive Protein Levels Correlate with Mortality and Organ Failure in Critically Ill Patients." *Chest: The Cardiopulmonary and Critical Care Journal* 123:2043–2049.

Luce, John M., and Gordon D. Rubenfeld. 2002. "Can Health Care Costs Be Reduced by Limiting Intensive Care at the End of Life?" *American Journal of Respiratory and Critical Care Medicine* 165:750–754.

Lunney, June, Joanne Lynn, Daniel Foley, Steven Lipson, and Jack Guralnik. 2003. "Patterns of Functional Decline at the End of Life." *Journal of the American Medical Association* 289:2387–2392.

Mayer, Karl Ulrich, and Nancy Brandon Tuma. 1990. "Life Course Research and Event History Analysis: An Overview." Pp. 3–20 in *Event History Analysis in Life Course Research*, edited by Karl Ulrich Mayer and Nancy Brandon Tuma. Madison: The University of Wisconsin Press.

McGrae, Mary, et al. 2003. "Knowledge and Attitudes Regarding Cardiovascular Disease Risk and Prevention in Patients with Coronary or Peripheral Arterial Disease." *Archives of Internal Medicine* 163: 2157–2162.

Morgan, Myfanwy, Michael Calnan, and Nick Manning. 1985. *Sociological Approaches to Health and Medicine*. London: Croom Helm.

Morris, David B. 2002. "Narrative, Ethics, and Pain: Thinking *with* Stories." Pp. 196–218 in *Stories Matter: The Role of Narrative in Medical Ethics*, edited by Rita Charon and Martha Montello. Chicago: University of Chicago Press.

Nolin, T., and R. Anderson. 2003. "Withdrawal of Medical Treatment in the ICU: A Cohort Study of 318 Cases during 1994–2000." *Acta Anaesthesiologica Scandinavica* 47:501–507.

Nuland, Sherwin B. 1994. *How We Die: Reflections on Life's Final Chapter.* New York: Alfred A. Knopf.

Osmon, S., D. Warren, S.M. Seiler, W. Shannon, V.J. Fraser, and M.H. Kollef. 2003. "The Influence of Infection on Hospital Mortality for Patients Requiring ≥ 48h of Intensive Care." *Chest* 124:1021–9.

Pardue, Lea. 1991. "Models for Ministry: The Spiritual Needs of the Frail Elderly Living in Long-Term Care Facilities." *Journal of Religious Gerontology* 8:13–23.

Pitorak, Elizabeth Ford. 2003. "Care at the Time of Death: How Nurses Can Make the Last Hours of Life a Richer, More Comfortable Experience." *American Journal of Nursing* 103:42–52.

Poullier, Jean-Pierre, and Sandra Wilson. 1993. *Organization for Economic Cooperation and Development (OECD) Health Systems: Facts and Trends, 1960–1991.* Paris: Organization for Economic Cooperation and Development.

Regehr, Cheryl. 2001. "Crisis Debriefing Groups for Emergency Responders: Reviewing the Evidence." *Brief Treatment and Crisis Intervention* 1:87–100.

Regehr, Cheryl. 2002. "Exposure to Human Tragedy, Empathy, and Trauma in Ambulance Paramedics." *American Journal of Orthopsychiatry* 72:505–513.

Rosner, Fred, and Rav Moshe D. Tendler. 1997. *Practical Medical Halachah.* Northvale: Jason Aronson, Inc.

Rubenfeld, Gordon D., and Stephan W. Crawford. 1996. "Withdrawing Life Support from Mechanically Ventilated Recipients of Bone Marrow Transplants: A Case for Evidence-Based Guidelines." *Annals of Internal Medicine* 125:625–633.

Schneiderman, Lawrence J., et al. 2003. "Effect of Ethics Consultations on Nonbeneficial Life-Sustaining Treatments in the Intensive Care

Setting: A Randomized Controlled Trial." *The Journal of the American Medical Association* 290:1166–1172.

Scott, H. Richard. 1992. *Organizations: Rational, Natural, and Open Systems.* Englewood Cliffs: Prentice Hall.

VandeCreek, Larry. 1991. "Understanding Physicians: An Educational History and Brief Practice Profile." Pp. 5–18. Binghampton: The Haworth Press.

Verbrugge, Lois, and Donald Patrick. 1995. "Seven Chronic Conditions: Their Impact on US Adults' Activity Levels and Use of Medical Services." *American Journal of Public Health* 85:173–182.

Warren, Tiffany, Shannon Lee, and Stephen Saunders. 2003. "Factors Influencing Experienced Distress and Attitude Toward Trauma by Emergency Medicine Practitioners." *Journal of Clinical Psychology in Medical Settings* 10:293–296.

Wastell, Colin. 2002. "Exposure to Trauma: The Long-Term Effects of Suppressing Emotional Reactions." *Journal of Nervous and Mental Disease* 190:839–845.

Williams, Carter Catlett. 1990. "Long-Term Care and the Human Spirit." *Generations: Aging and the Human Spirit.* Fall: 25–28.

Yan, Y., D.R. Hoover, R.D. Moore, and C. Xiong. 2003. "Multivariate Estimation of Cumulative Incidence, Prevalence, and Morbidity Time of a Disease When Death Is Likely." *Journal of Clinical Epidemiology* 56:546–552.

❧ 7 ❧
COUNSELING THE TERMINALLY ILL CONGREGANT

Phyllis Dvora Corn, M.Sc.
Benjamin W. Corn, M.D.

WHILE IT IS TRADITIONAL for rabbis to visit the sick and officiate at the funerals of congregants, it does not necessarily follow that rabbis are equipped to perform such tasks in the most effective and meaningful way. The role of the rabbi as a member of the support system for the dying patient and his family is complex. This complexity arises from the many factors that inherently beset families and individuals confronting terminal illness.

When getting involved in this kind of situation, the rabbi needs to investigate: his own self-awareness, the patient's preexisting family dynamics, the coping stage the individual and his family have reached, and the meaning — both symbolic and real — that illness and death has for the family, as well as definitions of death and the importance of viewing it from both a physical as well as psychological perspective. The rabbi fulfills a unique role as part of the supportive network for the patient and his family, as he may be able to facilitate a meaningful death for all involved.

DEFINING DEATH

Death is, by definition, the antithesis of life. Death, like birth, is common to all mortals regardless of gender, race, religion, nationality, or economic standing. All living creatures will experience death and many human beings will actually witness it. As King David exclaimed, "What man lives and will never see death?" (*Psalms* 89:49).

Although death can objectively be defined as the "absence of life", technology now allows us to more rigorously identify the moment of death. Traditionally, three major categories are invoked to define death:

- ▶ **Cellular or biological death** represents the actual cessation of the functioning of the organs.
- ▶ **Brain death** constitutes the specific cessation of the most critical organ in the body, ultimately due to the insufficient supply of oxygen (anoxia).
- ▶ **Clinical death** generally refers to the failure of the intrathoracic organs (i.e., cessation of the heartbeat and respiration).

It is not within the scope of this chapter to present the halachic definitions of death. To be sure, the task of defining death is not a trivial exercise and arguably continues to represent the most pressing concern in the entire field of bioethics today. The rabbi, most of the time, only needs to have a general ability to recognize death as it is physiologically unfolding. Although it is quite difficult to precisely appreciate the loss of the ephemeral components that maintain the human organism as a living being, the rabbi is capable of recognizing some telltale signs of impending death, such as the lack of response to external stimuli, the absence of movement or breathing, and even the absence of elicitable reflexes. The rabbi will not have the tools at his disposal to note flat or isoelectric lines on electro-encephalograms or electrocardiograms. At times he may be confronted with a patient who is rapidly dwindling; his role at this juncture is simply to contact the physician so that a medical assessment can be made and if necessary, death "pronounced". While there is a precise moment of death, it is the process of dying and the opportunities presented to the rabbi to add meaning to this process that are the rabbi's focus.

THE RABBI'S SELF-AWARENESS
AS A STARTING POINT

Superimposed on the complexity of working with the dying is the interplay between the thoughts, feelings, and beliefs of the rabbi, the patient, and perhaps the patient's family as well. These potentially differing positions may interact and even collide. The rabbi may be specifically sought as the person who can provide meaningful solace in this period of crisis and uncertainty. In order to optimally assist the patient in dealing with life's end, the rabbi must first take stock of his own relationship with illness and mortality — he must be keenly aware of the meaning of illness and death to him, personally. The rabbi needs to ask himself some of the following questions: "What have been my experiences with serious illness and death?" "How do I experience and cope with losses in general?" "What are the messages and stories that I have carried, either from my family of origin, close friends, or other life experiences that have colored the meaning of disease and the dying process?" "What has my anxiety level been when confronted with loss?"

All professional counselors are at risk of confusing their own feelings with those harbored by the patient. To minimize this potential blurring of emotions, the rabbi must remain cognizant of the multiple influences that affect him, including his own age, cultural background, socio-economic level, and especially his previous encounters with death and dying.

THE WORLD OF THE CENTRAL FIGURE: THE PATIENT

The dying process of a particular individual will directly and indirectly affect the person's family. A rabbi may be approached by the person diagnosed with a disease, or perhaps the family or close friends of that patient. At this point it will become important to understand the family's dynamics, as well as the rights of the ill person to remain autonomous.

When someone other than the ill person seeks guidance, that person is likely coming from an emotionally charged place that may include feelings of confusion, sadness, helplessness, shock, or anger. In virtually all situations, he or she has altruistic intentions on behalf of the sick person. The reactions that appear on the surface may be a mere glimmer of many underlying emotions and thoughts. It is important for a rabbi to bear in mind that the dying process, while experienced by family members and friends, is one that belongs primarily to the person who is dying.

The well-meaning intentions of others to be helpful or to play a particular role are best framed in terms of recognizing and respecting the desires of the dying person. For example, there is often a difference of opinion between the ill person and his family concerning how openly the person's illness and impending death should be discussed. It is not unusual for a family member to feel protective of his parent to the extent that he wishes to shield his parent and others from the dire prognosis. While there are rare situations where this might be indicated, the "right to know" and the "right to tell" really belong to the sick person, first and foremost.

As such, counseling family members about how best to

communicate during the dying process requires an exploration of the patient's wishes and needs. This may be done through a dialogue between the rabbi and the patient directly, or indirectly by counseling a friend or family member on how to explore these issues. Thoughtfulness, tenderness, and carefully chosen words are important in this setting. Usually, an ability to meet the patient "where he is" helps move the process forward in an unencumbered and honest manner.

The rabbi's discussions with family members and friends may best focus on what they are feeling. Assisting these individuals to sort out the complexity of their own emotions and to mobilize their internal resources and external support systems are important functions. Validating a family member's feelings and listening as an empathic outsider can be highly constructive.

It is important to encourage the family and friends of the dying to be available to the patient just to listen to him. That allows the patient to move through the dying process knowing that he is not alone. A rabbi can serve an integral role in bolstering family and friends at a time when they are quite fragile, but most needed.

THE STAGES OF DYING

While people have been dying for as long as life has existed, a careful study of the dying experience was not documented until the work of Dr. Elizabeth Kubler-Ross in 1968. Dr. Kubler-Ross, having worked with many dying patients, embarked on a project where a team of clergy, psychologists, and medical professionals met with people who were terminally ill and engaged them in frank and heartfelt conversations about their experiences. This project culminated in the watershed publication of *On Death and Dying*, and began decades of study into the subject of dying and communicating with those who are terminally ill.

The five stages of dying, according to Kubler-Ross are: **denial, anger, bargaining, depression, and acceptance.** These stages were initially thought to always occur in the same chronological order. Subsequently it was learned that they may, in fact, appear in varying order or even overlap or reoccur. Understanding the reactions of the dying within this framework may be helpful in deciphering what may appear to be confusing and even contradictory responses.

Denial and isolation. When the patient first hears that he is terminally ill, he usually goes into denial. Denial is a common and normal way of coping, and serves as a psychological buffer allowing the individual time to absorb the new reality. It allows the patient to collect himself before continuing. It is often followed by feelings of isolation and withdrawal from others as the recognition of a new, grim, and frightening reality sets in.

During this stage, as with others, the individual needs to know that he is not alone. Despite the fact that he may push others away and create a distance from those in his world, his basic need for love and support still exists. It may be tempting to maneuver a person away from denial, confront him with the reality, and attempt to move him toward acceptance. It is important however, to resist doing this, especially at this early stage, because he requires time and contemplation to assimilate this shocking news and the meaning it will have on his life. By maintaining a connection with him and being supportive, he will most likely, eventually, move himself to a place of acceptance (albeit partial at times).

Anger. An individual's anger may be potent, out of control, and displaced in all directions. The anger may be projected onto others in his life, such as family members, doctors, the health system, and even God. The family may feel unappreciated and others, such as health professionals, may feel abused by his constant outbursts and requests. The person begins to see his plans and hopes for the future disintegrate before his eyes. He feels a lack of control. This lack of control related to the disease process may be compounded by a highly bureaucratic medical system. Advances in medical technology have come with the price of a system that is challenging to navigate.

During this stage, the patient may risk alienating those who seek to help him, such as family, friends, and medical staff. The rabbi may be in the position to hear the patient's anger, accept it unconditionally, and then gently reflect back these feelings in an attempt to refocus this anger. Is the patient angry at those individuals on whom he is projecting these feelings? Or, in fact is this anger being displaced in an unhelpful way, simply because he is so understandably upset and there is no other place for it? It may be difficult for him to say that he has lost faith in God; the thought may be frightening for him to admit. The person may feel that he can no longer pray, for he is too angry at God. Validating the feelings of anger and the sense of unfairness that the person feels may be helpful. The rabbi can provide a safe place for the patient to vent his feelings without consequence.

Additionally, the person should be given every opportunity to maintain control and exert his right to make choices. Empathizing with his loss of control and finding opportunities for him to make choices may be very constructive in helping the patient to manage his feelings.

Bargaining. This stage is where the individual attempts to make a rational deal with God to change the course of his fate. What may be viewed as magical thinking and discounted as a primitive, unrealistic effort to alter the disease process may actually be a powerful coping tool that maintains the individual's hope — an essential ingredient for survival.

A rabbi might be asked to act as a conduit to God in the

bargaining process. While in Judaism we believe that each person has the unique, personal ability to relate directly to the Almighty, it is not uncommon for a person facing a life-threatening illness to rally additional troops into battle. It is at this stage that often people will take on additional mitzvot or make substantial contributions to institutions in the hope that the "decree" will be reversed.

The rabbi needs to take great care in this stage to examine his own agenda and issues with relation to the power projected onto him, as well as potential conflicts of interest. There is a high risk of his being pulled into the fantasy of being able to save the person. Yes, we do believe in the power of prayer and charity, and there have even been scientific studies to support the effects of prayer on healing (Byrd, 1988). But we also know that there are no guarantees that can be offered to the bargaining patient. A rabbi must be genuine and candid about his belief in the ultimate power of God to determine one's fate, and at the same time encourage hope and belief in the possibility for change in what appears to be a dismal prognosis.

Additionally, while a patient may gain a sense of control and empowerment by offering to make a large donation in the hopes of improving his health, a rabbi must be cautious, as there is the potential for conflict of interest in this regard. There isn't a Jewish community that could not benefit from a generous donation. It is vital for the rabbi to maintain his objectivity and propriety, considering what is best for the patient, what motivates him in his contribution, and what his expectations are of the contribution's impact.

Sometimes, there is a constructive element to the bargaining stage. For instance, dying patients may "will themselves" to live long enough to participate in an upcoming event (e.g., wedding of a grandchild). We view this as a positive form of bargaining that can instill hope.

Depression. As the disease progresses, depression often sets in. Depression may take different forms. One may experience a "reactive depression" or a "preparatory depression". The former may be related to previously unresolved losses and grief over past issues. This depression may be explored and addressed by gaining greater understanding of these past experiences in a supportive setting. Preparatory depression is a deeper and more profound depression, which relates to preparing for the final separation from life on this earth. The person realizes that his future hopes and dreams may be shattered and he becomes understandably saddened.

The tendency is for those around him to try to cheer him up. This is a human inclination to help people feel better, along with most people's inability to share for very long the sadness and pain of the dying person. Facing mortality in others is frightening; it provokes within us a sense of existential anxiety, which is disturbing and even alarming. However, cheering a person up (or attempting to do so) is usually not the best intervention here. The dying patient will often be unmovable and will want to stay in this sadness. He will resist attempts to be cheered up and, in fact, may resent such efforts and see them as alienating. It is advisable for the rabbi to accept the patient in this sadness, acknowledge it, and share it.

As professionals we are often asked: Don't you ever feel like you are going to cry in front of your patients? How do you hold back this seemingly weak and unprofessional response? The truth is, while boundaries and distance are essential, this is the time when tears may be shed by the professional. They are tears of empathy and they are perfectly appropriate. We are speaking here of sharing the greatest loss imaginable — the loss of being. When a dying person realizes that those around him share his anguish, he begins to feel understood and less alone.

Families will often seek guidance in dealing with this depression. They need to be counseled that this is a normal, healthy, and usually unavoidable response that requires their support and understanding. Sharing in this pain is not a sign of weakness; it is a sign of humanness.

Acceptance. Acceptance may follow depression, but may not constitute full acceptance. We often witness a sense of eternal hope that may function to maintain a delicate balance between resignation and perseverance. The dying person may have accepted the prognosis of imminent death as a reality on one level, yet continue to see the possibility of victory over the disease on another level. At this stage, the person may display what has been described as "quiet expectation." The depression of the earlier stage has somewhat lifted and much of the anger may also be gone. With acceptance comes a sense of calm and a diminishing of the struggle. Often times, the physiological needs and functions of the patient will begin to decline. He may eat less and engage in less activity. This may be extremely difficult for family members to witness. *They* may still be unable to accept this reality or to prepare for the person's death, yet the patient has already embarked on an agenda to accept the inevitable and make his departure.

Not all patients reach the stage of acceptance. The struggle to live may carry them until the very end of their lives. At the stage of acceptance, there is tremendous work to be done that can impact on the quality of the time left. The patient may want to resolve unfinished business from the past. Relationships may be reconciled; life goals may be pursued (such as writing a book or going on a long, desired trip). Repentance (*teshuvah*) is a task that takes on great meaning and encourages a sense of calm and closure at this time.

The rabbi may play a pivotal role in this final stage. Frank conversations with the patient about the people or issues with which he needs closure may bring about a willingness to gather these people back into his life for a final discussion. The rabbi could then contact individuals who have been important to the patient and bring them together for a final meeting. These sessions may bring a sense of ease to the patient and may be extremely beneficial to those who survive to mourn and grieve.

When the best medical resources have failed to save the patient, helping him to see the meaning of his life and to maintain faith (*emunah*) in God's plan may be extremely helpful. Maintaining a life of meaning until the last moment is possible when a person can come to appreciate the impact of his contribution to the world and to his family. If he is able to perceive himself as a link in a chain that began before him and continues onward, he may retain a sense of purpose and hope — even as he prepares to take his final breaths. The renowned psychiatrist and concentration camp survivor Viktor Frankl emphasized the importance of giving meaning to life, even in the absence of clear redemption from suffering. The opportunity for each man to leave his "footprint in the sands of time" and to choose what this "monument of his existence" will be gives even the most desperate hours a sense of purpose and meaning (Frankl, 1959).

A rabbi's ties to the family and an understanding of the relationships within the family can help foster conversations and interactions that can give deep meaning to the death of a loved one. The rabbi may also bring insight from the rich history of our ancestors, who often faced adversity but maintained their optimism, despite the great odds.

UNDERSTANDING THE FAMILY

Family development theories (also known as "Life Course Theory") (Bengtson and Allen, 1993) offer a framework for viewing the family's reactions over time. Families are also seen as progressing through developmental processes as the family as a unit moves through stages and events over time that will effect and change the structure, roles, and interactions within it (White and Klein, 2002). Each new stage acts as a virtual resting place after departure from an earlier stage, and represents a point or location within the family's life course. It is thought that the strength of any given family as a healthy and functioning unit is largely predicated on its "successful" passage through these various stages of family development.

Examination of the various family stages will provide insight into the possible expectations, stressors, strengths, and coping mechanisms that will present in the family. Is this a newly married couple adjusting to couple-hood, a young family with small children, a middle-aged couple with adolescents or children preparing to leave home, or a mature, retired couple planning their retirement years? Alternatively, is this a second marriage or blended family (such as those with children from previous marriages) in which some members find themselves at multiple stages simultaneously? A sensitivity to the challenges and resources that each of these stages introduce will provide an important backdrop against which the rabbi will relate to the patient and family.

Understanding the "personality" of the family and the way it functions under normal conditions is very important. A serious illness of a family member often disrupts the usual balance and activities within a family, but just the same, the manner in which family members cope under strain may be understood by looking at the family's history. When approached by a dying person or his family member, it is essential for the rabbi to talk with the family member to gain an understanding of the manner in which the family handles various life tasks during less stressful times. Areas to explore include the family's patterns in decision-making, sharing, or allocating the labor involved in running the home and knowing what outside support is available to them and can be called upon in times of need. Who usually takes the lead in performing tasks? Where does the sick person fit into this dynamic? What is the family structure? Is this a family that has rigid boundaries (parental group, children, grandparents) or does the family display flexibility in boundaries — or perhaps a lack thereof? The notion of the potential for change in roles and duties is particularly relevant, as regrouping and reassigning of tasks is often required for the family to manage when illness strikes a key family member, such as a parent.

Family members often draw upon coping strategies that may have been accessed in the past. Is this a family that tends to deny issues or employ taboos or secrets? Some family members prefer to take control by engaging in active fact-finding roles (especially through the resources of the internet) while others choose to "wait it out," withdraw, or isolate themselves.

COMMUNICATION PATTERNS

The work of Glaser and Strauss (1964, 1965) defined "awareness contexts," of which rabbis ought be mindful. They described two types of contexts — the "closed context" and the "open awareness context". The closed context exists when the system around the patient prevents him from knowing that he is dying. Family and friends collude with the health care team to hide the information from the patient. The open awareness context avoids any pretenses and allows the patient's terminal status to be known by all involved. While each context provides some advantage, the literature suggests that open awareness is preferable (Staton, Shuy, Byock, 2001).

The closed context offers the benefit of continuing life normally to a certain extent. This paternalistic arrangement theoretically liberates the patient from the anguish of facing a terminal illness and thoughts of impending death. Those who favor this approach indicate that social bonds are preserved with the patient when he is shielded, while those around him act with care and concern — as if the disease is temporary and remediable.

Seale's study of English patients (1998) who died of terminal illness related the sense of meaning that an open awareness context allowed them as they entered their final days. These patients talked openly about their illness and prognoses and exchanged intimate emotions with those in their lives, thus strengthening these bonds. These dying patients were aware and involved in planning their deaths and 79% were reported to have selected the place they would spend their dying days.

A family may choose the route of shielding the patient from knowing the truth. The rabbi may find himself in the midst of family dissonance regarding this issue, where some members would like full disclosure and others disagree. This may compel the rabbi to explore the advantages and disadvantages of each approach with the family. It is helpful to explore whether the family has had any previous conversations with the dying person prior to this time about his preference to know or not know. Occasionally, it will be reported that the patient once told a family member, "If something is seriously wrong with me, I'd rather not know." If this has occurred, it may still be gently explored to learn if anything has changed that may have altered that patient's wishes. It is important to gauge the concerns of the family regarding speaking about the illness. Precisely "who" is being protected is an important question to consider.

The critical issue to note regarding a closed context is that it is difficult to maintain successfully. The patient will find himself undergoing complex treatment, will most likely be seen by oncologists or other physicians who treat life-threatening diseases, and will reside in waiting rooms or be admitted to hospital wards with patients who are clearly ill and dying. The patient will decipher the facial expressions and emotional responses of those around him and deduce the seriousness of his situation. When this happens, he might then feel more frightened and emotionally isolated from those around him. He might feel that he has to maintain the secret of his diagnosis and prognosis to protect his family, even though he would like to further explore the reality of his situation.

While there may be specific circumstances where a closed context is indicated, the majority of individuals facing death benefit from hearing their prognosis. That being said, many patients will receive the news and then continue to carry on their lives in a way that avoids directly speaking about their fate. This too needs to be respected, and a rabbi counseling a dying patient is advised to listen carefully to the language employed by him and to mirror his coping and communication style.

If the patient speaks about his disease or his course of treatment and engages in an open way about his concerns, fears, or plans regarding his prognosis, he can be seen as a person who has reached a point where he has integrated the information and is able to process its impact on his life. A second type is the person who does not use the language of illness, but clearly has accepted the facts. He or she may have been raised in a culture that does not openly discuss illness or death, or it may simply be too painful for him to articulate the language. This person may speak about planning for when he is "gone" and refer to his cancer as "this situation," "this nuisance," or this "thing." He demonstrates his feelings of anger, frustration, or depression. The reality has set in. Conversation with some individuals may be characterized by use of medical terminology, but the majority of the content may be unrelated to his illness or impending death. He may discuss moving to a new home or redecorating the living room "when I get out of here." Finally, there are those patients who avoid speaking about their disease in any way, directly or indirectly. While they may have been informed of their illness and prognosis, these individuals are not ready to address it.

These positions are not static. While these responses often reflect the person's personality, as he passes through the emotional stages of dying, his patterns of communication may change. The rabbi should take great care to listen to the patient and attempt to understand where along this spectrum he is choosing to communicate. Once again, respecting the idiosyncratic communication style and following the patient's lead in this regard engenders a sense of closeness and empathy. Maintaining the use of metaphors ("this nuisance") and symbolic language that the patient may employ ("I will be going") fosters feelings of safety for him. By adopting the patient's style and language, the rabbi conveys a message that the patient is in control and the discussions that ensue will be on his terms. In creating an environment that conveys respect for the patient's wishes, the rabbi offers an opportunity for the patient to progress along the continuum towards acceptance at his own pace.

The general guideline of speaking to individuals at the level and in the manner that they communicate is also applicable to communicating with children. Whether it is the child who is the patient or a relative of the patient, the child will make known to others (subtly or directly) what he is ready to hear and discuss, and how. Communication with children needs to take into account the cognitive level of the child and his maturity. As with adults, attempting to shield children from the reality of a terminal illness is rarely successful. Children are both resilient and perceptive and will sense that the family is in crisis. A lack of open communication and reluctance to respond to the child's concerns will often raise a child's level of anxiety and fear. In such cases, the child will imagine that not only is something terrible happening, but also that the family can not provide the most important thing that families need to provide for children — the maintenance of a safe place. The home needs to be a place where one can safely speak, ask questions, and, at times, cry.

HOPE

No discussion of coping with dying is complete without consideration of the role that hope plays. *Webster's Dictionary* defines hope as: "Desire accompanied by expectation of or belief in fulfillment." When a cancer patient is told that his prognosis is terminal, at some point, he is faced with a choice. He can see his life as having ended at that moment or he can view this as yet another stage (albeit challenging) in his life. Even in this stage, desired expectations can be fulfilled. If the patient perceives the prognosis as an immediate death sentence, where the ensuing days will be devoid of any meaning, then he will abandon all hope. With that, he will retreat from life's tasks and the relationships that have been the fabric of his existence. In contrast, the person who retains a sense of hope is able to harvest enormous strength and ability to do what is required in this final stage. As such, people at the end of life begin to hope for different things. They may hope to participate in particular family events, to complete a particular project, or to experience less pain. As long as this sparkle of hope glimmers, one is embraced by life.

Byock (1996) describes the developmental milestones involved in dying. These include: bringing completion to relationships and worldly affairs, identifying the meaningful messages of one's life, gaining self-forgiveness and forgiveness of others, and connecting to enduring legacies. These tasks require deep introspection. Such introspection is often based on the under-lying notion that there is not only a purpose to one's life, but there is also a function and purpose to one's death as well. By seeing the dying person attain these milestones, those around him have enormous treasures to gain. The dying person, often liberated from many of life's trivial endeavors, now focuses on those values that are most sacred — family, friendships, beliefs, and principles. His evolution through the developmental pro-cess of dying allows others to renew their appreciation of these values as well. Subsequently, upon recognizing his value to oth-ers, the dying person may feel his life has even greater mean-ing during his plight. When a rabbi becomes involved in this reciprocal process, he has the unique opportunity to be part of a *chesed* that engenders inner growth and development for all involved.

TERMINATION: SAYING THE FINAL GOOD-BYE

Witnessing the ultimate departure from this world is both pow-erful and humbling. If a person who is dying has the chance to say goodbye prior to his final breath, this can provide comfort and solace to those who survive him. Likewise, when a friend or family member can say his or her goodbyes in return, a sense of closure is more likely felt. This is seen when we contrast the coping responses of those who suffered sudden traumatic losses with those who experienced losses that were anticipated (Barry et al, 2002).

The termination process may be brief or lengthy, formal or informal. Fundamental components of this process include: sharing the meaning of the relationship (often through remi-niscing about old times or recalling significant life events), resolving past disputes or clarifying unsettled issues, and ex-pressing appreciation for the rewards that each has gained from the relationship. For some, having the dying person wish them well can be very comforting. A young widow reported to us that after she and her dying husband embraced one last time, the most consoling words he uttered were his wish for her to rebuild her life and remarry after his death. These words, while painful and "even unthinkable" (her thoughts at the time), later allowed her to grieve for her husband and remarry with the feeling that his blessing enveloped her new home.

Rituals can be most helpful in aiding the termination process. A rabbi is in a particularly strong position to assist in structuring such events and to imbue them with religious meaning. Jewish sources and liturgy offer a wellspring of material. These may include the study of texts dealing with those who suffered, such as Job, or the Psalms of David, or the recitation of particular prayers and readings to offer comfort and inspiration. Embarking on a project of study has tremendous potential to provide a sense of empowerment and meaning to the dying patient. By investing time in teaching and learning cooperatively with a terminal patient, a message is conveyed that he is of value and "matters". Such study may also include other family members and may act as a bonding and sharing experience for a family that is at a loss for words or avoids speaking about their feelings.

Music, particularly prayers set to familiar melodies that resonate for the patient, may bring about a sense of calm. They may also help elicit memories that can be shared in passing on a legacy to future generations. A sixty-year-old grandfather who was close to death tape-recorded the *haftarah* cantillation for his eleven-year-old grandson. Hoping that he would live to see the bar mitzvah, he realized that this would likely not occur. By offering his grandson this gift, the grandfather gained a sense of connection to the future. He did not in fact make it to the grandson's bar mitzvah, but in a very real way, he was there on the *bimah* while the boy chanted his portion.

Establishing a set time to regularly participate in rituals provides structure and a sense of control for the dying person, who may have little else to effectively spend his time on during the late stages of disease. Rituals should be initiated with the input of the patient and in a way that allows him to choose what has personal meaning. The rabbi should show flexibility and alter or discontinue such activities if the patient desires, without taking personal offense and supporting the choice (perhaps one of the very few that the dying person may exercise).

CASE STUDIES

We have chosen two illustrative cases from our practices that highlight some common themes that arise when patients grapple with potentially terminal conditions. In both cases we suggest some possible interventions that may be offered by a rabbi providing counseling.

Case I: "Don't Tell My Daughter!"

Miriam, a nineteen-year-old young woman, had been experiencing headaches for three months. The headaches did not respond to aspirin or migraine medication. The family physician ordered a Magnetic Resonance Imaging study (MRI), which showed a large mass in the patient's brain. A referral was made to a neurosurgeon, who wanted to bring the patient to the operating room for a biopsy and removal of what was apparently a malignant tumor. The parents asked to meet privately with the surgeon and demanded that the doctor refer to her tumor as a "non-malignant cyst". They explained that they did not want to frighten their daughter by informing her of the seriousness of her condition. The physician reluctantly yielded to the parents' request, indicating that he would do his best to comply with their

wishes. Upon explaining the procedure to Miriam, the surgeon re-
vealed that the operation would result in a permanent scar and hair
loss that most likely would be temporary. Miriam listened and said, "I
don't understand why all this fuss is being made about a cyst. I refuse
to undergo disfiguring surgery just to remove a benign cyst!"

This is a common situation. A relative, usually a first-degree
relative, instructs the physician that the patient is not to be informed of the likely diagnosis of cancer. However, when this
happens, it is very reasonable for the patient to refuse to undergo a major procedure for some apparently minor purpose.
This family, with the best of intentions, has led the patient, an
adult who must sign the release form, down a path that endan-
gers her health.

At this point, a rabbi may be in a position to counsel the
family and patient. By exploring the parents' concerns, he may
assist them in managing their emotions. What is it that they
fear? Perhaps they fear exposing their state of worry and distress to their daughter. As parents, they see themselves as her
protectors. But at the same time, they face the fear of losing
their hopes and dreams for their daughter's future.

In what other ways can they protect or support their daughter through this crisis? In what way can they maintain their role
as parents, but also allow their daughter to be effectively involved in her own care? The rabbi may help the parents by
role-playing a scene in which Miriam is informed. What do
they think will be her reaction? How might they prepare themselves to respond to their daughter in a supportive way? What
are the parents' own beliefs regarding illness and death? How
have their experiences influenced the way they are coping with
the current situation? Clearly, they want what is best for their
daughter. How may they move toward more healthy, open, and
honest communication while still feeling safe?

The rabbi can discuss the Jewish view of suffering and pain. By being with all of them in their doubts and fears, the rabbi can support them and help them to build their faith. The trials of Abraham, for instance, can be discussed as a way of understanding the role that suffering may play in our lives. Helping the family move through the challenge together may provide them with an opportunity to strengthen their bonds with one another and God.

Case II: "We Can't Give Up on My Father"

Shoshana, the youngest of five children, has just learned that her 72-year-old father's prostate cancer has spread to his liver. A CAT scan disclosed that most of his liver is diseased. It is now obvious that Mr. Berkowitz has not responded to his hormone treatment. What's more, the only successful chemotherapy against prostate cancer cannot be considered here, since it causes significant liver damage. Her father is already hospitalized and they recommend that he be transferred to the local hospice for palliative care. Mr. Berkowitz has accepted this recommendation. Shoshana, on the other hand, is furious. She meets with the social worker and the attending physician and pleads with them to allow her father to remain in the oncology unit. She instructs the medical team that under no circumstances are they to give up on her father. While she initially had a friendly relationship with the nurses, the medical staff of the hospital is beginning to find Shoshana annoying and disruptive. They avoid her incessant calls throughout the day, which further exasperates Shoshana.

It is common for family members to refuse to accept that there is no cure to be offered to their loved one. This may leave them angry, frightened, and feeling powerless. When this occurs, they often vent their anger on others, often the health care staff. Rather than working collaboratively with these professionals, the family member begins to perceive them as adversaries.

This brings on an additional sense of panic and isolation.

Shoshana needs to sort out these feelings with someone. A rabbi would be in an excellent position to counsel her. Clearly, Shoshana is angry and fearful of losing her father. Being able to find less destructive ways of expressing this would be helpful. By providing an open, nonjudgmental ear, the rabbi may be the very person who could be most helpful. He can review aloud how much the medical team has already done on her father's behalf. His perspective as a person outside both the family and the medical system enables him to view things differently and share this view with Shoshana. He can also point out to her the value of working in collaboration with the medical staff, since they are necessary for her father's care at this time.

Furthermore, Shoshana's behavior and inability to accept reality merits further exploration. She may feel a strong obligation to control the situation, partly out of a sense of obeying the fifth commandment — honoring one's father and mother. The rabbi can clarify the obligations of this commandment and reflect on the ways that Shoshana has and may continue to honor her father, despite his terminal diagnosis. Reviewing the role of palliative care and understanding it as an active form of intervention — one that spares undue pain, as opposed to "giving up" — is important. Almost certainly, the medical team has already introduced this concept. The rabbi can be helpful here by reinforcing the change in management that is now evolving. Perhaps by listening to Shoshana's concerns, restating some of the medical facts, and reinforcing all she has done, the rabbi can help unburden her from the guilt she may feel regarding her father's condition.

It is not uncommon to observe dissonance between the patient's state of mind and that of his family. Often, the child is worried that her father may be overwhelmed by information that the patient has, in fact, already accepted. By calmly engaging the family and helping them process the facts, the rabbi can help them accept and better cope with the new reality.

BIBLIOGRAPHY

Barry, L. Kasl, S. and Prigerson, H. 2002. "Psychiatric Disorders Among Bereaved Persons: The Role of Perceived Circumstances of Death and Preparedness for Death." *American Journal of Geriatric Psychiatry* 10(4); 447–57.

Bengtson, V.L., Allen, K.R. 1993. "The Life Course Perspective Applied to Families Over Time." In Boss, Doherty, LaRossa, Schumm and Steinmetz (eds.) *Sourcebook for Family Theories and Methods: A Contextual Approach,* pp. 469–98. New York: Plenum Press.

Byock, I. 1996. "The Nature of Suffering and the Nature of Opportunity at the End of Life." *Clinics in Geriatric Medicine* 12, no.2: 237–52.

Byock, I., Staton, J., Shuy, R. 2001. *A Few Months to Live: Different Paths to Life's End.* Washington: Georgetown University Press.

Byrd, R. C. 1998. "Positive Therapeutic Effects of Intercessory Prayer in a Coronary Care Unit Population," *Southern Medical Journal* 81: 826–29.

Frankl, V.E. 1959. *Man's Search for Meaning.* Revised and updated, 1984. New York: Simon and Schuster Inc.

Glaser, B. G., and Strauss, A. L. 1964. "Awareness Contexts and Social Interactions." *American Sociological Review* 29:669–79.

Glaser, B. G. and Strauss, A. L. 1965. *Awareness of Dying.* Chicago: Aldine.

Kessler, D. 2000. *The Needs of the Dying.* New York: Harper Collins Publishers.

Kubler-Ross, E. 1969. *On Death and Dying: What the Dying Have to Teach Doctors, Nurses, Clergy and Their Families.* New York: Scribner/Simon and Schuster Inc.

Kubler-Ross, E. 1981. *Living with Death and Dying: How to Communicate with the Terminally Ill.* New York: Touchstone/Simon and Schuster Inc.

Kuhl, D. 2002. *What Dying People Want*. New York: Public Affairs, Perseus Books Group.

McDaniel, S.H., Hepworth, J., Doherty, W. 1997. *The Shared Experience of Illness: Stories of Patients, Families and Their Therapists*. New York: Basic Books.

Seale, C. F. 1998. *Constructing Death: The Sociology of Dying and Bereavement*. Cambridge: Cambridge University Press.

Webster's Ninth New Collegiate Dictionary. 1991. Massachusetts: Merriam Webster, Inc.

White, J.M., Klein, D.M. 2002. *Family Theories*, 2nd ed. Thousand Oaks: Sage Publications.

Zal, H.M. 1992. *The Sandwich Generation: Caught between Growing Children and Aging Parents*. New York: Plenum Publications.

❧ 8 ❧
COUNSELING PARENTS OF A DYING CHILD

Yisrael N. Levitz, Ph.D.

THERE IS NO MORE devastating an experience for parents than the shock of learning that their child has a fatal illness. Since the diagnosis alone implies a sense of doom and hopelessness, it most commonly elicits a response not just as a future threat but also as an experience of actual loss. For the rabbi called upon for support and counsel, it is essential that he understand the coping and grieving processes that parents go through during these terrible times.

Every parent reacts to the tragedy of a dying child in a unique manner. Each adjusts and copes in his own way, first to the knowledge of his child's impending fate and then to his actual death. Parents' responses will vary considerably as a function of their individual personalities, experience with previous crises, and the psychological implications this particular child has for them. A rabbi needs to be mindful of the different coping patterns of grieving parents and sensitive to the fact that there is no one correct way of dealing with this overwhelming tragedy.

Grieving, the process by which an individual copes with his feelings of loss, sadness, and helplessness, is experienced by many parents long before their child's death actually occurs. This anticipatory grief is indeed comparable to the process observed in persons actually experiencing the death of a loved one.

Parents whose children survive more than four months from the time of fatal prognosis tend to move through three characteristic psychological phases (Natterson and Knudson). Because the dreadful diagnosis is so unthinkable and unbearable, the most characteristic initial response is that of "denial". Parents will often take the ill child from one specialist to another, or go from clinic to clinic in the hope that someone can give them a more hopeful diagnosis.

There is also a tendency to use all forms of rationalization in order to avoid coming to grips with the diagnostic edict. The child's weakness may be explained by an insidious virus and leukemic bruises may be rationalized as a vitamin deficiency.

During this phase, parents tend to want to be with their children as much as possible, manifesting a tendency to cling to them physically. This time-consuming involvement with the sick child is often done at the expense of the rest of the family.

It is also common at this stage for parents to feel a sense of guilt and self-blame. It is here that a rabbi can play a key role in helping them examine any irrational guilt-provoking thoughts or unreasonable self-condemnations, such as when parents begin to tell the rabbi that the child's illness is their fault because, had they not been so busy with other matters, they might have noticed the child's symptoms sooner. It is often helpful for the rabbi to ask these parents what they would say to another caring parent who came to them with these self-recriminations. "Would you be as harsh and unfair to them as you are to yourself?" The rabbi's objective should not to be to attempt to convince them with logical arguments that the child's illness is not their fault. They are locked into a mind-set of irrational, blameful thinking that logic cannot reach. It is often more effective to prompt them to externalize their perspective by suggesting that they consider what they would say to another set of parents who were similarly harsh on themselves. "What would you say to these parents who have always been caring and devoted to their child and then began to blame themselves when their child became ill? Would it be reasonable to blame them?" It is important that the rabbi encourage them, if possible, to actually verbalize what they would say in such a case.

The second phase of coping is that of "confronting" reality. During this confrontational phase parents begin to psychologically internalize the reality of the child's illness; they experience and start coping with the anticipatory grief reaction aroused by that reality. It usually follows an exhaustive attempt to confirm the original diagnosis and is characterized by an active, realistic effort to prolong the child's life. Conscious denial is relinquished and the parents begin to face the hard reality that their child may likely die. Emotionally, they begin anticipating the loss and a process of mourning now begins.

During this phase, parents are not only interested in those measures which involve treatment of the disease, but also in the child's comfort and general emotional needs. At the same time, parents find that they are able to mobilize themselves sufficiently to be able to once again meet the needs of other family members.

The final phase of adjustment, the "terminal" phase, usually coincides with the final onslaught of the disease and the imminent death of the child. Mothers tend to be with their children whenever possible, but with adequate consideration for the needs of other members of the family. For the first time, wishes for the death of the child may be expressed openly to a rabbi and he should not be surprised if a wish for an end to this agonizing experience is confided with relatively little guilt.

Certain parents begin manifesting qualitative changes in focus and attitude at this phase. They show a more general interest in the suffering of others and express concern for all humanity, not specifically focusing on their child. It is not unusual to find parents becoming involved in the care of other children in the ward and expressing the desire to resume a more normal life and return to their other children at home.

Some researchers have observed that in cases of long terminal illness, the child's actual death was generally taken calmly, albeit with an appropriate expression of grief and sorrow. With a sense of relief that the child is no longer suffering, there tends to be a more muted expression of grief and a lessening of self-blame.

In follow-up studies of parents who have lost children through long illness, Sanford Friedman and his colleagues found that intense grief reactions tended to become much less pronounced following a three- to six-week period following the child's death. It is interesting to note that in follow-up observations, seven out of twenty-four mothers who had lost children were either pregnant, trying to become pregnant, or in the process of adopting a child.

It is clearly evident that a rabbi needs to maintain close contact with the bereaved family during this period of intense grief immediately following the child's death and to be aware that the grief for these parents, albeit less intense, never really ends.

THE EMOTIONAL COMPLEXITIES OF PARENTAL GRIEF

For parents suffering the loss of a child, the pace of grieving varies enormously as a function of a wide range of emotions. Undoubtedly the primary emotion is sorrow. It is interwoven, however, with a constellation of other emotions, particularly

anger, guilt, and anxiety. For the ministering rabbi, it is important to understand the underlying emotions of the grieving
process.

While grieving, parents tend to feel anger and resentment
that they are being forced to suffer a loss. Understandably, their
child's death is the cause of acute anguish and pain. However,
parents may also become aware that they have angry feelings
(with its concomitant guilt) toward the dying child, who is seen
as the cause of their anguish. Since they cannot vent their anger
against the child, they often turn on one another or express anger toward other family members.

It is also common to find parents turning their anger inward
and becoming depressed, or turning it against the physicians,
other attending medical professionals, or even the rabbi — blaming him harshly for even the slightest infraction or insensitivity,
real or imagined.

Particularly in the early stages of adjustment, reactions of
guilt are extremely common. A parent might reproach himself
for not having been more sensitive to the child's needs prior
to the illness. Before the diagnosis, for example, the child may
have been the cause of anger and rebuke. Many fatal illnesses
first appear with the kind of behavioral symptoms that cause
the child to be punished at home or at school. After the illness is diagnosed, parents and educators tend to feel intensely
guilty.

In the throes of self-recrimination, a parent experiences a
significant diminution in self-esteem and may begin a frenzied
effort to make up for his errors. Unrelieved guilt very often
leads to overindulgence of the child and a breakdown of discipline and boundaries.

The anticipation of a child's death often arouses in the parent a latent existential anxiety about his own mortality. Although this can be said regarding the death of any relative,

the parent-child relationship is generally regarded as the most reciprocally intense of all interpersonal relationships. Identification with the child poses a symbolic threat of death to the parent. In a sense, the parent confronts death, engages it, is defeated by it, and yet survives. The parent's feeling of apprehension is even further amplified by his sudden awareness of profound helplessness coupled with an overwhelming burden of responsibility. Parents experience a sense of engulfment and fear a loss of capacity to go on with the awesome task of maintaining a meaningful relationship with a child whose anticipated loss they are already grieving. They feel intense separation anxiety along with their grief.

Premature Parental Withdrawal

The characteristic adjustment of parents to the loss of a child is a process of withdrawing their emotional investment from their dying child and reinvesting in other people and other things. It is a gradual process, which begins with the onset of illness and is finalized after death. Very often, however, the grief process does not take place in a helping, supportive, or beneficial manner.

In cases, for example, where a strong conscious denial of the gravity of the child's illness persists, parents may show a very abrupt and profound mourning reaction when the child actually dies and reality can no longer be denied. At the other extreme, however, parents may complete most of the mourning process even before death occurs. In his book *The Dying Child*, W. Easson describes a particular instance of early parental withdrawal:

> While he was still alive, the family withdrew their emotional investment in the youngster and really had very few meaningful emotional ties to him...The child's toys, clothing and

other belongings were given away before the child was actually dead.

Although he may still be physically alive, he is in fact dead to them emotionally. Finding himself mourned too early and too completely, the child experiences a tragic sense of isolation and loneliness. In such instances the rabbi can play a significant role. He can engage the grieving parents in a discussion about the life and meaning of this particular child to them, as well as explore how they are coping at this juncture. If there are any unfinished issues between the dying child and his family, the rabbi is in a unique position to help the family with closure. "Has everyone had the opportunity to say goodbye?" he might ask family members. "Have you told him how much you love him?" While the dying child is still alive, the rabbi could ask the family if they want to express their love and appreciation, share a secret, or ask forgiveness. Though encouraging closure is important, the rabbi should nevertheless not pressure them. There are those who actually cope much better by being distracted rather than by focusing on the tragic reality. (See "Counseling Congregants in Crisis" in this volume.)

The rabbi, by visiting both the child and the parents, can serve as a bridge to the already severed relationship. He can invite family members to join him in his hospital visit to the child and be available following the visit to talk about how they are feeling.

Strategies for Coping

Becoming aware of the many ways in which parents of dying children cope psychologically can help a ministering rabbi be more sensitive, supportive, and understanding. Every grieving parent chooses a strategy most suitable and effective to his own personality and style. There is no one best way of coping. Each style of coping is the best psychological response that an individual can foster in order to survive a tragic and overwhelming situation.

Some parents cope by pursuing a strategy that is purely intellectual. They try to gain mastery over the situation by engaging in the intellectual pursuit of information gathering. Parents will research every aspect of the illness, via the Internet, scientific research, books, and consultations with experts worldwide. Others will appear to be in denial of the severity of their child's illness. They will minimize the seriousness of his condition and speak as though it is not fatal. For others there will be a marked increase in the amount of time spent in physical activities, such as sewing, knitting, or sports, which serve as a diversion from the threatening situation.

For many parents there is a compelling need to understand the meaning of their child's impending death within some theological or philosophical context. As tragic as their situation is, it is can be even more intolerable to think of it as mere "chance" or meaningless occurrence. These parents need to find a framework of meaning in which to better understand the dreadful event.

A rabbi can play a key role in helping these parents in their search for meaning so they can put the loss of their child into a more acceptable context. In order to help, however, he must use all the skills of effective rabbinic counseling (described elsewhere in this volume), especially active empathic listening. What for these parents is so special about this child? What has this child given them in the brief years of his/her life? What impact has this child had on others? Siblings? Friends? Grandparents?

The rabbi will likely be asked, "Why did God do this to our child and to us?"

It is incumbent upon the rabbi to respond honestly here.

Despite the expectation that he is expert in understanding God's ways, he should not attempt to explain the great mysteries of God's intent. He, after all, is also in the dark and stands defeated by the tragedy of the child's death. He can do no more than to help the parents find their own way. It is unlikely that a rabbi would ever be faulted for not knowing God's intent. If he is trite or simplistic in trying to explain the unexplainable, however, he will not be seen as either wise or understanding.

Though it can often be helpful for a rabbi to draw upon Biblical, Talmudic, Midrashic, or other religious sources as a framework for meaning, he must be careful not to make analogies or give metaphors that do not accurately reflect the experiential framework or beliefs of the parents. He needs, as well, to avoid banal explanations, imposing his own interpretations, or as was said, hypothesizing about Divine intent regarding their child's illness and death. He needs instead to engage in a process whereby grieving parents can feel heard and understood and safe expressing their emotions, and one that enables them to explore the meaning of their tragedy.

Finally, hope is an essential psychological defense in coping and should not be confused with denial. Unlike denial, hope does not interfere with taking appropriate action. Since we are never completely certain of any outcome, no matter how grave the situation, a rabbi can help parents sustain their sense of hope. This does not mean fostering denial of the seriousness of their child's prognosis, but rather holding onto the possibility that there is a chance their child *might* not die.

He can, for example, join with them in prayer, or guide them in the recitation of *tehillim* (psalms), or confirm that all outcomes are in God's hands and that miracles sometimes happen. By supporting their hope he is also playing a key role in helping them cope. It is not unusual to find grieving parents moving beyond their own child's situation and sharing hope with other sick children and their parents.

THE SOCIAL WORLD OF GRIEVING PARENTS

Another major factor affecting the process of parental bereavement is the quality of their family relationships and social contacts. Many studies have noted the importance of social contacts as a buffer against stress and anxiety. Human social interaction is known to provide anxiety-reducing properties. Yet, not all social contacts provide either relief or a reduction of grief for bereaved parents. The reason for this often revolves around the tendency of friends and relatives to unceasingly question or deny the reported seriousness of the child's condition and the inevitability of his death. In expressing their disbelief and questioning the validity of the diagnosis or the competence of the physician, friends and relatives often persist in maintaining a position of doubt and denial. This then forces parents into the uncomfortable position of having to defend their child's diagnosis and prognosis as well as to assure everyone that their child is receiving optimal medical care. Consequently, parents often feel that others perceive them as not doing enough to save their child from a tragic death.

Parents are often not permitted the open expression of hopelessness, yet are paradoxically expected to appear grief-stricken, sad, withdrawn, and sullen. Any deviation from this social expectancy, any attempt at temporary relief or escape, which entails enjoyment, levity, or lightheartedness, brings on implicit if not explicit condemnation. Parents of a seriously ill child who dare laugh or joke too freely risk being condemned and socially ostracized. Lightheartedness in the face of tragedy is not socially acceptable.

The dying child's mother is likely to be judged as dressing inappropriately if she wishes to wear more colorful clothes in order to bolster her spirits, as the child's father is likely to be viewed as callous, unfeeling, or uncaring if he chooses to work off some of his stress on the tennis court. Parents are not expected to be interested in any form of diversion, entertainment, leisure, or social activities. A rabbi can be very helpful not only by accepting and understanding this need for a period of relief, but also in encouraging parents to in fact take a break from the draining routine of the hospital ward and find some relief and escape in other areas.

Parents of dying children at times suffer from another kind of ostracism that is particularly painful. People might avoid them just when they are most in need of social support. Just as the dying often feel isolated in our society, so do their relatives. People fear that associating with someone suffering a tragedy might bring tragedy upon them. Bereaved parents often experience this as a bitter pill, indeed.

This is why the most critical source of social contact and support for them is frequently derived from other grieving parents. As parents observe and become involved in the loss and grief experienced by other parents, it helps facilitate their own grieving as well. For by virtue of grieving over the deaths of other sick children to whom they have become attached, they, in effect, rehearse for the death of their own child.

The grieving process constitutes a major task for parents of a fatally ill child. The process is a constellation of emotional responses from shock, confusion, helplessness, anger, and guilt to feelings of overwhelming sorrow and bereavement. Invariably, rabbis who counsel individuals in such dire circumstances come away with a large measure of personal growth. They discover the extent to which people are resilient and learn to respect the ability of human beings to mobilize themselves in the service of others. However, some community members might choose to distance themselves from the family of a dying child in order to shield themselves from the pain of the tragedy by not getting involved. Rabbis cannot, in good conscience, exercise this option. They need to be the anchor in a storm of emotions, a source of counsel, support, meaning, and hope, as well as facilitators of spiritual connection. In the end, experience has shown that they will receive back as much as they give.

BIBLIOGRAPHY AND SUGGESTED READING

Chodoff, P., Stanford, B., Friedman, B., and Hamburg, D. "Stress, Defenses and Coping Behavior: Observations in Parents of Children with Malignant Diseases," *American Journal of Psychiatry.*

Easson, W. 1970. *The Dying Child.* Springfield: Charles C. Thomas.

Edelstein, Linda. 1984. *Maternal Bereavement: Coping with the Unexpected Death of a Child.* New York: Praeger Scientific.

Friedman, S., Chodoff, P., Mason, J., and Hamburg, D. "Behavioral Observations on Parents Anticipating the Death of a Child," *Pediatrics* 32, 610.

Hamovitch, M. 1964. *The Parent and the Fatally Ill Child.* Los Angeles: Delman Publishing.

McCollum, Audrey T., ed. 1974. "Counseling the Grieving Parent," as found in *Care of the Child Facing Death.* London: Routledge & Kegan Paul.

Richmond, J. and Waisman, G. "Logical Aspects of Management of Children with Malignant Diseases," *AMA American Journal of Disease* 89: 42.

Natterson, J. and Knudson, A. "Observations Concerning Fear of Death in Fatally Ill Children and Their Mothers," *Psychosomatic Medicine* 22: 456.

Rosof, Barbara D. 1994. *The Worst Loss: How Families Heal from the Death of a Child.* New York: Henry Holt Publishers.

SUICIDE: THE RABBI'S ROLE

Rael Strous, M.D.

THE PARAMETERS OF SUICIDE

The word "suicide," derived from the Latin "self-murder," is defined as a self-induced fatal act representing an individual's desire to die. "Suicidal behavior" ranges from the individual's reporting of suicidal thoughts (ideation) to the actual carrying out of the act. The nature of the suicidal act may be an impulsive one or may be planned significantly in advance. While the act is often clearly self-evident, at times it may look like a car accident, work accident, drug overdose, or chronic self-neglect — such as with chronic alcohol abuse. Many suicidal acts among the young are often misinterpreted as accidents. Reasons for suicide usually include severe depression with feelings of a need to escape, feeling trapped with no foreseeable solution to problems of unbearable stress, feelings of hopelessness, loneliness, or a sense of abandonment.

Suicidal ideation and "gestures" (suicidal-like behaviors) should be seen as a cry for help and should always be taken very seriously. The popular notion that "those who threaten don't do it" is dangerously false.

While suicide is a very unnerving concept to contemplate and to understand for many, it is unfortunately not an uncom-

155

mon phenomenon. The suicide rate in Israel is approximately 8 per 100,000 and in the USA, approximately 12.5 per 100,000. In many countries around the world, suicide remains one of the 10 most common causes of death. Approximately 15% of individuals with untreated severe depression commit suicide and even many more (10–20 times that number) attempt suicide unsuccessfully. Suicide rates appear to be highest in the spring and fall, the reasons for which remain unclear.

Women attempt suicide more than men, but men more often succeed in completing the act. In addition, the suicidal act in males is usually carried out by more violent means. Although acts of self-harm such as burning with cigarettes, arm cutting, intentional self-mutilation etc. are not precisely the same as suicidal acts, they nevertheless should be considered a form of suicidal behavior. These acts need to be attended to with the utmost seriousness, since they may lead unintentionally to successful suicide. Sometimes, the intention may be to mutilate and not necessarily to die. An individual, for example, may believe that mutilation will help him feel that he exists, as opposed to his underlying feelings of unreality and depersonalization.

RISK FACTORS ASSOCIATED WITH SUICIDE

While suicide may often be an impulsive act, there are more than 40 identifiable "risk factors" that are strongly associated with the act. A rabbi, who may be consulted or asked to intervene in a situation where the threat of suicide is expressed, should keep this in mind. Several of these risk factors are considered to be more important than others. These include a history of psychiatric illness, where the risk increases 6–11 times that of the general population. In addition, approximately 25% of successful suicides are among the elderly, particularly single, divorced, or widowed white males. Men over the age of 65 exhibit the highest rate of suicide. Some studies have reported the feeling of intense hopelessness to be even more associated with suicide than depression alone. For these individuals, the pain of living is too much to bear and in order to end the pain, suicide becomes an option. Obviously, the two in combination (depression and hopelessness) are most dangerous.

The mode of suicidal intent is important to clarify. The more violent the plan, the greater the risk of suicide. The rabbi should be more concerned about a congregant who shares suicidal thoughts accompanied with a plan to shoot himself, jump off a building, hang himself, slash his wrist, or cut his throat, than a plan of a minor overdose of aspirin or to superficially cut his wrist.

Rates of suicide are also highest when depression is associated with recent loss, severe and disabling anxiety, chronic feelings of failure and low self-esteem, physical illness (present in 25–75% of suicide), substance abuse (suicide risk is 50 times higher when there is alcohol dependence), marital separation and divorce, or criminal behavior. Paradoxically, individuals may be at a slightly greater risk for suicide following the beginning of successful treatment for depression. In the depths of depression, individuals often lack the needed energy for a suicidal act. When energy and drive start to return, suicidal ideation may be acted on. The family should be alerted that their watchfulness should not stop when the person begins to feel a bit better. It should be remembered that approximately 15% of individuals with severe depression commit suicide.

Other risk factors include the sudden stopping of psychiatric medication — particularly for individuals requiring management for bipolar (manic-depressive) disorder, experiencing sudden demotion, job loss or even promotion at work. The additional responsibilities that go with promotion may be overwhelming to someone with low self-esteem who is terrified of failure. Severe illness for which no long-term cure is expected (e.g. cancer, AIDS) and a family history of suicide (especially of the same gender) are significant risk factors. Single individuals have double the rate of suicide compared to married individuals, and married individuals with children have the lowest rate of suicide. While rates among Jews are lower than most other religions, it is clear that Jews are not immune from suicide and rates appear to have increased over the past few decades. Perhaps the most important indicator of someone's increased suicide risk is evidence or a report of a previous suicidal attempt. It appears that approximately 40% of depressed individuals who successfully commit suicide have made a previous attempt. This risk is highest within 3 months of the previous attempt. All this notwithstanding, a low statistical incidence should not decrease one's alertness to suicide.

Although suicide is most common in adults, it may occur in youth as well, particularly when associated with family dysfunction, psychiatric illness, loss of interest in activities, parental arrest, lack of social/family support, early parental separation, child abuse, and self-directed aggression. A relatively rare but important factor in young people is the suicide of their "hero," someone whom they greatly respected or idealized. Suicide by important cultural or media figures has even led in some cases to epidemics of suicidal "copycat" behavior.

It is important to remember that serious depression may occur in the absence of obvious precipitating circumstances in the individual's life. These depressions may be due to chemical changes in the body. Any depressed person should be considered a suicidal risk, even if everything else in his life appears to be going well.

Warning signs of suicide demand expedited referral to a competent mental health caregiver. Among these are: sudden disposal of personal property (particularly if it meant a lot to the individual), lack of or discarding of future plans, recent severe loss, and showing a sudden interest in setting up life insurance policies or writing a will.

SUICIDE PREVENTION AND MANAGEMENT

Education

Perhaps one of the most important factors associated with the prevention of death by suicide involves community education with respect to identifying early signs of depression and reducing the stigma of treatment so that those requiring help obtain it early. A rabbi may play a particularly vital role in this area, both in terms of individual contact with suffering individuals, their families, and close friends, as well as through more general community outreach and education (sermons, *shiurim, derashot* etc.)

Inquiring

A critically important principle in the detection and management of individuals with whom the threat of suicide is suspected is not to be afraid of asking the individual whether he has been thinking of killing himself. It is simply not true that asking this "will give him ideas." However, sensitivity should be exhibited in the process of inquiring. Thus, it may be useful and advisable to begin with questions such as, "Do you ever have any thoughts that life is not worth living?" or "Do you ever wish that you would not wake up in the morning?" From there the rabbi may very gradually move on to more probing questions such as, "Do you have any intention now to harm yourself?" or "Have you thought about how you might carry it out?"

Suicide Management

Once the threat of suicide is expressed or suspected, the most important initial consideration is to determine whether observation or restraint is necessary. If the risk of self-harm is immediate and real, the need for hospitalization and prompt medical care becomes necessary, despite the potential protest from the individual and/or his family. This judgment and process is primarily the responsibility of the physician, but the rabbi may be called upon to help facilitate the course of action and/ or mediate optimal conditions. This may include, but not necessarily be limited to, reassuring the individual and his family that management is in their best interest in the long run. The recommendation to hospitalize an individual should be made in conjunction with a professional mental health caregiver and based upon current diagnosis, intensity of depression and/or suicidal ideation, presence of a suicide plan, current available support, and identification of risk factors as described above. Short-term treatment in a hospital may include medication, "talking therapy," and even electroconvulsive therapy for immediate response in an acutely "difficult to manage" suicidal individual. These treatments are all safe despite the stigma and obvious fears associated with them, and the rabbi may be called upon to reassure the individual and family. Within the bounds of confidentiality, the rabbi should feel comfortable questioning the treating physician/psychiatrist in order to help clarify issues for the family, if necessary. Finally, the rabbi should support and encourage follow-up with a mental health caregiver following hospital discharge. In general, as underscored so often in this volume, it is important for a rabbi to cultivate a relationship with one or more mental health professionals in order to enable him to receive direction and support in such situations.

Maintaining Support

It is important for the rabbi to maintain contact with the individual even after hospitalization. While the rabbi may find it difficult to instill hope and a desire to live in an individual suffering from acute depression of biological origin, he remains a vital part of the support structure. If the suicidal intention emanates, rather, from the person's feelings of loss or rejection etc., the rabbi could play a vital role in terms of instilling hope to carry on. In such a situation, hopelessness, rather than just depression, should be recognized by the rabbi as the risk factor for suicide and, in conjunction or partnership with competent medical management, the aim should be to work with the individual to clarify or restructure the current situation in a different light in order to regain hope for the future.

Crisis Intervention

The aim of crisis intervention in cases of suicidal ideation includes the building of a healthy rapport and optimal communication, identifying potential outside resources, ensuring the best environmental support and resources available under the circumstances, and initiating professional therapeutic intervention. These interventions may include medication management, individual and family psychotherapy, and an assessment of the individual's environment. The core of crisis intervention, in essence, encourages the individual to learn how to integrate alternatives and healthier, more adaptive mechanisms, to cope with the current stress, which is precipitating or prolonging the crisis leading to suicidal ideation. Along these lines, it is hoped that the individual will arrive at the understanding that what happens is not as important as how one deals with it.

If called upon to help in a suicide-related situation, the

rabbi should provide the individual with an opportunity to ventilate pain and frustration, so he can feel understood and, as a result, more willing to explore different viable options. The rabbi should allow the individual to freely explore his reason for wanting to die and allow for the open expression of anger, unacceptable thoughts, and feelings of hopelessness and rejection. In addition, the rabbi may assist in building realistic supportive social structures in the community for the individual at risk.

The rabbi should help dissuade the individual from making major life decisions when severely depressed — decisions which, in such a state, are likely affected by impaired judgment and which he may deeply regret once he recovers. It is advisable never to agree to keep a suicide plan confidential and thus exclude various avenues of assistance. Among mental health professionals, the sacred rules of confidentiality do not apply whenever there is a likelihood of suicide or murder. This is general practice and in most places, it is the law. When confidentiality needs to be broken, the rabbi should say something like, "I care too much not to seek help for you at this time."

Supporting the Family and Close Friends

In the worst of scenarios, where an individual succeeds in carrying out his suicidal intentions, the rabbi needs to be available to help the surviving family and close friends. Once again, this calls for the rabbi to give support, understanding, and the reassurance that they are not to blame. Guilt, it seems, is the most common feeling experienced by those close to a suicide victim. Losing a loved one to suicide leads to pain that is incomprehensible to those who have not experienced such a loss; and it is a pain that is never fully forgotten or resolved. Other common reactions, which should be recognized by the counseling rabbi, may include disbelief, anger, shame, anxiety, deep sadness, and physical symptoms. In addition to helping them explore these emotions, the rabbi can assist the family by recommending a support group that includes others who have experienced a similar loss.

Recognizing Your Own Needs

Since suicidal ideation and attempts are intense events, often the rabbi who may be called upon to help mediate or counsel in this life-threatening situation will commonly experiences anxiety himself. The rabbi should recognize that it is normal to feel many things when dealing with such a crisis, and he should feel comfortable seeking supportive help for himself, without fear of stigma. It is important to note that while most suicides are preventable, some are not. Thus, it is essential for the rabbi to invest all he can in helping out in the situation to the best of his ability, according to professional limitations. But ultimately, the rabbi needs to accept the fact that he has no control over the outcome.

COUNSELING THE BEREAVED

Rabbi Maurice Lamm
Dodi Lee Lamm, M.S.W.

THE DEATH OF A loved one is undoubtedly one of life's highest ranking stressors. A mourner presents himself to the rabbi in his or her most vulnerable moment, when the rabbi can become a source either of life-sustaining benefit or of life-shattering abandonment.

Rabbis need, therefore, to better understand the dynamics of grief, as well as the impact of effective rabbinic intervention during these stressful times. The Torah's goals for comforting the bereaved make this one of the greatest mitzvot in the category of *chesed*—greater than *bikkur cholim* (visiting the sick) and *hachnassat kallah* (dowering a bride). So in order to perform this mitzvah, it would be advisable for the rabbi to understand the purpose and rationale behind the mitzvot of mourning, and how, with the benefit of psychological insight, he can best assist the mourner.

ENGAGING THE MOURNER

The rabbi speaks at a funeral, visits the bereaved almost daily, and thereby gains a unique impression of the mourner in his or her own environment. The bereaved will most often show signs of depression, impatience, anger, and irritability, but occasionally he will talk about suicide, giving up on life, or his feelings that the deceased abandoned him. He will do so with a resignation that is close to capitulation, prompted by his frustration over his utter inability to control events. What may be at stake in such extreme cases are the person's marriage, family, school, job, and surely his or her self-image. The intensity of the mourner's despondency could become overwhelming for family and friends, whose attempts at support appear futile and who are left feeling helpless and concerned about the mourner's well-being. The rabbi is the most likely person in the community to be called upon at this time. It is important for him to be aware as he begins to engage both the mourner and his/her family and friends that most mourners are resilient despite the intensity of their initial grief reaction.

NORMAL GRIEF PATTERNS

Rabbis ministering to the bereaved need to be mindful that most grief reactions are normal and most mourners will return to normal functioning. Grief reactions may exhibit all the symptoms of pathology yet be no more than a normal manifestation of mourning. Do not become alarmed and rush into therapeutic intervention. The grief syndrome can be contradictory. On the one hand, most mourners are traumatized and can show excessive expressions of grief, yet in a short space of time their grief will diminish to the range of normalcy — for some as soon as *shiva* is over. Research studies indicate that most people overcome this initial reaction without any permanent aftereffects.

Rabbis should, therefore, not be quick to label the early behavior or reactions of distraught mourners as pathological and ship them off to the local psychiatrist. Bereavement needs to play itself out. After a reasonable period of time, if the syndrome of weeping, not eating, not working, and not sleeping continues, it should be handled with appropriate professional intervention.

It is important to remember that underneath it all, grief is perfectly natural. Indeed, the absence of grief is suspicious. It is not simply an expression of pain or regret. Grief is characteristically obstinate, conflicted, and resistant to being resolved.

Grief nevertheless does at times seem irrational, and its common symptoms—depression, guilt feelings, hostility to innocent bystanders, apathy, and social withdrawal—suggest mental breakdown. Yet to treat grief as an illness early in the process would be profoundly misguided. The burden of grief represents, rather, an intense effort to recover from the loss and to reintegrate into society. That is what Freud meant by the "work" of grieving, and it is what we should help mourners to accomplish.

It is literally a rabbinic mandate for the mourner to be *mekabel divrei tanchumim* (to welcome support and healing intervention)— to get well. Indeed, mourners are bidden to hear out the advice of comforters, despite some of the inanities uttered in the name of *nechamah* (comforting the bereaved).

THE GRIEVING PROCESS

A well-known paradigm of mourning — famously articulated by Dr. Elizabeth Kubler-Ross—describes five stages a mourner may experience. They are fluid stages in that they don't last for a specific amount of time, they do not necessarily come packaged in a sequential order, and once experienced they might be revisited. (These stages are also discussed in this book in "Counseling the Terminally Ill Congregant.")

They are: *denial, anger, bargaining, depression, and acceptance.* The mourner may appear to have reached a stage of acceptance and everyone might breathe a sigh of relief only to see that anger sets in once again or even for the first time. Saying goodbye and accepting the loss is not a linear progression.

- ➤ **Denial** is a logical first response. No one wants to hear bad news and at first it may seem like a dream or surreal. This is also a protective measure to keep from feeling deep shock and pain. The mourner turns away from reality and clings to the deceased. Unless the denial is causing difficulties, let it go. Allow the mourner his last fantasy. When he is ready, he will move on.

- ➤ **Anger** may arrive with a thud; this isn't a comfortable stage for the rest of the family. It relieves some emotional pressure for the mourner and aids in keeping the actual mourning at bay. This reaction may need to be watched so that it does not cause any irreparable damage to the family.

- ➤ **Bargaining** is a stage that gives the illusion of control in a world that has gone awry. It may be used as an attempted corrective measure, it may be associated with guilt, and it may aid in the adaptation of the death.

- ➤ **Depression** is the combination of a sense of helplessness, hopelessness, and powerlessness in the face of insurmountable odds. Reality has set in. Depression in the face of a loss is called "reactive depression". Sometimes reactive depression does not appear until months later. It is characterized by a loss of interest in the outside world and a change in the person's sleep patterns and appetite. The mourner may feel out of sync with the rest of the world and not care very much to rejoin the fold. Anger at the deceased for abandoning him/her may be turned inward and manifest itself as depression. Despair can also ensue, and when it does it may worsen into suicidal feelings. Suicidal feelings may be brought on by the desire to end the pain of the loss, and in severe cases to join the deceased in a fantasized hereafter. Should a family, friend, or rabbi feel concerned, a mental health professional should be contacted immediately. All threats should be taken seriously.

▶ **Acceptance.** The last and most peaceful stage is that of acceptance. In the halachic literature, it is most closely associated with *yishtakach min ha-lev*, and is the functional objective of many mitzvot designed for mourners.

COMPLICATED BEREAVEMENT

Despite the resilience of most mourners, a rabbi needs to recognize that there are those whose grief cannot be managed without professional help. There are individuals who live their entire lives in unresolved grief, as evidenced by a former congregant who recently asked me to help him resolve the grief of his father's death — some 45 years ago.

Grief demands that the mourner deeply experience its angst and discomfort, and then share it. The feeling associated with death and loss is daunting. One of the tools a mourner uses to avoid feeling the bite of the pain is to repress the emotion, thereby preventing the anxiety and conflict that follow. This is often associated with the fear that if the pain were felt it might be too overwhelming and intolerable. Over time, if there is no cathartic expression of grief, the loss may begin to manifest in ways that are unhealthy. The mourner may then enter a phase called *complicated bereavement.*

Someone experiencing complicated bereavement can't move

past the symptoms of initial grief, and is emotionally stuck. The difference between normal grief and complicated grief is that of duration. There are certainly individual and cultural differences regarding the normal duration of acute symptoms of grief. According to the *Diagnostic and Statistical Manual of the American Psychiatric Association,* however, acute symptoms of mourning are expected to subside after a period of two months. This of course does not mean that grief is expected to be resolved in two months — just the symptoms that usually manifest in the initial stage of mourning.

There are many possibilities why complicated bereavement occurs. One might be the nature of the relationship of between the deceased and the mourner prior to death. When death occurs before any coming to terms with issues, estrangement, or discord, it may be hard to accept that there can no longer be any resolution in life. Complicated bereavement may be intensified because of previous losses that were not resolved. This may impede the task of mourning. Resolution of unfinished business may need to be dealt with first.

Completing the mourning process may be affected by the person's level of emotional maturity, his ability to tolerate painful emotions, his degree of dependence on the deceased, and the circumstances of the death. Someone in this state may be oblivious to any problems and it might take some sort of intervention by a family member, rabbi, or trained professional to address it.

The symptoms of complicated bereavement are:

- ► Uncontrollable crying for long periods of time
- ► Isolation from friends and relatives
- ► Decreased performance at work or in school
- ► Talking often about death in unrelated conversations, and also its opposite — never mentioning any loss or death

and possibly not talking about the deceased in any form.

► Engaging in uncharacteristic behavior, such as substance abuse, heavy drinking, or promiscuity

► Drastically changed sleep habits

► Suicidal ideation (persistent thought about committing suicide)

► Strong grief as a result of insignificant events or conversations

► Displaying symptoms of severe depression

DIFFERENTIATING NORMAL GRIEF FROM DEPRESSION

According to the DSMIV (the Diagnostic and Statistical Manual of the American Psychiatric Association), there are several symptoms that are not characteristic of normal grief. If after two months these symptoms are still manifesting, then it is important for the rabbi to suggest that the individual seek professional help. These symptoms are not characteristic of a "normal" grief reaction and would suggest a major depressive episode. These include:

► Guilt about things other than actions taken or not taken by the survivor at the time of the death

► Thoughts of death other than the survivor feeling that he or she would be better off dead or should have died with the deceased person

► Morbid preoccupation with worthlessness

► Marked psychomotor retardation (slow movement, especially walking)

► Prolonged and marked functional impairment

► Hallucinatory experiences other than thinking that he or

she hears the voice of, or transiently sees the image of, the deceased person.

COUNSELING THE BEREAVED

Hypocrites's advice to medical doctors holds true for rabbis as well — "first do no harm." There is need for strong precautionary language in this regard. Mourners are very sensitive to what is said to them. Only words can help them through the pain of missing their beloved. The maladroit use of phrases during a crisis can be devastating, just as they can be creative and calming.

As rabbis, we must be doubly careful at such moments to check our tendency to be authoritative, overly confident, and judgmental. Beware of some pitfalls of the profession:

- ► Quoting Torah when the words are inappropriate and out of place
- ► Offering pleasantries that are fatuous
- ► Preaching in place of suggesting
- ► Being hypercritical of those who don't practice the mitzvot
- ► Issuing unthinking and inappropriate platitudes

Worse is using well-known folk expressions which we assume to be correct only because they are spoken in Hebrew or Yiddish, especially religious-sounding ones.

The Halachah and the Aggadah, the wisdom of *Chazal* and luminaries, the sagacity of the Chasidim and contemporary *gedolim* hold so much compacted brilliance that it behooves us all to study the ideas that underlie their stories and statements for clues as to how to truly console post-modern Jews. People have been dying forever, and ancient wisdom is to be highly prized, especially if it is supplemented with contemporary psychological research.

COUNSELING GUIDELINES

The rabbi's first encounter with the mourner usually comes upon hearing the news of the death. The mourner may not have yet completely absorbed the finality of what happened. In that first encounter with the newly bereaved, the rabbi needs to connect both empathically and concretely. "When?" "How?" and "Where did it happen?" are appropriate questions. They are concrete and they simply seek information, but they allow the mourner to verbally relay a story that often feels surrealistic, even when the death was expected.

Other informational questions are also important to explore at this time. "Where were you when it happened?" "How did you find out?" "Do the other family members know?" "Have any arrangements for a burial been made?" This begins to connect the rabbi to the experience of the mourner. The mourner may not come to grips with the reality of the loss for a while, but this concrete stage is an important beginning.

This is also the time to let the mourner know that everything that can be done to give the deceased a respectful, honorable funeral is being done. At a time of total helplessness in being able to bring the deceased back to life, it is comforting for the person to know that an honorable funeral is being arranged. The mourner might even find that helping with the funeral arrangements is a great source of comfort.

During the funeral service, the rabbi is often the one called upon to deliver the eulogy. The eulogy should begin the mourner's search for closure, although it is halachically spoken for the benefit of the deceased. The eulogy is, of course, not a therapy session, not a *shiur*, not a peroration, not a *mussar shmuess*, but a description and a panegyric that can assist the mourners in seeing a pattern to the deceased's life which is uplifting.

Following the funeral, the rabbi needs to assess the mourner's desire for solitude upon returning from the cemetery and the immediate days following, and respect his preference. Solitude gives the mourner space to think and get past many perceived obstacles to the problem of continuing life after experiencing the ugliness of death and its shocking finality.

It is similarly important to respect the mourner's wish for silence. This is the reason why consolers traditionally need to wait for the mourner to speak first, thereby allowing him or her to set the agenda for their *shiva* call. Many mourners express their clear wish for everyone to "stay away." This should be honored. Silence gives mourners the space to reflect, feel what they need to feel, and collect themselves. Sometimes silence speaks volumes. Just being with the mourner sans speaking banalities and trivialities is exactly the support the mourner needs.

There are several other important considerations that a rabbi needs to be mindful of when counseling and consoling the bereaved. Narrative, for example, is the quintessential agenda of all religious consolation strategies. This means that mourners should be encouraged to speak of their loss. Perhaps the most helpful words of consolation are: "Tell me what she was like." The mourner's repeating of this narrative, sometimes with a new twist or emphasis (depending on the listeners and the person's own new insights) brings him closer to closure. By the end of a successful *shiva*, the mourner has packaged a cogent story, with a beginning and an end and a logical progression of events to store in his mind for safekeeping. Slowly it dawns on him that he now understands what happened and that he can place it in its proper proportion. He is, of course, still bereaved.

Encourage the retelling of stories—about the deceased, about his death, about his final days—and the feelings that accompanied these events. The more one tells the story, the more one is able to make the death more real. Telling the story with all its pain is a partner to the healing process.

There is a counseling approach called *active listening* that will contribute greatly to the bond between the mourner and the rabbi. Communication comes in all forms, including speech, emotional response, and body language. For example, it is important to maintain good eye contact. It conveys to the mourner that you are not uncomfortable dealing with death and listening to the mourner's unvarnished feelings. Empathy can often be conveyed with a calm presence, eye contact, attentiveness, and a display of genuine interest. These are very effective in establishing a connection with the mourner and are also central components for consoling the bereaved.

Reflecting back is a way of letting the mourner know that you understand correctly what has been said and that you are listening with interest. The mourner may tend to contradict or even repeat himself because he is in the process of working through difficult emotions. When you reflect back, you make it permissible for the mourner to revisit and clarify his thoughts and feelings once again. It is a way of showing respect for the process of grieving and consoling. Paraphrasing a mourner's most important comments lends them importance while checking them for accuracy. Some emotions exhibited while grieving can be overwhelming and frightening to both the mourner and the listener. When a rabbi is able to "mirror feelings" and reflect back a sense that the emotions are significant, he makes it safe for the mourner to express all that he is feeling. A mourner might say, "I don't know what to do," and the rabbi might reply, "It sounds like you are feeling a bit lost right now." The rabbi helps put a name to the person's feelings.

It is important for the rabbi to ask questions rather than to toss out stock answers. Mourners do not want to hear theological insights, justifications, apologetics, comparative war stories, or even the rabbi's personal approach on how to make peace with tragedy. Empathy and understanding are what is called for — active listening and mirrored feelings, not long discourses on why bad things happen to good people.

There are also things that shouldn't be said, because they show insensitivity and a lack of empathy. Don't say, for example: "It could've been worse," "You need to get on with your life," "You'll have other children," "Don't take it so hard," or "Other people have lost their beloved." Remember, too, that the word "beloved" may not be appropriate. The deceased may not have in fact been loved.

Handle memories deftly. Screened memories, those that are not remembered accurately but as the individual wants or needs them to be, are common for mourners. These memories may not be objectively accurate, but they are often comforting to the person who is telling them. We unconsciously choose what we can handle and avoid that which is too threatening, primarily because it hurts too much. Sometimes good memories become paramount to the exclusion of other memories that might threaten how the mourner wants to remember the deceased. It is not necessary to correct those memories. Again, we are there just to listen.

Refer the mourner to a mental health professional when you sense that you are in over your head or if there is even the slightest mention of suicide. When in doubt, even the slightest doubt, be prudent and consult with or refer to a mental health professional.

WORKING WITH THE GRIEVING CHILD

Children generally need to talk about the death of a loved one over and over. Grieving children, no less than their adult counterparts, need to be able to express their feelings of sadness and loss. The rabbi's role with children is to allow them to express whatever feelings and thoughts they have, whether they are fears, questions, or anxious concerns. This helps them process the trauma. Be supportive, sensitive, and sympathetic, but do not feel that as a rabbi you need to have all the answers. Telling a child that there are things that even adults do not understand serves to validate his or her questions. Be honest about the tragedy. Euphemisms like "going to sleep," make the child fear sleep. Children grieve and recover at their own rate. Help the family respect their process.

A child might not want to express his feelings to his grieving family for fear of causing them more pain. The rabbi can play a key role in providing a safe opportunity for emotional catharsis. Children might think that they are bad because they feel angry at the deceased for abandoning them, or worse, that they are to blame for the tragedy. It is not uncommon for a child to feel guilty because he/she didn't always obey the deceased.

Children should be referred to professionals when, following a death, they regress to a less mature level of behavior and begin acting in ways that are not age appropriate. Similarly, it is advisable to consult with a competent child therapist when a child demonstrates a persistent inability or unwillingness to speak of the deceased and spurns all attempts to talk about his loss. This is not necessarily a sign of pathology, but nevertheless warrants a consultation with a competent child therapist.

There are other instances when a grieving child might need professional attention. If, following the death of a loved one, a child becomes prone to accidents, is overly absorbed in daydreaming, manifests prolonged dysfunction in school, becomes extremely hyperactive, or expresses a desire to die just as the deceased did, you need to inform the primary caretaker and immediately refer to a therapist. In the latter case of suicidal ideation, if you feel the child is serious and has a plan, you must not delay. It is also advisable to encourage the family to consult with a competent child therapist when a child articulates persistent blame — on himself and others — or experiences constant anxiety, such as fearing the loss of a family member, friend, or pet, or demonstrating exaggerated clinging to survivors.

CONCLUSION

The intense grief associated with death and loss is daunting and typically does not lend itself to "solution", but only to "resolution" — accepting the grief and achieving closure. Though bereavement is a natural process of healing the deepest of wounds, an effective rabbi can significantly facilitate the process and help the mourner move beyond death into the flow of life.

BIBLIOGRAPHY

Cassell, E. J. 1991. *The Nature of Suffering*. New York: Oxford University Press.

Kubler-Ross, E. 1974. *Questions and Answers on Death and Dying*. New York: Macmillan Publishing Co.

Linzer, N. (ed.). 1977. *Understanding Bereavement and Grief*. New York: YU Press.

National Institutes of Health. 1984. *Bereavement: Reactions, Consequences, Care*. Washington D.C.: National Academy Press.

Rando, T. A. 1993. *Treatment of Complicated Mourning*. Champaign: Research Press.

Raphael, S. P. 1996. *Jewish Views of the Afterlife*. Northvale: Jason Aronson.

Zunin, L. M. & Zunin, H. S. 1991. *The Art of Condolence*. New York: Harper Perennial.

SUGGESTED READING

Fumia, M. 1992. *Safe Passages: Words to Help the Grieving Hold Fast and Let Go.* Berkeley: Conari Press.

Cousins, N. 1983. *The Healing Heart.* New York: Norton.

Kay, A. A. 1993. *The Jewish Book of Comfort.* Northvale: Jason Aronson.

Krauss, P. & Goldfisher, M. 1998. *Why Me? Coping with Grief, Loss & Change.* New York: Bantam.

Lamm, M. 2004. *Consolation.* Philadelphia: JPS.

Lamm, M. and Kinzbrunner, B. 2004. *The Jewish Hospice Manual.* Miami: National Institute for Jewish Hospice and VITAS Healthcare.

Lamm, M. 2004. *The Jewish Way in Death and Mourning* (especially the chapter on "Discretionary Mourning" added to the revised edition). New York: Jonathan David.

Levine, A. 1994. *To Comfort the Bereaved.* Northvale: Jason Aronson.

Meier, L. 1991. *Jewish Values in Health and Medicine.* Lanham: University Press.

ॐ 11 ॐ

IN THE AFTERMATH OF DISASTER: COUNSELING CHILDREN AND THEIR PARENTS

David Pelcovitz, Ph.D.

THE CHINESE WORD characters for "crisis" consist of two symbols: danger and opportunity. Parents looking for guidance from their rabbi on how to help their children during a time of instability are understandably concerned about the physical and emotional risks that their children are facing. At the same time, periods of crisis present numerous opportunities for the counseling rabbi to help parents become more attuned to the central role they play in helping their children. Whether a rabbi is educating parents in the aftermath of a crisis or directly counseling children and adolescents, it is important for him to become aware of the impact of traumatic disaster on the young and the role that he and their parents can play in the healing process.

CHILDREN'S REACTIONS

In the aftermath of any major traumatic event such as that which occurred on September 11, 2001, parents can expect a wide range of reactions in their children. Among the factors that determine the intensity of a child's response are the child's prior history of loss, the child's temperament, and the intensity of his parents' reactions. Since, in the aftermath of any horrendous trauma there is a perceived threat to the child's protective shield which, until then, was taken for granted, children may react in a number of ways. Some children may express overt worries about their safety and that of their family members and friends. Some may be afraid of how a war might directly affect them, particularly high school seniors, many of whom voice concerns about having to become soldiers. Other children may display a heightened mistrust of those who are different, stigmatizing them as the "enemy".

Sometimes the effects on children are more subtle. They may start experiencing increased difficulty in their interactions with others. If a child exhibits increased irritability, more aggression against siblings or peers, or more noncompliance with parental requests in the aftermath of a recent disaster, parents should consider the possibility that this is an indirect reaction to the traumatic event. Sadness and anxiety may present in the form of vague physical complaints or changes in sleep or eating patterns. Some children may have difficulty concentrating or sitting still. All of these problems are in the realm of a normal reaction during the weeks that immediately follow traumatic events. The general guideline, however, is that if symptoms are interfering with normal functioning, particularly if they last for longer than a month, then parents should consider seeking professional help.

CHILDREN'S VIEW OF DEATH

In order to understand how a child may be affected by exposure to an event in which thousands were killed, it is helpful to review how children of different ages respond to death. Of course, infants have no understanding of death; they do, however, react to parental emotions and may respond to parental upset by becoming more cranky or clingy. Preschoolers view death as reversible, akin to sleeping. It doesn't take long to realize when discussing death with preschoolers that they view death in concrete and temporary terms. In such discussions, a preschooler will tell you that people wake up in the morning, go to sleep at night, die, and then get up again. The following incident illustrates this.

> A four-year-old boy was friendly with an older man who lived in the apartment next door. When the man died, the four year old appeared to accept the news of his friend's death with relative equanimity. About six months later the man's widow told the boy's parents that their son had stopped by to ask if he could play with his friend. When the widow gently reminded the boy that his friend had died, the boy complained, "But that was a long time ago."

The preschool years are also dominated by magical thinking, when children are more likely to blame themselves for a death, imagining that it happened because of something they did or said.

During the early elementary school years (ages 5–9), children view death as something that can happen, but not to them. As they approach their middle school years, they gradually come to see death as universal and irreversible. These children often take great interest in the biological aspects of death, but are often not able to fully grapple with the emotional impact of losing somebody close to them.

The capacity for abstract thought that develops in adolescence allows for a more adult-like understanding of death. Since adolescents are at an age where they are trying to figure out their place in life, death has a profoundly emotional impact on them. Research has shown that adolescents often have more difficulty with such loss than they would have had in their pre-adolescent years.

Sometimes children do not appear to be affected in the immediate aftermath of a death of someone they are close to, but they later show a delayed reaction.

> A father came to my office with his two daughters shortly after the death of their mother. After a few meetings, it became apparent that this loving father and a supportive extended family were helping the girls deal with the loss of their mother without any need for professional help.
>
> Several years later the father asked me to meet with his younger daughter, who had, uncharacteristically, become a behavior problem at home and in school. After a few sessions, the following story emerged. Her teacher had told the class a story that had as its moral, "Be careful what you wish for." Her mother, who had cancer, spent the last few weeks of her life at home, since there was little that the hospital could do for her. The morning her mother died, the girl remembers spending time in her mother's room. She sat down on her mother's bed and her mother cried out in pain. The girl, who was only eight at the time, remembered thinking, "I wish she would die already." When her mother died later that day, the girl was convinced that her wish was responsible for her mother's death. Unable to deal with the guilt that accompanied this belief, the girl pushed the memory out of her mind until the teacher's admonition, "Be careful what you wish for," triggered the unresolved guilt. Once this concern was brought into the open and the girl was reassured, her behavior quickly returned to normal.

TEMPERAMENT

Some children are more vulnerable to the effect of traumatic events than others. Children who are most at risk for having difficulty during uncertain times are the 15% of the population whose "wiring" makes them more prone to anxiety and causes them to have a greater biological reactivity to stress. When exposed to frightening events, their heart rates become elevated for longer and they remain on the alert for danger longer than their non-anxious peers. These children react more strongly during periods of instability. They are more likely to cling to adults for reassurance and support, and have difficulty sleeping and concentrating. Although initially, anxious children need more parental support than their calmer counterparts, in the long run, children with anxious temperaments respond very well to support and reassurance, and parents can expect to get their "old" child back when a sense of stability returns.

Children with "Type A" personalities also may respond strongly to periods of instability. Such children, who are intense and have low frustration tolerance, tend to have heightened cardiovascular responses to threat. They are most likely to respond to frightening events by becoming more irritable, aggressive, and noncompliant. Here, too, a combination of reassurance and firm, but calm, limits on defiant behavior should lead to a quick return to pre-trauma functioning.

COPING STYLES

As with adults, when it comes to coping with stress in children, one size doesn't fit all. There is no one correct way to deal with upsetting situations. Children often deal with stress and anxiety in ways that are qualitatively different from adults. Some children may show little reaction to upsetting events. Parents should not assume that it means that the child's coping mechanisms are not working. On the contrary, a child who is showing no symptoms and is not willing to discuss the situation may be doing just as well as a child who is openly discussing his/her feelings.

Research on how children cope with painful medical procedures or other stressful situations finds that each child's coping style is on a continuum from "attenders" to "distracters" — active information seekers to information avoiders. Children who are "attenders" deal with stressful situations in an active manner. For example, if they are about to get an injection from their pediatrician, they want to understand why and they prefer to assist the doctor in preparing for the injection. In contrast, "distracter" children prefer to distract themselves when getting the injection. They aren't interested in why the shot is necessary — they prefer to look the other way and perhaps play an electronic game. Interestingly, research shows that if you try to turn a distracter into an attender or vice versa, i.e., if you try to force the distracter to talk about his understanding of why the injection is necessary or if you try to force the attender to play a game while getting the injection, each child will cope much less successfully with the stress of the medical procedure.

These two approaches are echoed in two views expressed in the Talmud on how to cope with worries. *Mishlei* 12:25 says: "Anxiety in the heart of a man weighs him down, but a good word makes him glad." Based on this verse, the Talmud discusses two views of how to handle anxiety. R. Ami and R. Asi differ in the interpretation of this verse. One explains it, "Let him banish the anxiety from his mind," the other, "Let him discuss it with others" (*Yoma* 75a). The differing views of Rav Ami and Rav Asi echo the "attender" versus "distracter" approach to dealing with anxiety. Distracters follow the interpretation of banishing the worry from one's mind; attenders deal with worry by verbalizing their fears to others. In helping a child deal with serious stress at times of violence and instability, it is important to tune in to whether he is more comfortable using distraction as the preferred approach (*yasicheno meda'ato*), or whether he is more comforted by verbalizing his anxieties (*yasicheno le'acharim*) in discussion with others.

COUNSELING GUIDELINES

If you are counseling a child who has experienced a traumatic event, it might be helpful to ask him directly: how well he is coping, who, if anyone, can help him to cope, and what has he found to be most effective and ineffective in coping with his anxieties. Don't try to force a style on any child that doesn't work for him. If a child is an attender, he will do best if allowed to discuss his concerns openly. Your role as a counselor, and this is true for parents as well, is to be honest and direct, while at the same time reassuring the child that the adult world is doing its best to keep him safe. A child who is a distracter will almost certainly prefer not to hear too many details about unpleasant topics. Your job is to respect his right to remain silent and to try to find "teachable moments" when he might be more receptive to brief discussions aimed at reassuring him and providing him with information.

Parents whose child's coping style differs from their own may find it hard to deal with his preferred mode of processing difficult information. A rabbi can play an important role in making parents aware of the importance of letting their child find his own way. Parents will often need the rabbi's assurance that they are doing the right thing and being most helpful to their child.

Most children are resilient. If they show little in the way of obvious emotional or behavioral difficulties after events such as the September 11th attacks, parents should not assume that they are hiding their true feelings.

In some cases, there may be a delayed reaction. Research shows that most parents are not aware when their children are having difficulty dealing with the impact of traumatic events. Consequently, even if a child is doing well in the aftermath of tragedy, it might be advisable to occasionally check with him to make sure that there are no concerns that require clarification.

Approximately six months after the bombing of the federal building in Oklahoma City, an eleven-year-old girl, who lived over a thousand miles from the site of the bombing, seemed upset and preoccupied shortly before the family was to go on a vacation. In a discussion with her mother, she confided that a picture of the hotel where they would be staying reminded her of the federal building. She felt safe as long as she stayed near home, but in her mind, staying in a place that was reminiscent of the building that was bombed triggered fears that had remained latent until the family planned to leave the safety of home. Once she was able to voice her concerns, she responded to her mother's reassurance and was able to manage her anxiety.

Creating an atmosphere that allows children to voice their hidden anxieties requires a relaxed, indirect approach. It is fine to occasionally pose such questions as, "I'm wondering how you feel today," "You seem quiet today. I'm not sure what your thoughts are," "It sounds like...." Keep in mind, however, that parents are far more likely to engage their children in meaningful conversation about the children's apprehensions if they don't question too insistently.

Although it may be difficult for parents not to be able to fully discuss upsetting issues during troubling times, parents must separate what is in their control from what isn't. What is in the realm of parental control is to let the child know that they are available to discuss any concerns. For many children this is enough. Deep discussions are not necessarily best for them or needed.

There are a few guidelines to keep in mind when children start discussing their concerns. Research on children's responses to upsetting situations consistently shows that they do better when their parents answer questions honestly and directly. Evasion in the name of protecting the children tends to heighten their anxiety. On the other hand, reassuring children that they live in a strong country with powerful resources to protect them constitutes honest discussion that validates children's concerns about the threat of terrorism, while at the same time calming their fears.

Researchers on the psychological impact of traumatic events have long noted that even the most intelligent people may have difficulty understanding and processing information about anxiety-provoking situations. Consequently, it is important for parents to recognize that children's cognitive and emotional regression in response to frightening events may necessitate repetition regarding what happened, as well as frequent reassurance.

A woman whose child was being treated for leukemia made herself an expert on every aspect of her child's treatment. One day she received a call from her child's doctor saying that her son was in remission (meaning that the cancer was under control and was no longer active). Under normal circumstances she knew exactly what remission meant, but this time she was too paralyzed with anxiety to ask the doctor whether her child was going to live or die. Eventually she called the mother of another child being treated in the same center. Her friend reassured her that the doctor was giving her good news.

As noted earlier, when young children try to make sense of traumatic events, they are more likely than older children to personalize and think in concrete terms. Consequently, they are particularly prone to misinterpret the meaning of upsetting events.

Five-year-old twins were not responding to parental reassurance in the weeks following the attack on the Twin Towers.

Three weeks after the attack, as her mother was putting her to sleep, one of the twins asked, "Mommy, why do people hate twins?"

Finally, at times parents won't know the answer to a child's question. When children ask difficult questions such as, "Why do bad things happen to good people?" it may be more comforting for the child when the parent answers, "I don't know." Sometimes children prefer parental honesty about not having all of the answers. When Aharon was told about the death of his two sons, the Torah tells us that his response was silence: *Vayidom Aharon* (*Leviticus* 10:3).

The Abarbanel asks why the Torah uses the word *vayidom* instead of the more commonly used word for silence, *vayishkot*. He answers that the Hebrew word *sheket* is used when people know something, but choose not to share their knowledge. In contrast *demamah* is a term that describes a silence that comes from being truly speechless, not knowing what to say.

RECOMMENDATIONS

In discussing upsetting events with children, keep in mind that good listeners are generally more comforting than good talkers. It is often helpful for you to wait before answering a child's question, in order to make sure the child's true, underlying question is clear. If you aren't clear about the underlying meaning of a question, it might be helpful to ask the child, "What made you think of that?"

In dealing with adolescents, remember that even though many will not verbalize their fears, they may need to be reassured about their safety and security. In the weeks after the September 11th attack, many parents noted that teens who had long felt comfortable being home alone asked that their parents stay home with them at night.

It is particularly important to monitor childhood exposure to the media in the aftermath of terrorist attacks. Young children, in particular, may respond to each television replay of the Twin Tower attacks as if it were happening for the first time. It is also important to supervise young children's exposure to upsetting pictures in newspapers or news magazines. Also, keep in mind that children may be affected by repeatedly hearing adult discussions about the impact of the attacks.

Helping children take an active role in response to traumatic events is often therapeutic. Some of those who lost family members in the crash of TWA Flight 800 reported that the only comfort they found in the days following the crash was in looking at the hundreds of drawings that children from around the country sent them, in offering their condolences. Encouraging one's child to help raise money or send letters of support to families who lost members in the attacks is an opportunity to teach children that taking an active role in something can function as an antidote to feelings of helplessness.

Studies of children who lost their father in the Yom Kippur War found that their mothers' ability to talk of their sadness in front of their children played a crucial role in their children's recovery. A rabbi should encourage parents, therefore, to feel comfortable in occasionally discussing their sadness and concerns with their children. If this is done in a way that conveys a sense of loss mixed with reassurance and hope, children will learn a valuable lesson on how to deal with their own upsetting feelings.

≫ 12 ≪
HELPING THE ADDICTED
CONGREGANT

Abraham J. Twerski, M.D.

WHY SHOULD A RABBI BE FAMILIAR WITH
CHEMICAL DEPENDENCY PROBLEMS?

An appeal to the rabbi for help with a chemical addiction problem will generally come from a close family member rather
than from the addicted congregant himself. It is not often that
a person with an alcohol or drug problem will seek help. This
is because the person is usually engulfed in "denial", a psychological mechanism operating in the subconscious mind, which
blinds a person to one or more aspects of reality. An alcoholic's
life may be crumbling physically, emotionally, domestically,
socially, and occupationally, yet he may see no connection between this deterioration and his use of alcohol. Hence, he is unlikely to seek help for his drinking problem.

Denial operates within the community as well. The adage
shikker is a goy has lulled the Jewish community into a false
sense of security that it is immune to alcoholism and drug addiction. Only in recent years has this myth begun to be dispelled. Persistence of this misinformation only prevents the
recognition of an addiction problem.

Addictive chemicals are used to obtain an emotional change, and they do so by affecting brain cells. They can cause any and every affective or cognitive symptom. There is no way that one can accurately diagnose a psychological disorder when the brain tissue is affected by a mood-altering chemical. Therefore, the possibility of an alcohol or drug problem should be entertained whenever there is any recurring behavioral problem.

Being alert to this possibility will enable the rabbi to better evaluate a problem. He may be told of marital discord, job difficulties, financial crises, poor school performance, depression, anxiety, disobedience of children, or another dysfunction. Abuse of a mood-altering chemical may be the underlying cause for any of these problems, but is likely to be concealed.

One of the reasons why addiction is concealed is because it is viewed as shameful, "a *shonda*." This is also the reason why a rabbi may be hesitant to inquire about the use of alcohol or drugs. "This person is a respected member of the congregation. He attends minyan daily as well as the Talmud *shiur*. He is generous with *tzedakah*. How can I insult him by asking him whether he drinks too much or uses drugs?" Yet, if there is a chemical dependency, then whatever the rabbi tries to do to resolve the problem is likely to be futile. We must, therefore, address the question of how a rabbi should inquire about a chemical dependency problem. First, however, let us explore the nature of addiction itself.

WHAT IS ADDICTION?

There are numerous definitions of addiction. A practical, working definition is: *the continuing, compulsive use of a mood-altering chemical despite physical and/or psychological harm to the user and/or society.* Psychological dependence is the subjective feeling that the user needs the drug to maintain a feeling of well-being; physical dependence is characterized by tolerance (the need for increasingly larger doses in order to achieve the initial effect) and withdrawal symptoms when the user is abstinent.

An exception to this definition is the "periodic drinker," whose use of alcohol is not continuous but appears compulsive. This is a person who may abstain from alcohol for several months, but once he starts drinking, loses control and/or may experience a severe emotional disturbance as a result.

WHO IS VULNERABLE TO CHEMICAL ADDICTION?

Addiction is an "equal opportunity destroyer." There is no immunity. Alcoholism and drug addiction can occur in both men and women, no matter what age, level of intellect, socioeconomic level, religious or secular, professional or layman. The thought that "it could never happen in my family" is dangerous and may allow the addict to progress undetected or to go untreated.

WHAT ARE THE MORE COMMON ADDICTIVE CHEMICALS?

The more common addictive chemicals include alcohol, heroin, cocaine, oxycontin and other synthetic narcotics, stimulants, and hallucinogens, marijuana, tranquilizers, and sedatives. There are a variety of names by which these drugs are known on the street.

Some of the most difficult addictions are to prescription drugs. Sometimes addiction may develop as the result of persistent insomnia or a chronic pain problem when the use of the medication gets out of hand. The fact that a person is receiving the chemical by virtue of a doctor's prescription does not prevent addiction. A person may obtain the prescriptions he wants from several doctors.

There is public controversy about the dangers of marijuana use, with some people advocating legalization of marijuana. The excellent paper by Dr. Robert Dupont, who was an ardent advocate for decriminalizing marijuana when he was drug-czar in the Carter administration, dispels the illusion that marijuana is safe.

CROSS-ADDICTION

An important phenomenon that is unfortunately overlooked is *cross-addiction*. This means that once a person develops an addiction to any chemical, he is extremely vulnerable to become addicted to any other mood-altering chemical. Thus, a cocaine addict may abstain from cocaine, but may think he can use alcohol or tranquilizers. Experience has shown that he is likely to get addicted to alcohol or tranquilizers as well.

If a person who has recovered from any chemical dependency develops a medical condition that calls for a narcotic-type pain medication, special precautions must be taken to avoid his relapse into addiction.

WHY DO PEOPLE USE CHEMICALS?

People may take drugs for many reasons: to relieve stress, to relieve pain, to relax, to sleep, to escape reality, to feel more self-esteem, to feel euphoria, to keep alert, for increased energy, or because of peer pressure.

Chemical dependency is so prevalent that a rabbi can be certain that he will have to deal with such problems sometime. The idea that "it doesn't exist in my congregation or school" is misleading. It is important that the rabbi become knowledgeable about chemical addiction by reading informative literature, by taking courses on the subject, and by attending open meetings of Alcoholics Anonymous, Narcotics Anonymous, and the corresponding family support groups, Al-Anon and Nar-Anon.

The rabbi's effectiveness in dealing with chemical addiction will depend to a great degree on his own feelings about the problem. If the rabbi feels that alcoholism or chemical dependency is a sin, a moral failure, a character weakness, or anything that reflects on the value of the person, he is unlikely to be of much help. Even if he uses all the right words, his attitude that the condition is a *shonda* (shameful) will convey itself to the person and reinforce the person's denial and resistance. If the rabbi believes the addict to be suffering from a disease and that he is essentially a victim rather than a villain, he can help him recover.

But in what way is alcoholism a disease? The addicted individual willfully and voluntarily puts the glass to his lips. The fact is that some people drink a *l'chaim* and are not negatively affected while others are.

Alcoholism is the end product of a combination of factors: genetic, physiological, psychological, and social. The genetic propensity to alcoholism has been proven by many research studies over the years. The disease manifests itself in three principal ways: dependence, loss of control, and/or emotional upset.

A person who breaks out in hives every time he eats strawberries soon recognizes the cause and effect, and he avoids strawberries. He can do this because the abnormal reaction affects his skin but leaves his brain and thought processes intact so that he can make the cause and effect connection. Alcohol, however, affects the brain — the very organ that must make a judgment — and if the person's makeup (genetic, physiological, psychological, and social) is such that the effects of alcohol are abnormal, these effects on the brain render him unable to make the cause and effect connection. He cannot realize that alcohol is having deleterious effects. His dependence, loss of control, and/or emotional upset occur without his implicating alcohol. He thinks that there is nothing wrong with his drinking. Convincing, logical arguments that alcohol is damaging him tend to have no impact.

We can hardly fault anyone for taking a drink. Our culture is an alcohol "pusher". Anyone making a wedding or bar mitzvah without serving alcohol will be thought of as a tightwad. One's first use of alcohol is usually quite innocent, and when its harmful use takes over, the person cannot see it.

Much the same is true of prescription drugs. Some people can take a tranquilizer, painkiller, or sleeping pill without becoming dependent. Others become dependent, but the effect of the chemical on their thinking precludes their seeing that they are developing a problem. If and when they do recognize that they have a problem and try to stop or reduce the amount of drug they use, the withdrawal symptoms can be so severe that they cannot help taking more.

The beginning use of illicit drugs is not so innocent. It is foolhardy to introduce an illicit chemical into the body. Yet, marijuana use is widespread, epidemic on the campuses and widely used socially. Furthermore, people feel a false sense of security that marijuana is not a dangerous drug. "Here, try this" often entices someone to do just that out of curiosity. If the effect is pleasurable, the person may see nothing wrong with repeated use.

Many people naively experiment with heroin or cocaine. Some people will say "it's not my thing" and not use it again. Others like the effect and may think that occasional use is harmless. Even brief use of these drugs causes dependence in vulnerable people.

GUIDELINES FOR RABBINIC INTERVENTION

If an older person suffers a heart attack while shoveling snow, we do not say, "It's your own fault. You should have known better." We do everything to restore his health and we do not refuse to treat or help him because of his poor judgment. Our attitude toward addicts should be no different.

If the problem is presented as one of substance abuse, e.g., the wife says, "Rabbi, I'm afraid my husband is an alcoholic," the rabbi should ask for the reasons she thinks so. In many cases, she may have pleaded with her husband to reduce his drinking, but the husband denies that there is a problem. In such cases, telling the wife, "Have your husband call me," or taking the initiative to approach the husband is of little value. The husband will dismiss the allegation as absurd.

Unless the rabbi has become expert in alcoholism counseling, his response should be, "If your husband does not see his drinking as a problem, he will not avail himself of help. However, his drinking is obviously a problem for you. I suggest that you meet with a family counselor for alcoholism and attend Al-Anon meetings for families of alcoholics. These people are veterans in dealing with this kind of situation and can give excellent guidance."

"But Rabbi, my husband has great respect for you," she may say. "I'm sure that he will listen if you talk to him." Don't fall into that trap. All the respect he has for you may disappear if you challenge his use of alcohol. What the wife of the alcoholic wants is for somebody to change him. The Al-Anon principle of the "three C's" holds true for everyone. "You did not Cause it, you cannot Control it, and you cannot Cure it."

The wife of the alcoholic is often referred to as being "codependent". There are many definitions of codependence. The easiest to understand is that "the alcoholic plays the fiddle and the codependent dances to the tune." Codependents, with every good intention, often act in a way that actually encourages continuation of the drinking.

Codependents do not *cause* a person to become chemically dependent any more than oxygen *causes* a fire. However, just as oxygen *enables* a fire to burn, the codependent may *enable* the development or continuation of the chemical dependency.

An "intervention" may be necessary to break through the alcoholic's denial that he has a problem and get him into treatment before he does irreversible damage to himself and his family. An intervention is when a number of people who are significant to the alcoholic join together to speak to him. An intervention is not a "do-it-yourself" approach. It should be done only with the guidance and involvement of an addiction counselor with expertise in interventions. Otherwise it could be counterproductive.

The rabbi should have the names and phone numbers of people who can provide proper counseling for the wife. It is likely that the wife may continue to want to discuss the situation with the rabbi. Allowing her to do so only prolongs her codependency. The rabbi should be empathic but firm. "Mrs. B, this is a serious situation which is not going to be helped by telling me how much you are suffering. I believe you. Now you must go for help to the person who can actually provide what you need."

If and when the alcoholic accepts help, the rabbi can play a vital role in his recovery. Spirituality is crucial in recovery, but it is not the same as religiosity. It is important to understand just what spirituality is as it applies to recovery.

The human being is a composite creature, comprised of a body and "something else". The body is essentially an animalistic body. The primary features of the "something else" that are unique to man and hence define humanity are (1) greater intelligence; (2) the ability to learn from the past; (3) the ability to define one's goal and purpose in life; (4) the ability to volitionally improve oneself; (5) the ability to predict the consequences of one's behavior; (6) the ability to delay gratification, and (7) the ability to make ethical and moral decisions in defiance of bodily urges.

The sum total of these unique features may be termed the human "spirit". These features are "abilities" which a person may or may not put to use. If a person implements all the components of the spirit, he is "spiritual". Theoretically, a person may be spiritual even if he does not practice any religion. Religion plays a part when considering one's goal or purpose and in determining one's values. It says that there can be no meaningful personal purpose in a world that was not created for a purpose. It also teaches divinely determined moral and ethical values for the human mind to adopt. In active alcoholism and drug addiction, all of the components of the spirit wither away. Long term recovery cannot occur without development of one's spirituality.

It is essential that the rabbi understand the way an addict thinks. Although not as manifestly absurd as the thinking of the psychotic, the thought processes of the addict are no less unrealistic. The difference is that the unreality of the psychotic is evident, whereas the addict can make his argument sound so reasonable that one may not detect its fallacy. Even seasoned psychiatrists and psychologists can be taken in by the addict.

Under pressure, the addict may reluctantly concede that he has a problem and promise never to drink or use drugs again. He can cry tears of remorse and appear so sincere that one is tempted to accept his promise. The point to remember is that *the addict has a compulsion which he cannot resist* and his promises are of no value whatsoever. He may be most sincere in swearing off alcohol or drugs, but he is making a promise that he cannot keep. He may abstain for a period of time, but without treatment, relapse is virtually certain.

Rabbis are firm believers in *teshuvah*, and it may be difficult to reject the contrition of the addict. However, the only effective *teshuvah* for the addict is recovery with treatment.

Occasionally, the addict may be so frightened by the consequences of his addiction—loss of his job or his wife leaving him—that he may abstain for an extended period of time. Without treatment, this abstinence is referred to as "dry drunk", i.e. all the negative behavioral traits persist, although the person is free of chemicals. (It is interesting to note that the first reference to "dry drunk" can be found in *Isaiah* 29:9, "They were drunk, but not from wine; they staggered, but not from liquor."). Some family members have said that as difficult as it was to live with the active drinker, it was even worse when he was a dry drunk.

HOW TO INTERVIEW

If the complaint is one of obvious alcohol or drug abuse, the rabbi should direct the person to a therapist with established expertise in chemical dependency. Even the finest psychiatrists and psychologists may not be qualified to evaluate or treat an alcohol or drug problem. In my three years of psychiatric training, there was no teaching about alcoholism or drug addiction—and this is still true of some training programs. A mental health specialist who has not been adequately trained in chemical dependency may mistakenly diagnose the condition as some type of mental disorder and prescribe medications or psychotherapy, without addressing the chemical problem. As noted, this delays recovery and may further complicate a difficult problem.

When the person who approaches the rabbi is a spouse or family member complaining about someone's behavior without reference to any substance abuse, the rabbi should listen attentively and give consideration to all possible factors that may be responsible for the problem behavior. The possible causes of any problem are legion. After listening thoroughly, the rabbi may ask, "Have you noticed whether your husband's behavior is any different after he has had a drink?"

Some people can be adversely affected by even small amounts of alcohol. One person realized that the arguments with his wife occurred only Friday night and Shabbat afternoon. When he substituted grape juice for wine, there were no further arguments. Hence, an alcohol-related problem may not necessarily be due to *heavy* drinking.

Making *kiddush* on Shabbat morning is not a problem for a non-alcoholic. However, some men take several drinks at the "*kiddush* club," then take several more drinks when they get home. After this, the Shabbat meal can become very unpleasant.

A wife may report that her husband often returns home inordinately late. He may come back at 2 A.M. with a plausible explanation. Repeated tardiness with plausible explanations is a red flag. The rabbi should inquire whether she notes alterations in his mood. People who use chemicals can experience radical mood swings from day to day. The mood changes in bipolar disorders are much more gradual. Abrupt changes may be chemically related.

"Does your husband appear to be secretive about some of his phone calls? Is he isolating himself more than usual? Have you found that he has lied to you? Are you having financial problems that are not well accounted for?" Whereas alcohol is cheap, cocaine and heroin can be very costly.

If, after careful questioning, the rabbi feels that there may be an alcohol or drug problem, he may ask the wife, "Do you think your husband would agree to talk to me? May I call him?" The wife may say, "Oh, no! I don't want him to know that I've spoken to you." In that case, the rabbi should refer the woman to a therapist competent in chemical dependency problems for further consultation. If the conclusion is that there is no evidence of a chemical problem, the rabbi may see the wife for several sessions of rabbinic counseling or refer her to an appropriate therapist.

If the wife says, "Yes, I wish you would talk to him," the rabbi must make it clear that he will have to tell the husband that the wife is concerned about his behavior. The wife may say, "Talk to him, but don't let him know that I spoke to you about it." If the rabbi has no grounds for approaching the husband except for the wife's complaint, this is untenable.

If the husband does consult the rabbi, the rabbi should bring up the problem which the wife described. Assuming that the husband does not totally deny the problem, the rabbi may ask, "Does this tend to occur after you have had a drink?" He also may ask, "How does a drink affect you?" or "Have you ever found that you drank more than you intended?" One does not ask, "Do you drink excessively?" To the alcoholic, even the copious consumption of alcohol is not excessive.

Heavy drinking may result in a "blackout". This is a phenomenon where the person may behave in a normal manner, but has no recollection of what happened. An alcoholic physician may perform several difficult operations perfectly under the effects of alcohol, but not remember having done so. A blackout is evidence of heavy drinking.

If the rabbi has reason to suspect that there is a chemical problem, he may say, "I'm concerned that you may have a problem with (alcohol, marijuana, pills) and I think you should look into this further." Chemical problems are not static. They always progress, and if not attended to early, they can have very serious consequences. The rabbi should have a list of competent chemical dependency therapists to whom he can refer the congregant.

CHEMICAL PROBLEMS IN AN ADOLESCENT

The use of chemicals among young people is epidemic. A teenager may be using and even selling drugs. Parents may not recognize that their child has a chemical problem.

Unruly and defiant behavior in youngsters is not necessarily chemically related, but it is grounds for considering chemicals as a possible cause. Youngsters who use chemicals may be doing poorly in school. They may have rapid mood swings. They may stay out late at night and give a variety of excuses for their behavior. They may hang up the phone suddenly when the parent enters the room. They may stay in their room for long hours. The parents may discover that money or other items of value are missing.

The greatest difficulty with a teenager who is drinking or using is that often the parents have little control over him. The youngster may defy all rules and disciplinary measures. With an adult, one can say, "These are the rules of the house. Excessive drinking and use of drugs is forbidden here. We cannot control what you do, but we can control who lives in this house. If you are unable to comply with the rules, you are free to find a place to live elsewhere." You cannot say this to a fourteen year old. He knows that you will not evict him. Since you will not evict nor physically restrain him, a youngster may do as he pleases.

The frustration of being powerless while your child is harming himself with chemicals can be devastating. It is crucial that the parents receive guidance from a counselor with expertise in juvenile chemical problems, and that they attend family support meetings. They must learn what they can and should do, and what behavior and actions to avoid.

Youngsters who use chemicals often reject religion. The primary concern of the parents may be that their son has deviated from religious observance. The rabbi should help the parents realize that there is no point in trying to get the youngster to be religious as long as he is using chemicals. Treatment of the chemical problem must take priority.

TREATMENT OPTIONS

There are a variety of treatment approaches, and the appropriate treatment must be individualized. In many cases, detoxification is necessary. Many chemically dependent people try to withdraw from chemicals on their own. Sometimes this is dangerous, because the withdrawal reaction can be very severe. Even when there is no danger, the chemically dependent person may find the withdrawal symptoms intolerable and he will resume use of the chemical. Detoxification or withdrawal in a hospital or rehabilitation center is often necessary.

Residential treatment is usually the most desirable and effective strategy. However, the addict may resist going into a residential program. Furthermore, third party coverage for residential treatment is generally inadequate. Depending on the evaluation by a therapist, an out-patient program may be tried first. If that fails, residential treatment becomes necessary.

Out-patient programs vary in intensity and frequency. The appropriate schedule should be recommended by the therapist. It is important that the rabbi familiarize himself with the available treatment resources.

12–Step Programs

We do not speak of "cures" for chemical dependency. Rather, we say the condition has been "arrested." "Cure" would imply that the person is no longer an addict and that he may, therefore, drink or use an addictive drug again. Virtually every attempt of a recovering alcoholic to drink "socially" results in full relapse. People recovering from alcoholism or other chemical dependencies should avoid any use of alcohol. Grape juice should be substituted for wine, and there should be no exceptions to this rule.

Life-long abstinence from alcohol may appear so formidable to the alcoholic that he may see an attempt at sobriety to be futile. The best approach is that taken by Alcoholics Anonymous (AA) to "take one day at a time." Abstinence for today is feasible. Inasmuch as one cannot predict today about tomorrow's drinking, there is no reason to worry about it now. Tomorrow's challenge can be dealt with tomorrow.

The "one day at a time" method has proven to be effective. One recovering person wrote the number of his sober days in his calendar daily. The night before his death at age eighty-four, he entered the number 16,425. Although he was sober for forty-five years, he was very sincere about taking "one day at a time."

Some Jews have resisted joining Alcoholics Anonymous because they see it as a Christian program. They cite the fact that it originated with a Christian group, that AA meetings are generally held in churches, and that the meetings close with the Lord's Prayer. They also point to the AA concept of "turning my will over to a Higher Power, God as I understand Him" to be alien to Judaism.

The preponderance of AA meetings in churches is simply because synagogues have not welcomed them. Efforts to bring AA meetings into synagogues have generally met strong resistance. The myth "alcoholism is not a Jewish problem" is unfortunately still prevalent.

Nothing in the AA principles requires saying the Lord's Prayer. A person may say whatever prayer he wishes. The term "God as I understand Him" was chosen to accommodate people of all faiths. If one wishes to say "I turn my will over to Hashem," this is perfectly acceptable. The idea of turning one's will over to Hashem is found in *Ethics of the Fathers* (2:4): "Treat His will as if it were your own will...." The 12–step recovery programs of AA and Narcotics Anonymous (NA) are compatible with Judaism. The real resistance to these programs is because addicts refuse to accept total abstinence. Using religious reasons for refusal to attend AA or NA meetings is nothing but an attempt to legitimize one's resistance.

Rabbis would do well to attend open meetings of AA, NA, Al-Anon and Nar-Anon family groups, where observers are welcome. The information about chemical dependency and recovery that can be gained at these meetings is invaluable.

Jews in Alcoholics Anonymous (JACS)

A number of years ago, several Jews from Alcoholics Anonymous, feeling uncomfortable being in the minority, sought to share their recovery with other Jews. From this nucleus there developed an organization called Jewish Alcoholics, Chemically Dependent and Significant others. This organization provides helpful information for chemically dependent Jews and their family members. JACS holds two weekend retreats annually, as well as educational sessions on spirituality. Although JACS is headquartered in New York, local groups have been formed in other communities and countries. JACS is a very helpful resource.

ADDICTIONS BEYOND DRUGS AND ALCOHOL

Tobacco

Rabbis have long since recognized the addictive nature of cigarettes. As Shabbat draws to a close, some congregants become visibly agitated, and at the first permissible moment, they make a mad dash for the package of cigarettes they stowed away on Friday.

The rabbi is not usually consulted by people who wish to break their smoking habit. However, the rabbi may have a role in discouraging youngsters from picking up the habit. The rabbi may address the youngsters on the subject, utilizing information from the vast literature on smoking and its effects. Brochures on smoking-cessation should also be made available to congregants.

Compulsive Gambling

As with alcohol, many people buy lottery tickets and, yet, do not develop an addiction to gambling. Others may experience a progressive dependence from the first time they make a bet or visit a casino. While accurate statistics of the incidence of compulsive gambling among Jews is not known, the problem is by no means uncommon. The compulsive drive to gamble overwhelms all logical reasoning and arguments to the contrary. Compulsive gambling could destroy an individual and family and even lead to suicide attempts.

The compulsive gambler usually keeps his gambling a secret from the family. He constantly has a need for more money, and the compulsive drive may make him do anything to get it, from embezzling to mortgaging the house, to forging his wife's signature in order to withdraw money, to selling her jewelry, to gambling away the children's savings accounts. Eventually the need for money is so great that he appeals to everyone possible, concocting a story about why he is in dire financial straits.

A person may run a business while involved in gambling. He may tell family and friends that he needs money to save his business from bankruptcy. People may believe him and give him money. There are likely to be several such "crises" before the truth comes out.

Even when it is discovered that the person is deeply in debt because of gambling, family members and friends may still try to bail him out. He may convince them that with just another $10,000 or $30,000 he will be able to get the $500,000 he needs to get out of debt. A compulsive gambler can be very manipulative and adept at getting people to believe him.

A gambler may have written bad checks or committed other crimes to get money for his habit. Fearing damage to their reputation if this is exposed, the family may pay off the gambler's debts in exchange for his promise that he will never again gamble. As with all addictions, his promises are absolutely worthless, regardless of how sincere he seems. His sincerity may be due to the fact that he actually believes that he can stop his addictive behavior.

The addict may say that he is in debt to loan sharks, and he has been threatened with bodily harm or death if he does not pay the debt. The family might panic and bail him out, only to discover later that he is again deep in debt.

The rabbi can be extremely helpful, particularly in providing guidance for the family who feels guilt-ridden for not "helping" the son or brother. They must be made to understand that giving money to a compulsive gambler is like giving whisky to an alcoholic.

Whether the rabbi is approached by the gambler himself or the family, there is only one approach to recommend: treatment, not promises. And the treatment must be by someone competent in gambling addiction. Treatment resources can be found on the internet under "Compulsive Gambling."

Gamblers Anonymous (GA) and Gam-Anon family groups are indispensable resources for both the gambler and his family.

As with alcoholism, it is not unusual to find that there is resistance to attending these support groups. The rabbi should strongly urge attendance. The wife may persist in asking, "What can I do about my husband?" and may not be able to understand that as the victim of this condition, *she* needs help. In fact, as long as she keeps the focus on getting her husband to change, nothing is likely to happen.

The rabbi's attendance at GA and Gam-Anon meetings can give him insight into a world that is totally alien to him. Only when one has had personal contact with people in recovery can one believe that such a lifestyle of recovery is even possible.

Recognizing Compulsive Gambling

In the later stages, there is little difficulty in recognizing that something is drastically wrong and further investigation will reveal the gambling problem. In later stages, the compulsive gambler may be run-down and weary. Sleep is poor and with nightmares. He has no interest in his health or hygiene. He is jumpy, edgy, and cannot sit still. He may be depressed or exhibit acute anxiety, and may experience uncontrollable weeping. He jumps whenever there is a knock on the door or the telephone rings. He may drink or use tranquilizers to quell his agitation. He may have periods of explosive rage, breaking or throwing things. He also may walk about aimlessly, muttering to himself.

However, in the early stages these signs are absent, and it may be difficult to detect the condition. There tends to be a drop-off in his usual activities and interests. He spends more time away from home and misses work, explaining both with a variety of excuses. He may use the telephone more to call his bookmaker. He may withdraw from his wife and children. There may be a diversion of family funds with attempts to explain them or cover them up. As gambling debts increase, he may redeem securities or bonds, cash in insurance policies, and sell things of value.

These "soft signs" are a red flag. They should not be ignored, and the wife should insist on an explanation for these acts, bearing in mind that the compulsive gambler generally does not tell the truth.

When a person first begins gambling, he is usually fairly open about it. He may entertain others with his gambling stories and boast about how much money he won. When he starts getting into debt and tries to raise money in ways that he doesn't want his wife to know about, he begins to conceal his gambling.

If the gambling habit progresses, he might devote more time to it, staying at the racetrack or the casino longer, or going to out of town places instead of the local ones. An increase in the size of his bets is a warning sign. A sudden interest in football, for example watching three games a week instead of one, may indicate increased betting. He may boast about his winnings and be evasive about his losses.

The Rabbi as a Stabilizer

Even more than alcoholism, compulsive gambling may cause erratic fluctuations within the family. One day a wife is ready to file for divorce and the next day she loves her husband so much that she decides not to leave him and feels she must rescue him.

With a thorough understanding of the behavior of the compulsive gambler and family members, the rabbi may be the only consistent and rational voice. The vacillation of family members between sympathy and anger makes recovery impossible. The compulsive gambler is an expert at manipulation and will pull every trick to keep the family supporting his behavior. The rabbi can help the family resist the manipulation and enable eventual recovery.

His relatives will ask, Should we make his mortgage payments and buy food for his family? A competent therapist will guide the family on how they can be of help without inadvertently being "enablers".

Access to Treatment

Initiating treatment in a residential program is ideal. Ironically, the gambler has thrown his family into such dire financial straits that there is no money to pay for residential treatment. This is one time where relatives, if possible, are encouraged to make money available. It goes without saying that the money should be given to the treatment center directly.

Chronic Debt

It is not unusual for a family to be in debt. There are people who seem to have no control over spending money, although they may not gamble. They are chronically in debt and may repeatedly borrow money from family and friends. This compulsion is somewhat similar to gambling and is most effectively addressed by the 12–step program, Debtors Anonymous.

Eating Disorders

Eating disorders are similar to other addictions in that the person knows that his eating pattern is harmful, but he is unable to stop. Furthermore, when food consumption exceeds nutritional needs, the food is invariably being used as a "tranquilizer". This essentially converts food to the status of being a drug.

Obesity is now considered to be the major health problem

in the United States. Every month there are new "miracle diets" that are guaranteed to work. They all result in weight loss which is invariably followed by regaining the weight. Sustained weight reduction is best achieved by ongoing participation in a support group (e.g., Overeaters Anonymous, Weight Watchers). Surgery is advised only when the degree of obesity is life-threatening.

A serious eating disorder that is far more prevalent than suspected is "anorexia-bulimia". It is thought that one of four adolescent girls has this condition, which is generally characterized by binge eating followed by radical attempts to prevent weight gain, such as induced vomiting, fasting, purging with laxatives, or extreme exercising. Young women conceal this problem from their parents and even from therapists.

Anorexia-bulimia results in the young woman being so preoccupied with eating and losing weight that it tends to impair her school work and social functioning, and may cause her to feel depressed. The rabbi can help the family overcome their denial of the problem and seek competent therapy for the young woman.

Sexual Addiction

If alcoholism and compulsive gambling are concealed under a cloak of secrecy, one can imagine how much greater is the concealment of sexual addiction. The humiliation involved if it were to be exposed keeps it under wraps and away from treatment.

"Voyeurism" has become much more widespread with the availability of pornography on the internet. Prior to this, some men were deterred by the fear that they would be caught outside someone's window ("peeping Tom") or be seen in an adult shop. However, this deterrent was eliminated with the privacy afforded by the internet. Wives have been horrified by the accidental discovery that their husbands have been regularly viewing pornography.

As with other compulsive behaviors, there may be gross inconsistencies. A man who is a devoted husband and father and an exemplary religious person may fall victim to sexual compulsions. And as with other addictions, remorse and promises are of little value.

Wives may also stumble across evidence of extramarital affairs. These are not necessarily of an addictive nature. Addiction is essentially a compulsion, where the individual engages in a behavior he wishes he could stop, but feels helpless to avoid. He succumbs to this drive against his better judgment. A person who feels there is nothing wrong with an extramarital affair is a person with impaired morals, rather than an addict.

Although there are no definitive guidelines, demanding excessive sexual relations even within marriage may be unreasonable and evidence of an addiction problem. If a husband complains that his wife is denying him sexual relations, she should be asked for her version of the situation. Unless the full spectrum of the situation is understood, she may be erroneously considered cold and withholding.

Whether or not a person's sexual behavior is compulsive or simply morally loose requires evaluation by a therapist with expertise in sexual addiction. Treatment should also be provided only by therapists qualified in the treatment of sexual addiction and sexual disorders.

As with other addictions, ongoing participation in a support group is essential. The addict may object, "How can I take a chance being seen in a support group of sexual addicts (Sex and Love Anonymous [SLA] or Sex Anonymous [SA])? If word gets out, it will ruin my reputation and bring shame to my children." As logical as this may sound, there is no option. Unchecked sexual addiction will bring greater ruin to the family.

Referral to Treatment

If the rabbi takes an interest in the various addictions, he will generally make the acquaintance of people who are in recovery from alcoholism, drug addiction, compulsive gambling, or sexual addiction. It can be most helpful if the rabbi can arrange contact for the addict or family members with someone who is already in recovery. Such contact can significantly decrease their resistance to treatment.

Many addicts suffer from "terminal uniqueness," believing that no one else in their position has had a similar problem. Just the awareness that they are not alone—that others have been in the same situation and that there are people who can understand—is an important step toward recovery.

In sum, with addictions of all kinds being prevalent among Jews of all ages, socio-economic levels, and religious or secular orientation, the rabbi may be in a pivotal position to help combat these problems. The rabbi's role is important because Jewish communities tend to deny these problems and resist treatment for them. A thorough awareness of addictions can enable the rabbi to provide an invaluable service to the addict, his family, and the community.

❧ 13 ❧
COUNSELING THE SINGLE CONGREGANT: STRATEGIES FOR RABBINIC INTERVENTION

Rosie Einhorn, M.S.W.
Sherry Zimmerman, J.D.

THE PLIGHT OF modern Jewish singles who yearn to marry, but for psychosocial and cultural reasons are unable to, has reached crisis proportions. There are ways that the Jewish community can help alleviate this problem, including creating more opportunities for singles to be introduced to each other or to meet on their own in an appropriate environment. However, at the same time, there is a tendency for the community to judge singles unsympathetically, believing that to some degree they are at fault for being single (either they are negligent in something they should be doing or in something they should not be doing). Also, contemporary American social values negatively influence the modern Jewish mind-set to the point that married people believe that older Jewish unmarrieds have chosen to remain single. They are viewed as independent, self-sufficient, and neither needing nor wanting help in finding a life partner.

It is often difficult for the community rabbi, who is generally preoccupied with ongoing congregational responsibilities, to perceive the magnitude of the "singles' crisis" in his own community and to be sensitive to the pain of the Jewish single. Yet the statistics provided by the 2000 National Jewish Population Survey in the United States are most disturbing for all who are concerned about the future of the Jews in America. Nearly 40% of all Jewish adults are unmarried and 25% of all Jewish adults believe that they themselves will never marry. Furthermore, Jews who marry tend to do so later than non-Jewish Americans.[1]

While these statistics cover the general Jewish population and are not broken down according to the different affiliations in the community, the truth is that every sector has already been affected by this phenomenon, without exception. It is threatening Jewish survival and continuity, with Jewish birthrates below that of other Americans and falling rapidly.[2] When we add to this the fact that the majority of Jewish singles are indeed eager to marry and have children, but simply do not know how to go about meeting the right person for them, we begin to grasp the extent of the personal suffering that lies beneath the surface of this crisis.

The community rabbi needs to recognize that he is in a unique position to address this alarming trend. Over the past several years rabbis have been increasingly challenged by singles, who feel alienated from synagogue life and Jewish communal life. Rabbis now are being increasingly approached by parents with unmarried children or by singles in search of more networking contacts and opportunities to meet other singles.

Parts of this chapter discuss approaches that are more applicable to westernized singles than men and women raised in more traditional communities, who are accustomed to following a more focused approach to marriage-oriented dating and to utilizing a selective networking process to facilitate their search for a potential spouse. Nevertheless, most of the difficulties that singles face are universal. Furthermore, rabbis of more traditional congregations will find that most of the content in this chapter can be adapted to the needs of their own congregants.

Demoralized by encounters with insensitive matchmakers, scarred from being paired up with people who clearly were not a good match, or depressed that their dating experiences have been unsuccessful on the whole, singles are turning to their rabbis for counsel. To know how to respond to each appeal for help, a rabbi must understand the primary reasons why such a large percentage of Jewish adults are not married.

UNDERSTANDING THE PHENOMENON

Contemporary western social values are adversely affecting many modern American Jews. In American society, marriage is no longer viewed as necessary for achieving social acceptability, financial stability, a sense of personal accomplishment, or a physically satisfying relationship. Marriage is now considered to be just one of several valid lifestyle choices,[3] and many Jewish adults have also adopted this attitude. They no longer feel any urgency to marry.

American society's changed view of marriage has had an impact on the more traditional Jewish community as well. While the vast majority of traditional singles plan to marry and build homes and families that are devoted to Torah values, many have been influenced concerning at which point they will be ready to marry, the role marriage will fill in their lives, the qualities they seek in a spouse, and the nature of the relationship they will have with their husband or wife.

In addition, with western society's emphasis on personal fulfillment and instant gratification, fewer adults view their single years as an important developmental stage that provides them with the opportunity to:

> ► Achieve independence
> ► Assume responsibility for their own day-to-day living
> ► Clarify their values
> ► Gain a strong sense of who they are.[4]

Instead, their passage into adulthood becomes just an extended adolescence, and they are no more ready for marriage at age 29 or 35 than they were at age 20. Even individuals who plan on marrying someday first want to finish their education and achieve financial well-being, professional advancement, social status, and enjoy general life experiences.

To further exacerbate the problem, Hollywood's version of romantic love and Madison Avenue's version of physical perfection have colored people's expectations concerning courtship and marriage. As a result, many single Jews have adopted unrealistic ideas about who would be a good spouse for them or how to go about building a solid, healthy relationship with another individual that can lead to marriage. One person is as clueless as the next, and there are few models of successful courtship for them to imitate or advisors for them to turn to for guidance.

These same people, instead of viewing marriage as a commitment to build a life together and endure both life's ups and downs as a team, due to a lack of guidance, expect marriage to run smoothly at all times, with little conflict.

Another obstacle for modern Jewish singles is that they engage in casual dating for a number of years and then often do not know how to make the transition to courtship-for-marriage once they decide to go in that direction. They have no idea which changes they then need to make.

In addition, as a Jewish single gets older, venues for meeting a potential spouse tend to diminish.

Older singles also tend to suffer from psychological barriers that are not a factor for those who marry young. Older people tend to be more guarded than younger cohorts for several reasons. They may have been hurt or disappointed more, while younger people are still open to taking emotional risks. Older singles may have higher expectations of others, while at the same time they become less flexible. The longer singles live on their own, responsible for their own financial, physical, and emotional well-being, the more difficult it is for them to open up emotionally to a dating partner, or to be willing to alter their living arrangements, social life, career, and finances to accommodate another person's needs.

Many singles, both older and younger, fear what will happen if their marriage does not work out. Their fears may be based on seeing their parents not getting along. They fear they will repeat their parents' mistakes; they wish to avoid the pain and shame that comes with divorce, along with the financial aftermath of a broken marriage. Because some singles see a number of troubled marriages even among their own peers, and fewer successful ones on which they can model their own relationships, they lack confidence in their ability to be a good spouse, deal with the small and large crises that every marriage weathers, and to know how to make a marriage thrive.

Once a rabbi understands the possible reasons for people marrying late or not at all, he can take some practical steps that will begin to reverse this trend. Many of these steps require the rabbi to become proactive in establishing community infrastructures for singles and to mobilize members of the community to join in addressing this issue. This is uncharted territory for most rabbis, who seldom interact with the majority of unmarried Jewish adults who reside on the fringes of Jewish synagogue life.

ALIENATED SINGLES

There are a number of reasons why a significant portion of single Jewish adults feel alienated from synagogue as well as Jewish communal life. One is that most synagogues gear their activities toward married couples and families, and many singles feel that they are treated as second-rate because they don't fit in. Even when singles attempt to participate in services or run for board positions and committee chairmanships, they may be passed over due to their marital status.

Singles who feel alienated from Jewish communal life are likely to fill their need to socialize by going elsewhere. They may check out several different synagogues until they find a place where they fit in. (Sadly, some men and women who cannot find a niche will look outside of the Jewish community.) Occasionally a synagogue will schedule alternate services and programs for unmarried adults, so they can feel a stronger sense of belonging, but unless an effort is made to integrate them into the fabric of the community, these alternate programs only intensify their feelings of isolation.

Once a rabbi can acknowledge the fact that some Jewish singles will never marry and that others may not marry for a long time, he will hopefully take action to make them feel more important and welcome. Instead of fostering the feeling that singles and marrieds exist in parallel universes, the synagogue can encourage their singles to join committees, assume leadership roles, and interact more with the marrieds at social functions. Instead of segregating singles in their own services and social functions, invite them to: Shabbat dinners and holiday parties geared to different age ranges, same-gender programs that work together on community service projects, sports teams, young leadership programs, or pair them with married study partners in programs modeled after Partners in Torah.[5]

Doing this will reap the triple benefits of enabling singles to feel a sense of belonging, facilitating the formation of friendships between singles and marrieds, and encouraging singles who wish to marry to utilize these social connections to meet suitable dating partners.

All of these programs will help singles feel a closer connection to the Jewish community and the synagogue. Most probably they will then feel more comfortable approaching their rabbi for advice in personal matters.

DATING ISSUES

Many singles are embarrassed to approach their rabbi and admit that they are not succeeding in finding a mate. Usually they have already been on the receiving end of a fair share of unjust criticism ("You're too picky and that's why you're single," "If you really wanted to get married, you would," or "Why were you were working so hard to get your Ph.D.? You should have made an effort to get your Mrs. instead."), and if they do not view their rabbi as sensitive to their plight, they will not open themselves up to him. In addition, if they do not think the rabbi can actually do something to help them, they will be reluctant to ask him for advice.

Many times, a rabbi is approached by a congregant who is feeling anguished by the fact that his adult child has not yet married. A son or daughter may have been dating for some time without success or is having difficulty obtaining appropriate matches. Older singles, divorced, or widowed congregants often approach the rabbi with similar complaints and ask for help finding an appropriate dating partner or where to get suitable guidance or information. Each of these individuals is experiencing intense emotional pain, and it is imperative for the rabbi to respond to their dilemma with sensitivity and concern, and without passing judgment.

A rabbi who is approached by a single or the parent of a single who needs help finding appropriate dating partners can ask certain questions that will help clarify the issues he needs to address. These include:

> ➤ Does the single have a clear idea of his/her value system?
>
> ➤ Does the single have a clear idea of his/her goals for the next one to five years and how s/he intends to accomplish them?
>
> ➤ What personal qualities does the single feel characterize him/her as a unique individual?
>
> ➤ What qualities can s/he contribute to a marriage?
>
> ➤ What qualities is s/he seeking in her future life partner?

An individual who cannot articulate clear answers to any of these questions needs to explore these areas and develop a better sense of himself or herself before continuing to search. This is because common values, compatible goals, and similar directions in life are the prerequisites for enduring relationships and a starting point for any suggested match. Singles who have difficulty finding matches who are well-suited to them often have not yet clarified in their minds who they are, where they are headed, and what they need. Moreover, a single who focuses on characteristics or values that are unrealistic, not reflective of his/her own needs, or simply not important is wasting his/her time. A rabbi can suggest that this person begin by thinking honestly and carefully about his/her answers to the above questions.

Many singles have difficulty developing and maintaining a relationship that will lead to marriage and would benefit considerably from one-on-one guidance throughout their dating.

Although a rabbi should not be expected to provide this degree of involvement, he can encourage congregants who have been happily married for at least a few years and have good insight, judgment, and the ability to be discreet to mentor a single who is dating for marriage.

This invaluable service, in many cases, makes the difference between a successful courtship that leads to marriage and the failure of a promising relationship. A mentor can act as a sounding board for the single to voice his concerns. A mentor can also assist him in developing a network of people who can introduce him to appropriate matches, tell him how to develop a healthy relationship with the opposite sex, guide him through a courtship, and reassure him that he will reach his goal.

Successful dating mentors do not require specialized training; they can apply their own practical knowledge and common sense. However, they certainly might benefit from a workshop[6] that discusses the different problems singles face and effective solutions they can adapt to whomever they are helping. There are also self-help books for singles and on-line resources for mentors.

Rabbis can be extremely helpful by setting up a mentoring program in their area and referring individuals to it in appropriate situations. A mentoring program is most effective when one volunteer is paired with one single, so that the mentor never works with more than one single at a time.

Another way for the rabbi to be helpful to singles who have difficulty finding dating partners is to encourage his congregation, either alone or in conjunction with several other congregations in the region, to create opportunities for singles to meet. The assumed truth is that the further individuals are from their early twenties, the fewer opportunities they have to meet potential dates in a casual setting and through networking. Although many modern singles turn to clubs, mixers, and parties, these are not a viable answer for marriage-minded Jews, for several reasons. One reason is that most people do not "perform" well at mixer-type activities, where judgments are based primarily on physical qualities or charisma. Also, some singles' programs attract the same people over and over again and simply "torture" the participants into spending unproductive hours with the same unsuitable people they already met at a previous singles' event.

The success of a mixed-gender event for singles can be measured in the positive impression the event makes on its participants, the number of marriages that it produces, and the number of marriages that result from networking between participants after the event concludes. Keys to a successful program include limiting the age range of participants, balancing numbers of men and women, opening the program to singles from different geographic areas, limiting the size of the event, dividing participants into sub-groups for meals or discussions, and, above all, using a number of married volunteers to stimulate interaction at the event and to help facilitate arrangements for dates between interested parties in the weeks following the program. While more traditional communities rely primarily on matchmakers and networking to facilitate introductions between singles, some rabbinic authorities have approved of well-organized mixed-gender activities such as Shabbatons, Shabbat dinners with local families, and educational programs as a way for marriage-minded men and women to meet suitable dating partners.

In modern Jewish communities, another successful alternative to unproductive, large-scale singles programs can be for the rabbi to encourage a single to develop and utilize a network to find suitable dating partners. Networking is a particularly effective tool for singles, yet many singles do not know how to develop a network for this purpose or how to utilize it to their advantage. There are many Jewish singles who need more assistance than others in developing networks because they have limited personal resources within the Jewish community. Converts to Judaism, Jews who have recently become religiously observant, and even newcomers to the area often face the additional challenge of building a network from scratch, since many of their family members and friends cannot be helpful to them. The rabbi may be able to suggest individuals these singles can approach for help, or facilitate an introduction to a married couple or volunteer who can assist the single with networking.

A rabbi can provide guidance to all singles by explaining how to use a network and suggesting individuals the single can approach to help find suitable dating partners. These can include relatives, close friends, friends from the past, neighbors, co-workers, acquaintances, synagogue members, and former rabbis and teachers. The rabbi can also advise the single to provide the members of his network with a brief description of his best personal qualities, the direction his life is taking, and the qualities he is looking for in a future spouse.

> Lanie was in college when she took a course in comparative religion and decided that she wanted to learn more about Judaism. She felt a connection to the Jewish faith because her father's parents were Jewish, and the more she learned the more she felt that she was a Jew in her heart. Lanie's conversion to Judaism became official when she was 23, and she took a year off to study at a seminary in Israel. Several months after she returned to the United States, Lanie decided that she was comfortable enough with her Jewish observance to begin dating for marriage. However, most of her Jewish friends were in Israel, and she was just becoming acquainted with the members of her new synagogue. Her family did not know the type of people she would want to date, and she had no idea where to get started finding dating partners. She asked the rabbi who had taught her

conversion class for guidance. This rabbi knew that her predicament was a common one for newcomers to Judaism, and so he took the time to explain the manner in which Jewish singles develop networks of friends, family, former teachers, synagogue members, and others to introduce them to suitable dates. He put Lanie in touch with a couple who was active in Jewish outreach and was willing to help her develop a dating-referral network and serve as her dating mentors. He also encouraged her to ask the rabbi of the synagogue she had joined to introduce her to couples and singles her age with whom she could socialize and who could eventually introduce her to dating partners.

Another way for a rabbi to address the difficulty singles have finding suitable dates is to encourage the community to develop a region-wide, non-profit matchmaking service in cooperation with other synagogues. This is no easy venture, since the group must be well-organized and develop a uniform procedure of gathering and presenting information about singles, determining the best criteria for making matches, and providing follow-up assistance to couples. Committee members can model their own program after successful groups in other communities and utilize resources that are available on line.[7]

WHEN THERAPY IS NEEDED

Sometimes, a rabbi may determine that a single who consults with him needs more help than a dating mentor, networking, or matchmaking service can provide. An individual who appears to be clinically depressed or dysfunctional, or exhibits inappropriate conduct, should not be dating and should be referred to a therapist. Similarly, an individual with poor interpersonal skills or extremely low self-esteem will benefit from a program or therapist who can help him address these shortcomings so that he can come to date successfully.

However, most of the singles who seek the rabbi's advice are bright, personable, functional individuals who live very full lives. Some of them have difficulties dating for marriage successfully because they have not adequately dealt with an issue, even a seemingly minor one, that blocks them from moving forward in a relationship. After questioning an apparently emotionally healthy single about her dating history, the rabbi may get the sense that she can benefit from short-term intervention by a mental health professional because she has experienced one or more of the following:

▸ Dating for many years without developing a close relationship

▸ Developing one or more close relationships but not being able to follow through to engagement and/or marriage

▸ Engaging in a repetitive pattern of dating behavior, such as never getting past a second date, having trouble developing an emotional connection with a dating partner, or sabotaging each relationship as it becomes serious

▸ Seldom liking anyone she has dated

▸ Not appearing to have individuated from a parent (overly identifying with a parent or relying too heavily on a parent for emotional or financial support)

▸ Possessing an intense fear of marriage because of her own problematic background

In such cases, short-term, goal-oriented therapy with a mental health professional who has had prior experience working with marriage-oriented singles can be very effective in helping the single identify the reason she has not been able to build a relationship that leads to marriage and address it satisfactorily.

Some singles are reluctant to seek therapy because they believe that doing so is an admission that "something is wrong with me." The truth is that except for these unresolved issues, most singles who can benefit from therapy are emotionally healthy people, and a rabbi can influence them to seek professional intervention by emphasizing this fact. We recommend that rabbis develop a referral list of experienced therapists who use a short-term, goal-oriented approach to relationship development. The rabbi should bear in mind that the most effective therapists for individuals who want to overcome obstacles to marriage are themselves married, and are familiar with and supportive of the client's religious orientation.[8]

THE MARRIAGE DILEMMA

It is not uncommon for a rabbi to be approached by someone who cannot decide whether to become engaged or has doubts about going through with an upcoming wedding. This may be particularly true if the rabbi has been selected to perform the couple's marriage ceremony. The rabbi may wonder if it is just a case of cold feet, or if there are legitimate reasons why the individual seeking his advice should not become engaged or should call off an engagement. Our own experiences working with singles in similar predicaments has helped us formulate guidelines that can help a rabbi determine how to counsel such an individual.

Many singles merely seek a rabbi's assurance that they are making the right decision. A rabbi can advise the single to ask himself/herself the following questions about his/her relationship with the person she is contemplating marriage:

► Do we have compatible goals and values, and are we moving in the same general direction?
► Do we respect each other?

➤ Are there qualities in the other person that each of us admires?

➤ Are we attracted to each other?

➤ Can we accept our partner for who and what s/he is, including his/her family background and personal shortcomings?

➤ Do we have a mutually felt emotional connection and feelings of affection for one another?

When the answers to all of these questions are in the affirmative, it is a sign that the couple has a strong foundation upon which to build a happy and enduring life together. A rabbi can share his observation that the couple has these important ingredients for a successful relationship, and can offer the observation that the single's nervousness is an expression of general anxiety about marriage that many individuals experience before taking this major step in their lives. If the single suddenly fixates on a character trait or behavior that never was an issue earlier in the courtship, such as her dating partner's way of cracking his knuckles, the rabbi may be able to reassure her that this is a way many singles bind their general anxiety and does not indicate a problem in her relationship. He can encourage her to find a happily married friend to serve as her "hand holder" whenever she needs reassurance before her wedding.

Our experience has shown us that it is unwise to encourage a couple to become engaged under pressured circumstances, even where they seem perfectly suited to each other on paper. If a man and woman have not developed an emotional connection after eight or ten dates, in all likelihood the connection will not form later. Assuring such a couple that the connection, and love, will come later is unwise. The adjustment to married life is difficult enough. Two people who have never formed a connection to each other often cannot make the adjustment and end up divorced after a relatively short marriage.

Marriage may also be contraindicated when an issue that has always been present, but has never been resolved, will likely interfere with the relationship. Most young couples who are progressing toward marriage do not experience significant bumps along the road as their relationship develops, and are able to resolve or learn to live with minor issues they encounter. However, when a couple who has been dating for a period of time is unable to resolve important philosophical differences or conflicting goals or values, or if one party is unable to accept a character trait that has always bothered her about her partner, they are not well-suited for marriage. These significant "bumps" will not smooth out even if the couple invests more time in trying to resolve them, and they will not "correct" themselves after marriage. Rabbis who encourage an individual in these circumstances to become engaged, or to follow through with a wedding, may, in doing so, condemn that person to an unhappy marriage and a future divorce.

> Josh and Sandy had been dating for four months. He admired her career aspirations, felt that she was very pretty, and just "knew" that she would make a great wife and mother. Josh also liked Sandy's sense of humor, and he wanted to make their relationship work. He felt that he was ready to get married, and on paper Sandy had all of the qualities he has been looking for. Yet, something was holding Josh back from deciding that Sandy was "the one." Her insecurities had troubled him from the second time they met, and even though he thought he could get used to them, over time this just hadn't happened. Josh didn't want to discuss his concerns with either his friends or his parents, reasoning that if he decided to marry Sandy, he didn't want them to know the issue that had troubled him. Instead, he turned to a former teacher with whom he had remained close after high school. Rabbi S. encouraged Josh

to express what really bothered him about Sandy's personality and review the efforts he had made to accept this character trait. He then asked Josh if he wished this aspect of Sandy's personality didn't exist, or could be changed. When Josh answered yes, Rabbi S. told him that a person contemplating marriage should be able to accept the person he is dating as a "package" deal. He should be able to acknowledge and accept both her positive and negative qualities, and shouldn't marry with the expectation that he will later become used to a personality trait he now dislikes, or that this aspect of his partner will change. Rabbi S. also suggested that when a major personality trait or other significant issue doesn't resolve itself after four months of dating, it never will. Josh eventually chose to end his relationship with Sandy. Within a year, he met the woman he eventually married, and had to agree with Rabbi S.'s advice that a courtship with the right partner is generally not marred with major bumps in the road.

Older singles sometimes travel a rockier road to marriage than their younger counterparts, because they may have to deal with more personal "baggage" that slows the development of their relationship. These men and women may need the assistance of a dating mentor or therapist to help them navigate the bumps in the road to marriage. A rabbi who counsels such an individual can assure him that it is common for older singles in promising relationships to experience these difficulties and that many older singles need a dating advisor to help them advance their courtship. The rabbi should encourage the single to utilize a dating mentor and/or a therapist who has experience in guiding older singles through the courtship process.

Paul had been dating Renee on and off for three years. Each time, he couldn't make the decision to become engaged, and each time Renee broke up with him because he could not commit. Yet, because Paul liked Renee and they very well suited to each other, he could never completely let go. He would date other people after their break-ups and then go back to Renee. This time, however, Renee had no interest in taking Paul back. She figured that at forty-five, Paul was a lifelong commitment-phobic, and she did not want to waste any more of her time in a courtship that had no future. Paul asked his rabbi, "How can I know if Renee is really right for me? There are younger, more attractive women in the world — is Renee the reason I've stayed single for twenty years?" The rabbi felt that he was not experienced enough to appropriately advise Paul, and recommended that he see a clinical social worker who specialized in working with older singles. She was able to pinpoint Paul's pattern of approach-avoidance: when he came too close to commitment he pulled back. With the therapist's help, Paul was able to understand the reasons for this behavior and overcome his problem, and today he and Renee are happily married.

PARENTAL CONCERNS ABOUT AN UPCOMING MARRIAGE

A rabbi may also be approached by parents who believe that their adult child has chosen an inappropriate dating partner or fiancé. Parents appeal to the rabbi to intervene in order to prevent the engagement or marriage from taking place as a last resort, usually after the parents have made exhaustive efforts to persuade their son or daughter to break off the relationship. At this point, the rabbi's ability to influence the prospective bride or groom is very limited and often counterproductive.

A rabbi who is approached with this problem should first explore the situation without comment. He can ask the parents to describe their relationship with their child, the relationship between the child and the intended spouse, and the relationship between the fiancé and different members of the family, including the parents. The rabbi can also ask questions such as:

➤ What concerns you about the way your child relates to his/her intended?

➤ What effect has the relationship or the upcoming marriage had on your family dynamics?

➤ Are there any other concerns that you have about the situation?

➤ Why are you opposed to this relationship?

Answers to questions such as these can clarify the parents' true concerns. It may be that the opposition to the pending marriage is based on a legitimate point. The child or her intended may be irresponsible, immature, and incapable of making the necessary adjustments to married life. She may be too infatuated to see that her fiancé is controlling or does not respect her, or that the two of them do not have the same values and goals and are not headed in the same direction. The parents may believe that the relationship between the couple is strained and that they have difficulty resolving their own conflicts. The parents might identify other issues that indicate that the couple will likely have a problematic union. If the rabbi concludes that the parents' concerns have validity, he can agree to meet with the child and explain that he has been asked to intervene and that his primary concern is that every couple he marries begins their life together with a strong foundation and has the interpersonal skills to nurture their relationship over the course of time. Since the couple will likely view the rabbi as an agent of the parents, intent on breaking up their relationship, it is a good idea for the rabbi to explain that he will do his best to be objective, and would not discourage a couple from marrying simply because the parents are unhappy.

The rabbi should then ask each partner to describe their expectations about the marriage, their goals for the future as individuals and as a couple, how each person relates to the other's family members, and how they expect to deal with the inevitable conflicts or crises that arise in every marriage. If the rabbi is concerned about the marriage's prognosis for the future, he can recommend that the couple either address certain issues or reconsider their decision to marry. The rabbi can refer the couple to a couple's therapist, a premarital skills workshop, if one exists in the community, or adopt a policy of recommending that all engaged couples enroll in such a course. The rabbi can assure the couple that the ultimate decision to marry will be theirs, but the observations he makes after taking time to get to know them both may influence them to reconsider their decision to marry or to obtain intervention that can help them acquire marriage-building skills.

There will be times when a rabbi may conclude that the difficulty with a pending marriage has little to do with the quality of the engaged couple's relationship or their ability to sustain a lasting marriage, but is due to the parent's unwillingness or inability to accept their child's future spouse. Parents may object to a prospective wedding for many reasons: the future in-laws may not be from the social class they had expected; they may be uncomfortable with the fiancé's background; they might not like their child's intended even though the couple seems to get along well; they might not be pleased with the couple's economic situation; the child may be moving out of the area after the marriage; the age difference between the couple may make them uncomfortable; or the parent may not be ready for the child to individuate. After asking the same questions he would ask of two people whose relationship might be troubled, the rabbi might conclude that the parents, rather than the couple, are the ones who own the "problem". In such a case, the rabbi can suggest ways in which the young couple can establish boundaries between themselves and their parents. For example, the partner whose parents object to the marriage can respectfully insist that his parents always treat his intended and her family with respect and not say anything negative about her to him or others. The rabbi can then meet with the parents, offer his positive observations about the couple's relationship, and explain that even though the parents' expectations haven't been met, the couple has sufficient strengths for marriage, and can hopefully look forward to a happy and enduring life together.

NOTES

1. The National Jewish Population Survey (NJPS) 2000–01.

2. The National Jewish Population Survey (NJPS) 2000–01.

3. Waite, Linda J. and Gallagher, Maggie. 2000.*The Case for Marriage*. New York: Doubleday.

4. Hendrix, Harville. 1992. *Keeping The Love You Find*, New York: Pocket Books.

5. www.jewishworldreview.com/pit/.

6. One such program is offered *by Sasson v'Simcha*, www.jewishdating andmarriage.com.

7. See www.jewishdatingandmarriage.com.

8. Individuals seeking a therapist, who can help a religiously observant individual overcome obstacles to forming relationships that lead to marriage, can contact Nefesh International, The International Network of Orthodox Mental Health Professionals, at nefeshint@yisumit.com.

✑ 14 ✑
PREMARITAL COUNSELING

Lisa Aiken, Ph.D.

MARITAL DISCORD IS so common in the contemporary Jewish world that it has become one of the community's most pressing problems. Experience and research have shown, however, that premarital counseling can be very effective in helping couples to avoid many problems. Much of this premarital work can be done by rabbis, who can play a critical role in ensuring that couples are equipped to become husband and wife before they marry.

We assume that it is important for people to be trained in and get experience in a trade before they are allowed to practice without supervision. Marriage should be no different. It should also require both studying relevant information, as well as informed practice where possible. While most Orthodox Jewish couples take classes in the halachic aspects of marital intimacy, they rarely cover what couples need to know about the practical aspects of living together. This severe lack was noted by Rabbi Moshe Feinstein *ztz"l* decades ago. Prior to marrying a couple, he invariably sat with them for several hours and discussed practical and spiritual matters that he thought were essential to a harmonious home life.

Several goals can be accomplished by meeting with an engaged couple prior to their wedding. First, the rabbi can give them information that will encourage them to find meaning in the wedding rituals, build a Jewish home and marriage, and stay committed to the Jewish people and to a Jewish community. Second, the rabbi can explore important issues with them and delineate those that need to be worked through. Third, the rabbi can assess if the couple has areas of conflict or concern for which professional help is indicated. Finally, these meetings can help foster a relationship between the rabbi and the couple so that they might consider turning to him if they have troubling issues or questions after they are married.

SHARING INFORMATION: THE RABBI AS TEACHER

Every rabbi has insights and understanding about the meaning of marriage that he wants to share with engaged couples. These might include explaining the symbolisms of the wedding ceremony, the importance of Jewish continuity and the building of a Jewish home, the ways that religious ritual enriches a couple, and the Jewish values that need to be transmitted to their children. Jewish rituals give stability, predictability, and spiritual enrichment to a couple's marriage and children. Giving charity, studying Torah, and bringing sanctity into one's marital life make God a partner in the marriage and set the stage for marriage being a true partnership that helps two individuals transcend their self-centered interests and become one entity.

The rabbi will want to share Jewish ideas about how one relates to a spouse, the obligations each has toward the other in marriage, the importance of raising children who will carry on their heritage to the next generation, and the general concept of marriage as a viable framework within which to practice "love thy neighbor as thyself." Jewish marriage provides the opportunity for a person to grow emotionally and spiritually by working through the challenges of living with someone who is very different from oneself, with each viewing themselves primarily as contributors rather than takers. By placing the couple's marriage within a religious framework, the rabbi thereby fulfills his function as a teacher and helps the couple view their marriage as having a higher purpose.

EXPLORING AND ASSESSING COMPATIBILITY: THE RABBI AS FACILITATOR AND DIAGNOSTICIAN

While face-to-face sessions as well as formal classes are an excellent way to convey general information to couples, counseling one couple at a time is the best way to speak to a specific couple's concerns and needs. This usually involves a minimum of two hour-long appointments. If the first meeting indicates that the couple is basically on sound footing, the second meeting might be scheduled two to three weeks before the wedding for further discussion and to formalize last-minute wedding plans. If a couple has issues that aren't readily resolved in the first meeting, a second meeting should be scheduled as soon as possible.

The objective of this phase of rabbinic premarital counseling is to explore with the couple issues of compatibility. The rabbi can begin by asking the couple if they have any questions or concerns about marriage or about anything that they learned in their premarital or laws of *taharat ha-mishpachah* classes. If they do, this is the time for the rabbi to clarify and resolve their questions. It also opens the door for the couple to express their fears and hopefully have their concerns addressed. The objectives of this phase of premarital counseling are two-fold. On the one hand, it gives a couple the opportunity to explore and discuss issues that they might not have previously discussed or thought about. Secondly, it is an opportunity for the rabbi to assess the health of their relationship.

In cases where a bride and groom get instruction in *taharat ha-mishpachah*, the rabbi should find out who is teaching each of them and ask if they have discussed any differences in perspective. If there are differences, the rabbi should advise the couple as to how to resolve them. Keep in mind, however, that not all differences are problematic. There will undoubtedly be differences, both in terms of personality, personal preferences, culture, style, beliefs, and values. It is only if these differences are problematic to the couple, intolerable to one or the other, or ignored prior to marriage, that they need further exploration.

What follows is a suggested protocol of areas to be explored by the rabbi with the engaged couple. These questions should not be posed to the couple in a mechanical, verbatim manner, but rather should serve as a guide to the kinds of issues that would be beneficial to explore. They are meant to alert the rabbi to the couple's areas of strength and weakness. Prior to marriage is the best time to explore these areas.

The rabbi can also serve as a facilitator to clarify the very important topic of what each person's expectations are of married life. The following are other suggested topics for the rabbi to explore with couples in premarital sessions.

What are your expectations of marriage in the following areas:

Love and Attraction

- ► Of all the people in the world, how did the both of you decide to choose each other?
- ► How did you meet? What were your first thoughts? Feelings?
- ► What attracted you to each other?
- ► What do you value and love about each other?
- ► What do you expect to be fulfilling and make you happy in your marriage?

Living and Working Together

> ▶ Where do you plan to live? Are you both comfortable with this decision?

> ▶ What kind of neighborhood and house do you each want to live in? How much personal space and time alone do you each need?

> ▶ What kind of work do you each intend to have? Who will support the family?

> ▶ How do you plan to manage your personal finances, such as paying the bills, balancing the checkbook, making investments, and using credit cards? Are you both comfortable with this arrangement?

> ▶ How will housework and child-rearing tasks be divided or accomplished?

> ▶ How much time do you expect to spend together every week, and when do you expect to do this?

> ▶ Where/how do you expect to spend the Jewish holidays?

Handling Differences

> ▶ What do you expect to be challenging in your marriage?

> ▶ What stresses you and how do you deal with stress?

> ▶ What makes you and your partner angry and how does each of you respond when that happens?

> ▶ When you disagree with each other, what happens? How do your disagreements get resolved, or don't they?

> ▶ How long do you stay upset with each other and what kinds of issues lead to those feelings?

> ▶ What do you do when you are feeling upset? How does that affect your partner?

> ▶ Do either of you lose your temper (throw objects or hit things or people) when you are angry?

➤ What have been the most difficult times you have experienced so far as a couple and how did you deal with them?

Family and Friends

➤ How do you feel about separating from your parents?

➤ How do your parents and friends feel about your marrying each other?

➤ How do you feel about your in-laws and how do they feel about you?

➤ What kind of relationship do you envision having with your parents, respective families, and old friends after you get married? Are you both comfortable with this?

Expectations of Change

➤ Is there anything that you think your partner would like you to change about yourself? How do feel about that?

➤ Are there any aspects of your behavior that you think you need to change for the sake of your marriage?

➤ What do you think will change in your relationship after you marry?

➤ What do you hope will not change and what do you envision having to do in order to keep those parts of your relationship present?

Religious, Cultural, and Value Differences

➤ What cultural/socio-economic differences do you have (Sefardi/Ashkenazi, Russian/American, wealthy/middle-class)?

➤ What do you know about your future spouse's culture and its likely impact on your life together?

➤ Do you anticipate differences in beliefs and values with

regard to how you will relate to one another as husband and wife?

► How will your cultural differences affect your approach to raising children? Which type of education will you choose for your children? How will your cultural or socio-economic differences affect your relationship to your and each others' parents? How will your differences affect your decisions about spending money?

► What religious differences do you have and how do you envision these differences affecting you?

► How do you anticipate religious values being expressed in your home (guests for Shabbat, home decorated with religious articles and paintings, no television etc.)? Are you both comfortable with this?

Finances

► How do you envision supporting yourselves over the next several years?

► Are there any differences in the way the both of you handle money?

► Do you plan to have credit cards? A checking account? Will it be a joint account? Separate accounts? Are you both comfortable with this?

► How will you make decisions about spending money?

► Will you be budgeting? How will the budget be decided upon?

► If you both received a gift of say $5,000, what would each of you choose to do with it?

Health and Genetics

► Have you discussed any medical or psychological problems you have that might impact on your marriage?

- ➤ Have you been tested for any genetically transmitted diseases, such as Tay Sachs?
- ➤ Do you have any questions or concerns about them?

Children and Parenting

- ➤ How do you each feel about having children? Do you agree about the general number of children you would like to have and when you would like to start a family?
- ➤ Have you discussed your ideas about disciplining and educating your children?
- ➤ How do you think your fiancé will be as a parent?

REMARRIAGE

If one or both partners were previously married, the rabbi should explore what each learned from his/her first marriage. What impact will their first marriage have on their present marriage? If there are children from either marriage, what is the couple doing to prepare them for their remarriage? What changes does the couple think will take place, especially with respect to the children, when they remarry? Is this realistic?

One of the most important roles that a rabbi can play when doing premarital counseling is to explore a couple's issues, how the couple communicates about their differences, and how their issues will play out in a marriage. The rabbi needs to get a sense of potential non-negotiable issues that may wreak havoc in their relationship. Every marriage has negotiable as well as irreconcilable differences. The question is: can one accept the other with these differences and live with them?

In this exploration stage, the rabbi should ask (and notice) how the couple handles their differences.

- ➤ Are they respectful in the way they discuss issues?

- ➤ Have they talked about their differences? If so, what has resulted?
- ➤ Does one stonewall the other or are they both engaged in a respectful attempt to resolve their issues?
- ➤ Is there a sense of defensiveness or unwillingness to discuss important issues?
- ➤ How does each view the things about which they disagree?
- ➤ Are there signs of hostility? Does one, for example, mock the other, insult, or use sarcastic humor?
- ➤ Do they blame or attack each other?

The rabbi should bear in mind that everyone is likely to have a few concerns about his intended spouse. That is to be expected. How those concerns are voiced can be very telling about the couple's future. A complaint is a legitimate expression of a wish that things be different. A criticism voiced by attacking someone's character or person should be a warning sign to the rabbi and the couple that something is seriously wrong. (See John Gottman. 1994. *Why Marriages Succeed or Fail*, New York: Fireside Books.)

ASSESSING POTENTIAL PROBLEMS

The rabbi should note and explore areas that seem problematic. If there seem to be significant problems, he should tell the couple what those problems might portend for the future and ask if they are concerned. If significant conflict is present or is likely to arise, a referral to a professional is indicated. A couple's ability to resolve conflicts is one of the best barometers for the success of their marriage.

The following should serve as red flags for the rabbi when he explores the couple's differences:

> ► If issues are shoved under the carpet, avoided, or are not otherwise resolved

> ► If one or both parties respond with contempt to the other's concerns

> ► If one person gets defensive instead of addressing the partner's complaint or concern

> ► If their communication styles result in increased conflict instead of resolution

When any of the above occur, the rabbi might ask the couple what it is like for them to have these differences and if it bothers them. If they are concerned about the problem, do not know how to fix it, and feel stuck, the rabbi could then suggest that they go for professional counseling.

Based on the research of John Gottman in his couples' laboratory at the University of Washington, it is possible to predict with great accuracy which couples will not have successful marriages. In observing the men's behavior, Gottman found that among the signs that were predictive of divorce were a man's seeming lack of fondness or affection for the woman he chose, his seeing himself as fully independent in marriage instead of as part of a team, his remembering few details of how he met his partner and what happened during their courtship, his being vague about what attracted him to her, his expressing negative feelings about her, disagreeing with her frequently, and withdrawing from problem-solving disagreements. In observing women in premarital or early marital relationships, Gottman noted the greater probability of divorce in instances where she had a harsh way of starting a disagreement, had little sense of togetherness with her partner, did not respect him, or felt disappointed in him.

If a rabbi notices any of these signs during his premarital counseling with a couple, he should refer them to a professional. Though he can share with them some of his concerns about their relationship, it is generally inadvisable for a rabbi to play prophet by informing an engaged couple that they are not well-suited for each other and are not going to make it. A competent professional couples' counselor can either help couples resolve some of their issues or help them disengage.

Rabbis do couples a great service when they address warning signs instead of ignoring them. If a rabbi is not sure whether certain whitewashed issues are likely to threaten a marriage, he should consult a seasoned couples' therapist and learn more about the issue in question.

The following are situations where an individual or a couple should be referred for professional help:

1. The primary reason one or both individuals got engaged is because

➤ Most of their friends are married and they feel that it is time for them to get married.

➤ There is a younger sibling who is ready for marriage and they are embarrassed to remain single.

➤ They were pressured to get married; everyone told them their intended spouse has wonderful qualities and they shouldn't pass him/her up, but they feel no strong attraction to one another.

➤ They feel lonely and know of no other way to deal with it besides getting married.

➤ They are not responsible with money or are having financial problems and think marriage is a way out.

Note that in each of these situations one or both of them are lacking the proper motivation, attraction, or emotional connection with the person they are planning to marry.

2. One or both of them believe that if things don't work out,

they can always get divorced. While it is true that divorce is always an option, a couple that is already thinking of divorce is probably in denial about their major differences.

3. One feels a lack of trust in the other, and perhaps for good reason. This is a serious flaw in the relationship. Trust, after all, is the basis upon which relationships are built.

4. When a new couple suffers from blowups, bickering, denigrating put-downs, or an overt lack of respect for the other. While most couples can learn what skills are essential for making a good marriage, this alone cannot solve fundamental attitude problems such as those described above. If a rabbi sees that a couple is unable to successfully negotiate their differences, or senses abusive behavior, or an intractable problem, he should refer them to a competent professional for further assessment and treatment.

There are times when a rabbi might be tempted to give simple intuitive advice. It would be more prudent, though, for him to instead explore issues, options, preferences, and strategies more fully with the couple, so that their conflicts, doubts, and concerns can come out into the open. As a rule, if individuals and couples arrive at their own realizations and conclusions, rather than hearing them from the rabbi, then the process tends to be more fruitful. Giving vent to suppressed doubts and apprehensions can be extremely helpful in putting each spouse's concerns into perspective.

The following is an example of an ill-advised discussion between a student who is concerned about marrying a particular girl and his rabbi.

A 25-year-old yeshiva student approached his rabbi and told him that he had met a nice girl who came from a good family, had nice character traits, and wanted to marry him.

"What should I do? the student asked.

"Do you like her?" asked the rabbi.

"She's okay, I guess," the student responded.

"Do you both have similar goals?" the rabbi continued.

The student nodded.

"Is there anything about her that you don't like?" the rabbi prodded.

The student shook his head, indicating that there was not, but added, "I just don't seem very excited about marrying her."

The rabbi then said, "Look, excitement will come later. As long as you don't find her repulsive in any way, then go ahead and marry her. The rest will happen in time."

Instead of advising the student to marry her, the rabbi should have explored with him how he feels in general about getting married and specifically about marrying this woman. Why does he want to marry her? Are there any positive reasons? Does he feel any emotional connection with her? Is he physically attracted to her enough that intimacy between them will be enjoyable? Does he have concerns or negative feelings about marriage that need to be explored, perhaps even with the help of a professional? How does he envision feeling about her in a year or in ten years' time? If not for social or other pressures, would he want to marry at this time?

Every helping professional experiences varying degrees of frustration in working with clients or congregants. There are times when a rabbi's assessment is very clear and his recommendations very appropriate and astute, yet his counselees choose to go their own way. This should be expected. Individuals have free will and the right to exercise it as they wish. Though saddened and frustrated at times, a rabbi needs to accept the fact that ultimately it is the couple's right to choose and make decisions about their own life. The following example demonstrates this.

A thirty-year-old woman called a local rabbi for help. She and her fiancé had been engaged for two months and she was having serious doubts about continuing their relationship. The wedding was two months away. He was procrastinating and had not yet given her a list of wedding guests. He had not yet bought her an engagement ring and he was always too busy to search for an apartment with her. He professed to care about her and wanted to marry her, yet she was beginning to think that he was too terrified of marriage to grow up and leave home. Could the rabbi, whom the fiancé respected and was willing to see, please meet with them?

The rabbi agreed.

First he saw both of them together and then he saw each one separately, for a total of about an hour. During that time, the man told the rabbi that his fiancée was pressuring him too much. He needed to take his time and not be told what to do.

The rabbi asked him what initiative he had taken with regard to planning the wedding, looking for an apartment, and preparing for marriage. The man's response indicated that he had done very little, yet he thought that what he had done was quite appropriate. He gave a series of reasons why he hadn't been able to do more. Apart from devoting himself to his job, the man shied away from all other personal responsibilities in his life. His mother still did his laundry and his shopping. He continued to live at home. He hadn't begun packing any of his belongings in anticipation of moving. With the exception of his working instead of going to school, his life essentially hadn't changed since he was fourteen years old.

The rabbi asked what the man thought were his responsibilities towards his fiancée, and what he expected to provide as a husband. The gist of his answer was that he would work hard to make a living and expect his wife to accept him as he was, without pressuring him to change. He was feeling a lot of anxiety because she expected him to do things on her time-table, and he didn't want to be controlled like that.

The rabbi interviewed the woman. Her expectations seemed perfectly reasonable. She had to send out invitations, and without his list, she could do nothing. She couldn't tell the caterer if they should prepare for 150 guests or 250 guests. She needed to put down money for an apartment and buy furniture, allowing time for it to be delivered. His entire input was to veto whatever she suggested. He hadn't even offered any concrete alternatives.

The rabbi then met with both of them as a couple and further explored the effect they were having on each other — his feeling pressured by her and her feeling alone and abandoned by him in making the marriage preparations. She spoke of her frustrations when he would veto her decisions, and her resentfulness at having to do everything alone. He spoke of his feeling resentful at what he perceived as her trying to control and pressure him.

The rabbi asked them how they thought this would affect their marriage if the pattern continued. They were both very concerned, but even more worried about jeopardizing their engagement.

The rabbi confirmed their concerns and realistically summarized the conflicts that faced them as a couple. He then suggested that it would be prudent for them to meet with a couples' therapist before they married in order to work out some of their issues together. They agreed to do just that.

However, over the next week, the man, fearful of breaking up, convinced his fiancée that he really was ready for marriage, gave her his guest list, and joined her in looking at apartments and furniture. She, feeling anxiety about the ticking of her biological clock, decided to suppress her concerns in the hope that her fiancé had magically changed. They both decided then that they did not need to see a couples' therapist. They married, and on their wedding night he confided to her that he really didn't think he was ready to be committed to her. After two years of great pain and suffering, they divorced.

One might argue that the rabbi should have been more forceful in trying to stop this couple from marrying in the first place. It seemed so obvious that this man was not ready for commitment. Perhaps the rabbi should have said this outright. It is, however, very risky for a rabbi to declare whether a match is or isn't suitable.* Generally, it is better if the rabbi points out the serious incompatibility, asks how the couple sees that issue playing out, and refers the couple to a professional couples' counselor. Even then, of course, there is no guarantee that the couple will follow through.

There are, nevertheless, times when a rabbi can be more direct and express his concerns about a forthcoming marriage in a more candid way. If, for example, one or both partners have a tendency toward violence, rage, reckless impulsivity, a need to control the partner (possessiveness), unwillingness or inability to hold a job, serious instability, irresponsibility, or drug/alcohol misuse, the rabbi should express his opposition openly and unequivocally. He can tell them that without serious professional

---

* To the extent that many engaged couples will not exhibit signs of a problematic relationship in premarital counseling, the most objective way of assessing their compatibility is by asking each party to complete a PREPARE (Premarital Personal and Relation Evaluation) questionnaire. This 125-item questionnaire is computer scored. The couple is then given feedback by a trained counselor. Information about the questionnaire and trained counselors can be obtained from PREPARE, P.O.B. 190, Minneapolis, MN 55440-0190, or from David Olson, its developer, at the University of Minnesota. It has predicted which couples are likely to get divorced with 80–85% accuracy, and has been used by more than half a million people worldwide. If used properly, it could become a valuable tool in the repertoire of the rabbinic counselor working with couples.

help the prospects do not seem very promising, and even with professional intervention such a situation does not bode well. Once again, however, a rabbi needs to be cognizant of the fact that his concerns do not automatically transfer over to the couple. They may choose to marry, without the benefit of professional help, and despite his reservations.

Minimizing the Problems

There are times when a rabbi might neglect to send a couple for professional help, believing that his intuition is sufficient. When a rabbi gets caught up in the emotions of a given circumstance, he can underestimate the severity of a problem and offer only his well-intended advice. The following is such a case, where a rabbi, overcome by a romantic notion of love and commitment, neglected to see the potential for problems down the road.

> An engaged woman in her thirties came to her rabbi because she was not sure what to do. She and her fiancé were both scientists who worked in the same research lab, and it was there that they had met. They had known each other for two years and cared for each other very much.
>
> He had suffered from clinical depression off and on since he was fifteen, and was taking antidepressant medication. The medication, however, didn't always help. She was worried about how his depression would affect their marriage and their future children.
>
> The rabbi appropriately asked to meet with both of them. He explored what they each valued about each other, and what they expected would be the strengths and challenges of their marrying.
>
> They had already consulted his psychiatrist about the likely course of his depression and his likelihood of passing on a predisposition to depression to his children. In exploring the woman's concerns, she told the rabbi that she always felt upset

that she could do nothing to help her fiancé when he was depressed. She spoke of how she felt helpless when he became so self-absorbed for days on end, and she worried that he would not be emotionally available to their children. The rabbi was very moved by her sensitivity and love for her fiancé and this caused him to minimize her very real concerns.

The rabbi told them that the woman had such beautiful character traits that she would be an excellent wife for the man. If anyone would be a good match, they would. Surely with all of the love the woman had to give, he would come out of his depression and be a great husband and father.

Needless to say, if any situation should have been referred to a competent professional, this was it. The couple married and suffered terribly because love alone cannot cure chronic depression. They finally went for professional help. The therapist recommended Cognitive Behavioral techniques for dealing with the husband's depression, recommended that he consult his psychiatrist whenever his medication wasn't helping, and stressed to the wife that it was not her job to fix her husband. In a few sessions of couples' therapy, both husband and wife were taught new tools to use in relating to each other, and they subsequently did have a great marriage. Had the rabbi initially referred them to a competent couples' therapist before they got married, they could have avoided much heartache.

ESTABLISHING A POST-WEDDING RELATIONSHIP

If the rabbi shows sensitivity to and empathy for the engaged couples that he counsels, they will tend to feel comfortable turning to him after the wedding, should problems arise. If the rabbi sensed areas of concern prior to the wedding, he can call two weeks to a month after the wedding and ask the husband and wife separately how things are going. This show of concern is likely to encourage the couple to share any difficulties they are having and open them to hearing advice that can keep the problems from ruining their fragile marriage. If more follow-up if necessary, the rabbi might want to suggest a professional referral, recommended reading, or meeting with helpful lay people in the community who can give ongoing advice.

If the couple did not seem to have areas of concern prior to the wedding, a follow-up call anywhere from one to three months after the wedding can be invaluable. "I just called to see how you two are finding married life," is a non-threatening opening line. If the rabbi senses the person hesitating a bit before responding, he might encourage the person to say more by sharing, "I know that when people get married, they usually have a lot of adjustments to make. Which are going smoothly for you, and which are you finding challenging?" Most people will open up when they hear that having problems is normal and not a sign of failure.

If the rabbi will be too busy to "check up" on couples and provide counseling if need be a few weeks after the wedding, lay advisors in a community can help the couple get past the bumps of the first year. The rabbi can make such a connection ahead of time, such as by having the advisors invite the couple to their house for a Shabbat meal. The rabbi can simultaneously set up the expectation that it is normal for couples to experience difficulties after the wedding and that these can be overcome.

GUIDELINES FOR RABBINIC COUNSELORS

The above examples show that a few caveats need to be observed when doing premarital counseling:

1. Know your limitations. Don't let your desire to see singles get married preclude you from exploring and acknowledging the depth and seriousness of a couple's

problems. Err on the side of referring to a professional, when in doubt.

2. Maintain a relationship with a competent professional who is knowledgeable and respectful of your religious values, and with whom you can consult about various couples. It is sometimes very useful to work in tandem, or at least in coordination, with one another.

   Rabbis should not assume that just because a therapist is licensed or busy, that he or she is effective. It is best to refer a couple to a therapist who is specially trained in couples' or family therapy. A therapist who is seasoned in working with individual clients is not necessarily trained or equipped to work with couples. In addition, some therapists are great at working with certain issues, but not with others. The rabbi should ask referred couples for feedback about the professionalism and efficacy of the therapist.

   Rabbis need also be aware that many therapists are disrespectful of Jewish values and rituals. It is best to find a qualified religious therapist or one who will respect the religious beliefs of patients you refer.

3. Don't impose your biases on the couples you see. Some rabbis with very loving marriages cannot understand how couples can't work out their differences, and they sometimes give poor advice as a result. Others are so cynical about certain issues that they inject unwarranted pessimism where it doesn't belong. In general, if a rabbi has an emotional response to what he is hearing from a couple, his response is known as *countertransference*. While a rabbi needs to be aware of his own feelings, he needs to be careful not to inappropriately bring them to bear when counseling others.

Barbara and Steve were in their early twenties. He was not a stellar student and was working part-time at a blue-collar job. Meanwhile, Barbara was studying for her master's degree in social work. She was obviously more ambitious, brighter, and more social than he was. Barbara's parents had informed the rabbi that they were opposed to the marriage, and had really hoped Barbara would find a better match.

When the rabbi met with the couple, Steve reminded him of his son-in-law. The rabbi had also wanted more for his daughter than the individual whom she had married. Despite the fact that Barbara loved Steve for qualities that were very real and lasting, and was perfectly willing to support the family if need be, the rabbi only saw those deficits that were so evident in his own son-in-law. For this reason, he did his best to break up their relationship.

The couple went and asked another rabbi to marry them, and he did. That rabbi and his wife gave the couple additional emotional support and advice during their first year of marriage, when they encountered difficulties. Despite the first rabbi's misgivings, the couple remained very happily married.

Therapists spend years going to school in order to learn counseling. If a couple requires more than a few meetings with a rabbi in order to resolve their problems, it is usually a sign that they need to see someone with professional training. It is not a sign of inadequacy to admit that, as a rabbi, you are not qualified to help people repair complicated relationships or to undo a lifetime of emotional baggage.

Rabbinic premarital counseling should usually be limited to helping a couple explore their expectations, compatibilities, and interaction style, educating them about the practical aspects of marriage and helping them achieve spiritual growth. When they have serious issues such as those mentioned above, the rabbi can help them see that these are problematic areas and that they haven't adequately or realistically resolved them. Such judgments should not be based on matters of taste, personal preference, and the like. For example, breaking up a couple because the man has poor social skills and you think the woman should marry someone more polished is abusing your position of power. If you do want to voice such a comment, you should be very clear in advance that this is your bias and it no way implies the unsuitability of a specific man for a specific woman.

PREMARITAL CLASSES

It is recommended that rabbis prepare different information to discuss with couples when they meet privately that is not otherwise covered by classes or readings. If the couple will not be attending such classes, the rabbi will want to cover many of the questions listed above, as well as some of the themes that are listed below. The rabbi should include details that are very down-to-earth and practical for the couple. For example, the rabbi might want to tell them about the importance of going out together and looking attractive even after they are married, creating emotional intimacy, or about specific issues involving sex or birth control, deciding where to spend the Jewish holidays (at home, with his parents, her parents, with friends, at a resort), deciding who is responsible for which tasks at home, the importance of helping whenever it is needed, flexibility, putting the other person's needs first, what each will contribute to the marriage, and when to call the rabbi.

Couples from more traditionally sheltered religious backgrounds may need concrete information about sex and physical intimacy. The rabbi may want a book or two at hand that he can recommend for this purpose.

It is important to stress to couples that a good marriage

does not mean that two people agree about everything. It is normal and healthy to have differences in temperament, emotional needs, likes and dislikes, even perspectives about life. It is also common for most couples to have some minor irreconcilable differences that do not severely diminish the overall positive feelings that they have for each other. John Gottman, in his research on marriage, found that a stable marriage needs a 5:1 ratio of positive to negative factors. There is always some incompatibility in a marriage. If, however, the positive aspects of the marriage are five times greater than the negative, the marriage can remain stable and satisfying.

It is important, therefore, to educate couples that a good marriage is not one without problems or differences. Couples should expect that having a good marriage takes lots of work, especially during their first year and after having children.

INTERFACING WITH PROFESSIONALS

When a rabbi engages in premarital counseling, he should bear in mind that the information he hears is confidential. He is not free to share it (unless there is a threat to someone's health or life) without the person's permission. If a rabbi has reason to contact a professional (such as for a consultation or evaluating the appropriateness of a referral), he should be sure to do so in a way that does not disclose the identity of the individual(s) involved. If the rabbi needs to identify the person to a third party, he should first obtain his/her consent, preferably in writing.

Rabbis should always know a competent psychiatrist to whom they can refer people with severe psychiatric disorders, a therapist who specializes in anger management (preferably a licensed professional with training in Cognitive Behavioral therapy), a skilled couples' therapist (preferably one trained in couples' and family therapy), and a professional who can treat sexual problems (such as victims of rape, incest, or sexual dysfunction).

The rabbi should ascertain in advance the range of the professionals' fees, and which insurance, if any, he or she accepts. For those couples who cannot afford private fees, have the name of one or two good clinics that charge according to a sliding scale.

COMMUNITY INVOLVEMENT IN
PREMARITAL INSTRUCTION

While this chapter has focused on how the rabbi can personally convey important information to a couple, a structured course attended by multiple couples has also shown itself to be invaluable. While there are no hard and fast rules for exactly what information should be conveyed in a course format, let's keep in mind that preparation for driving a car requires at least thirty hours of lectures and practical experience, plus several hours of reading. Marriage is far more complicated than driving. Most rabbis will need to find a middle ground between the ideal time that should be allotted for premarital counseling classes and the actual time that couples are willing to spend (and that the rabbi and/or therapist are available to teach.) Ten hours seems to be the bare minimum, not including detailed *taharat ha-mishpachah* instruction. Some ten-hour courses are taught in five two-hour classes, and include the following topics:

1. The Jewish View of Marriage
2. The Jewish Wedding — its legality and symbolic meaning
3. Differences between Men and Women (emotionally and spiritually) and how this plays out in married life, includ-

ing their needs for love and respect, differences in the way they communicate, and different ways of responding to problems

4. Men's and Women's Marital Obligations and Roles, including the husband's special obligations during the first year

5. Communication and Problem-Solving — how to say what needs to be said, the importance of expressing love on an ongoing basis, validating a partner, being a good listener, sharing feelings both positive and negative, how to differ with each other productively, and what to do with anger

6. Parents and In-Laws — Jewish obligations, where to spend the holidays, practical suggestions for dealing with common conflicts (when parents aren't religious or aren't Jewish, intrusive or divisive parents, cutting the apron strings, etc.)

7. Intimacy — including how to build closeness in marriage at times when one isn't physically intimate, Jewish perspectives on sex, the basics of *taharat ha-mishpachah*

8. Living Harmoniously under One Roof — forming realistic expectations, day-to-day life, delegating responsibilities

9. Building a Jewish Home — Jewish holidays, differences in religious customs, perspectives and behaviors, spirituality in the home, ongoing spiritual growth, the importance of Jewish values and rituals for children

10. Money and Budgets — Jewish perspectives on the husband's need to support his wife, joint bank accounts and tax returns, making sure the husband doesn't control the wife's spending of money, setting up bank accounts when the wife wants to retain her earnings, following a budget, basic record keeping. A financial planner or advisor

often co-teaches this session if it is attended by working couples.

The structure of the topics listed above is just one of many possibilities and will need to be modified to suit the needs of specific couples. Each rabbi will undoubtedly stress those areas that he perceives are most important to the couples he counsels. Time for questions and answers should also be included. A rabbi can use the information imparted through classes as a starting point, which he then supplements in his personal counseling.

If rabbis in a given community would all agree to make it mandatory for couples to take informational classes in conjunction with effective premarital rabbinic counseling, tremendous gains could be made in preparing Jewish couples for marriage. For example, twelve years ago, a woman approached several South African rabbis and asked them to require Jewish couples to complete a five-session, ten-hour premarital course. The rabbis agreed. The resulting course, called Jewish Marriage Encounter, presented practical and spiritual aspects of Jewish marriage, along with some basic laws of *taharat ha-mishpachah*. In its first five years, 350 couples met with volunteer, lay instructors (men teaching men, women teaching women) from their communities. Twenty percent of these couples decided to keep *taharat ha-mishpachah* as a result, and almost everyone who took the course found it helpful. Other communities today are emulating their model.

FURTHER INFORMATION ABOUT TRAINING

Rabbis who would like additional training in premarital counseling can enroll in a university counseling or psychology program (anywhere from one to two years full-time for a master's degree, four-plus years for a Ph.D.). In some places, institutes train rabbis and mental health professionals to do marital counseling. A common alternative is for a rabbi to pay a marital therapist to supervise his counseling work.

Attending rabbinic and outreach conferences that have sessions addressing couples' issues can also be very informative. A number of Jewish organizations have recently begun offering seminars on marriage, as well.

Finally, Marriage Encounter and Jewish Marriage Encounter offer retreats and local meetings for enriching couple's marriages. Rabbis might get some good ideas there to share with engaged couples.

Together with all the other considerations discussed in this chapter, the rabbi can indeed become a significant force in enhancing marriages and preventing divorce.

SUGGESTED READING

Aiken, Lisa. 2003. *Guide for the Romantically Perplexed.* Jerusalem: Devora Publishing. This is the only book of its kind that offers a comprehensive, practical marriage guide for Jewish couples that can also be used as a guidebook for premarital counseling. It combines techniques used in couples' therapy with practical advice, communication enhancement and problem-solving exercises, as well as Jewish perspectives about many aspects of marriage.

Gottman, J. 1994. *Why Marriages Succeed or Fail.* New York: Fireside Press. Based on decades of research with couples, Gottman describes how to recognize attitudes that doom a marriage and provides practical advice on how to avoid patterns that otherwise lead to divorce.

Notarius, C. and H. Markman. 1993. *We Can Work It Out.* New York: GP Putnam's Sons. Fascinating research on the centrality of conflict resolution in marriage and how different marital styles work for or against it.

Counseling Couples in Distress

Neal D. Levy, Ph.D.

MOST COMMONLY, people turn to their congregational rabbi when they are in distress about marriage and family problems. While some congregants feel that consulting with their community rabbi is too close for comfort and they go directly to a marriage professional, a large percentage of congregants feel that the rabbi already knows them and is trusted, so they turn to him with their initial request for help. These are generally congregants who have known the rabbi over a period of time and respect him for his wisdom, insight, and ability to relate to others in his community. Marital problems are a very private affair for most couples, and so they rarely turn to their rabbi unless they are in great pain.

They may officially make an appointment or pull him aside in an impromptu fashion. Sometimes a congregant may just appear at the rabbi's front door, if he is in the midst of a crisis. It is also not uncommon for concerned others to alert the rabbi that a couple in his congregation is in crisis. "Rabbi, you don't know me, but I must tell you that Mr. and Mrs. Schwartz in your community are in serious trouble. They have five children and their marriage is really falling apart. Something needs to be done quickly. Can you help them?" Sometimes even a school principal or teacher of one of the couple's children will alert the rabbi that a child recently shared something about a serious conflict at home.

Although in most instances requests for help are clear and compelling, there are times, however, when the request is communicated in disguised form. For example, a couple having a dispute about a religious matter may decide to ask the rabbi a halachic question. It may seem on the surface like a straightforward rabbinic question, but it soon becomes evident that the question is only a subterfuge and is hiding a deeper issue. In such a case, the rabbi, though introduced to the marital problem by way of a rabbinic question, may find himself enmeshed in a much more complex vortex of marital conflict. The real issue may not be the religious query at all. Rabbis need to be aware that couples will sometimes present problems in this camouflaged manner, or request a particular kind of help, when some other more essential issue should really be the focus of concern.

There are times when a rabbi will recognize symptoms of a couple's discord by the way they interact in communal functions. A spouse, for example, might seem antagonistic, sarcastic, or competitive with his/her partner while serving on a synagogue committee together. What should a rabbi do in such a case? Should he approach them, uninvited, with his concerns? Much depends, of course, on his relationship with them. Should he wait for the couple to request help on their own? On the one hand, if he does choose to say something, it clearly shows that he cares. On the other hand, the couple may not be ready to share their issues with him, and might not even be cognizant of their marital distress on a conscious level. If that is the case, then they will feel that their boundary of privacy was invaded. If the rabbi chooses to intervene by expressing concern about what he observed or by what he was told by others, he must do so with a clear understanding that the couple might not be ready to discuss any of their marital issues with him, and he will have to back down from further inquiry. On the other hand, if he feels sufficiently comfortable to approach them, it might be the very opportunity they need to begin to work on their marital issues. In essence, to intervene or not is a judgment call based on the rabbi's best projection of their response.

The myriad of problems that couples experience during the course of their marriage run the gamut from:

- ➤ Difficulties in communication
- ➤ Difficulties in reaching mutually acceptable decisions
- ➤ Disputes about finances and other economic concerns
- ➤ Difficulties in dealing with families of origin and other extended family
- ➤ Differences in religious and other lifestyle issues
- ➤ Parenting and child-rearing issues
- ➤ Balancing one's professional pursuits with the responsibilities of home and family life
- ➤ Problems with intimacy, both physical and emotional

and many others. Even if the rabbi should ultimately not be the one to do the full course of counseling, it is important for him to become familiar with the range of problems that couples encounter, as well as various methods and interventions that are utilized to help a couple improve their relationship.

How can the rabbi gain an understanding of where a couple is hurting in their relationship? What are some common foci that couples need to work on in order to improve and what are some interventions a rabbi can employ to help them do it?

GENERAL PRINCIPLES OF MARITAL COUNSELING

It is strongly suggested, despite the pressure that some couples might exert on the rabbi to hear them out individually, that he invite both spouses into the initial marital interview. Conducting a joint interview helps the rabbi avoid becoming a go-between, and puts him into a position to help them improve their relationship on an equal footing. In keeping with the purpose of conducting the interview as a joint meeting, it is important for the rabbi to also structure the form of this meeting to maximize open communication. For example, the chairs in his office should be set up in such a way so as to maximize eye contact between all participants in the meeting. This will help the rabbi not only to interact with each partner, but also to observe the ways in which they interact with each other during the conversation. Establishing a balanced relationship with each of the partners, from the moment he greets them and throughout the interview, is extremely important. What is called "balanced neutrality" in couples work is a critical element of counseling, and not always as simple to execute as it may seem.

This is of special concern when the rabbi has a closer relationship with one of the partners or when one spouse has a more positive religious outlook or level of observance than the other. A rabbi, however, should be extremely careful not to allow his own beliefs prejudice the neutrality of his relationship with both spouses. He must always be mindful of balancing his relationship with the couple so that neither spouse comes out of the counseling session feeling that the rabbi was biased or had a predisposition to support one side at the expense of the other.

THE INITIAL INTERVIEW

Within the scope of the initial interview, the rabbi should explore the following ares in an engaging rather than mechanical way:

1. Gain an understanding of the problems at hand according to the perspective of each partner (e.g., How would

each of you describe the difficulties in your relationship, from your own perspective?) During this discussion, it is helpful for the rabbi to ask each spouse for specific examples that illustrate the problem.

2. Understand what each views as precipitants to the problem (e.g., What events may have preceded or led to this problem?)

3. Determine when these difficulties began and what was happening in their lives at the time.

4. Explore relevant background information about their marriage, including their families of origin and any other family circumstances which impinge on the problem or are adversely affected by the problem (e.g., Are there any other family members who are involved in the issues between you? Are there events in your lives that are affecting this problem?)

5. Ask when and how often this problem surfaces, when does it not become a problem, and how have they already attempted to deal with this problem (successfully or unsuccessfully).

6. Examine how they react to each other in response to this problem and what are each of their hypotheses about why this problem exists?

7. Determine what is or has ever been positive in their relationship, and what their marriage was like before the onset of this problem.

8. Ask each spouse what he or she would like to see changed, and what role they would like the rabbi to play in helping them.

In addition to gathering this vital information about their situation, the rabbi should also observe the dynamics of their relationship as reflected in the way they communicate and respond to each other in the office. This includes both verbal and non-verbal communication.

Depending on such factors as the number of problems discussed, the complexity of the couple's circumstances, the couple's pace in presenting their problems, as well as the rabbi's level of interviewing skills, this initial process could span several sessions. Unless this is an emergency situation, it is better for the rabbi not to feel pressured to accomplish everything in a one-hour meeting. This also allows the couple some time to reflect upon the previous discussion before reconvening with the rabbi.

Towards the end of this exploration, the rabbi should offer some feedback to the couple about what he has heard and understood. This should include a brief summary or restatement of the problem in general terms and a reframed understanding of the problem. Reframing the problem helps to convert their understanding of their difficulties (which is usually framed in a more blameful way) into more "user-friendly" and constructive language. This changes the context of the problem while not altering the facts of their situation, and helps the couple to allow each other more latitude in the process of change. We will discuss the method of reframing in more detail later in this chapter.

Couples who have exhausted their every attempt at successfully dealing with their problems, will often feel the situation is hopeless and that they are helpless to fix it. A rabbi, however, can instill them with a sense of hope. It should not be dispensed superficially, as a way of minimizing their problems. It should also not be framed as a promise that "everything will turn out okay," but rather as a suggestion that if they are willing to approach their difficulties differently, it can lead to a better outcome.

PROBLEMS IN MARRIAGE

How do we define a problem in the context of marriage? It is helpful to draw a distinction between what is considered a problem and what could be described as turbulence. Turbulence is a rough patch of air that an airplane must fly through. If the pilot knows how to negotiate the winds and guide the plane through this, in time the flight will resume as usual. Turbulence may be defined as the normal pressures of life. This includes work stress, money stress, children, common illnesses, etc. They are the fabric of existence and should not be defined as problems. Life is filled with such situations. When a couple possesses the skills necessary to work through these, these difficulties will not escalate into problems and the couple will emerge intact. That a couple has faced turbulence in their life does not mean that their marriage is a problematic one.

However, if a pilot does not know how to fly the plane out of the turbulence, then a serious problem arises. So it is, too, when a couple lacks the ability to cope with normal turbulence or when the level of turbulence is so extreme that normal coping skills are inadequate. In this instance, the couple may need to enter a therapeutic process to help them develop more skills in their relationship. Couples who are not able to efficiently resolve issues arising from the common stresses of everyday life together may benefit from counseling. Its goal would be to help them get unstuck and enhance their abilities to deal effectively with more extreme situations. Either way, the rabbi should share his hope that the couple can learn to improve both the circumstances they face as well as their manner of approaching such situations more effectively.

Here again, instilling hope for the couple can be introduced only after the rabbi has a fuller understanding of the couple's difficulties together and the dynamics of their relationship.

Hope can then emanate from a realistic discussion of goals for change and a plan of action for how to achieve them. Prior to this, the offering of hope can be premature or unrealistic, setting up a false sense of what to expect.

THE RABBI'S ROLE AND FUNCTION

It is important for the rabbi to first define for himself what his role will be in the counseling situation, and then how he will carry it out. What role the couple would like him to play, the severity of the problem, and what the rabbi feels he can contribute to this situation (in light of his level of skill in counseling and his comfort level in working with this particular couple as part of the larger community) will help him determine all of this. Furthermore, he needs to delineate which forms of intervention he thinks will best help the couple. This analysis will help the rabbi decide whether he should do the counseling for the couple or just meet with them in order to refer them to a professional.

STRESS FACTORS

In understanding the range of stress factors that contribute to problems in marriage, it is often helpful to distinguish between external stress factors and internal ones. One should keep in mind, however, that this may be an artificial distinction, since it is unusual for these factors to exist in a vacuum and there are usually connections between them. "External" here means that the locus of stress is outside the relationship proper. Some common examples of these include:

▶ Families of origin. Some parents may have difficulty "letting go" of their married children and continue to control them, without allowing the married couple to develop their own relationship and resolve life's challenges on their own. Some individuals find it difficult to balance the needs of both the family of origin and the spouse, whether regarding emotional ties or concrete responsibilities. For instance, a spouse can be caught in a "tug of war" between his partner and his parents, with his parents making demands that, if he complied, would threaten his loyalty to his spouse. Sometimes the unwillingness of parents to help out when their assistance would be appropriate is another form of external stress, or when there is a serious emotional or medical problem in an extended family member.

▶ Vocational and career goals. The aspirations of one partner may conflict with or aggravate the needs of the other. Often one conflict brings into play many others, e.g. differences in values, communication styles, and cultures. For instance, one couple relocated to another state for the sake of the husband's job. This precipitated a string of problems: he now had to work late, his wife missed her old friends and social life, and he had no sympathy for her since he believed her priorities should be him and their home exclusively.

▶ Financial concerns. This is a common problem, which usually surfaces around the lack of adequate finances, the excess of it, family inheritances, and patterns of spending and budgeting. This factor is frequently the "straw that breaks the camel's back" and raises other marital problems, which were previously kept under control.

▶ Health issues. Even an accident or a sudden illness can be the external stress that activates a period of crisis for a couple, bringing out other underlying problems in their relationship. Certainly, this is true when a family member develops a chronic illness.

The following are examples of *internal* stresses where the locus of the problem is within the relationship itself:

► Communication problems. One or both spouses may lack the skills to understand the other's position, opinions, and feelings and/or the skills to make his or her position understood by the other.

► Negotiation difficulties. These include the reluctance or inability to negotiate with each other about decisions that have to be made, the roles of each spouse, and the division of household and other responsibilities. This part of marital life entails more than the ability to communicate.

► Lack of individuation. Dependence on a family of origin without the couple attempting to confront and resolve problems on their own first is another example of an internal stress. This is often accentuated when one spouse is more allied with his/her family of origin than with the spouse or where the partner's relationship with the in-laws is poor. In these cases, the stress is often experienced as resentment toward the spouse who takes "private" information outside the bounds of the marital relationship.

► Parent/child boundaries. Stress and a host of other behavior and relationship problems results when the boundary between the couple and their own children is either too rigid or too lax. Where there is an overly rigid boundary, the flow of open communication between the couple and their children is restricted, which can lead to an abnormal distancing or inability for family members to connect with each other in an emotional way. Where there is a lax boundary, the flow of communication is too fluid and areas of the couple's life that should be kept more private become an open field of interaction and mutual involvement. Here, children become inappropriately involved in their parents' marriage. When a parent becomes overly allied with a child, the parental team is weakened. In a healthy family, parents function as an effective parental team, which ultimately provides the greatest degree of emotional stability for the children and normal functioning for the family as a unit. When this overall functioning is not properly developed, or broken by one parent allying with a child against the other parent, a coalition is formed. This engages the child in an unhealthy closeness with one parent, usually at the expense of the other.

DEVELOPMENTAL LIFE CRISES

In a different vein, many theorists focus on the developmental stages in marriage and family life in order to understand where a couple is "stuck." These stages are distinguished by a typical developmental change or crisis, which a couple may have difficulty negotiating or overcoming. Some examples of these are:

> ► The birth of a child. Some couples, who previously enjoyed a stable marital relationship, seem to "come apart at the seams" when a child enters the picture. Other couples can make the necessary modifications regarding their lives together and their responsibilities to integrate this child into the family.

> ► When the youngest child enters school. This is not always a benign event. It can shift the balance in the marital relationship, particularly when the mother, who has

been home during the early child-rearing years, seeks to occupy her time differently In one family, for example, the couple had previously agreed upon a balance of roles whereby the husband was the breadwinner and the wife was the homemaker. After the youngest child began school, the husband had difficulty when his wife wanted to accept a job offer, since this would change their role definitions. In another family, the mother became depressed when her youngest child began to attend a full day of school. She had overly attached herself to this child for companionship and felt bereft without the child's presence at home.

► Adolescence. This stage often presents the parents, as a "parental team", with new and sometimes overwhelming challenges. If the marital relationship is already strained, the turmoil of the adolescent's struggle for independence tends to create enormous tension in the family.

► The emptying nest. When the children marry and leave home, the couple is forced to reexamine the quality of their relationship, which must now continue without its primary focus being on the needs of the children. Many couples who have not developed their relationship together, experience difficulty at this stage. When the last child leaves home, issues that went unresolved until then, may now reemerge.

One special marital issue, which has become more prevalent in recent years, is that of the "reconstituted marriage" or "blended family". When previously married spouses marry and join households, many challenges arise as they attempt to merge their families and integrate their children from their previous marriages. Issues of power and sharing surface — it is hard to reconstruct the old way of doing things in a new relationship and old patterns never fit the new family structure. One parent may have mixed feelings about allowing the new partner to exercise authority over "his" child. Children pick up on these power struggles and get involved, often to the point of pitting one parent against the other. It is an enormous challenge to reconstruct the boundaries in the new family, between the marital partners and each of their children, the couple and the children as a unit, and even between the children themselves.

By using his understanding of the types of marital difficulties discussed above, the rabbi will be better able to locate, in a diagnostic manner, what the nature of the problem is in the relationship. At no time should he consider a hypothesis where there is fault or blame placed on either spouse. Trying to figure out who is to blame is neither in the interest of the couple nor the counseling process.

INTERVENTIONS

What do couples need to focus and work on in order to improve their marriage, and how can the rabbi be most helpful? One of the most important areas of a marital relationship is the quality of the couple's communication. Patterns of marital communication are usually established in the very early stages of the marriage. Although the way a couple communicates is a function of their overall relationship, the blend of their communication styles has its roots in the level of skill previously developed by each individual. Effective communication is an asset that enables other components of the relationship to grow and develop. Ineffective or destructive communication is a major source of frustration for a couple and undermines virtually all areas of their relationship.

The two major components of communication are listening skills and speaking skills. These are areas in a relationship, which, with conscious effort, can be significantly improved and can become the access route for improving other aspects of the relationship as well. If the rabbi can learn to recognize the technical areas of communication which are deficient, he can then attempt to help the couple work on improving these through clear and direct counseling as well as effectively modeling good communication himself.

Communication problems tend to impede the ability of the couple to effectively discuss matters together. Some of the destructive patterns of listening that the rabbi might observe in a couple's communication include:

- ▶ Interrupting one another before the other has finished expressing his or her thought
- ▶ Ignoring the speaker in the midst of conversation
- ▶ Diverting or shifting the focus away from what was intended
- ▶ "Mind-reading" instead of allowing the speaker to convey the intended thought
- ▶ Analyzing the other person's intentions and motivations instead of taking them at face value
- ▶ "Yes-Butting", where a listener appears to agree with the content of what the other person is saying, but in essence disagrees with it. It can be most disconcerting to hear "yes" — indicating agreement — immediately followed with "but" — indicating disagreement.
- ▶ Defensiveness, such as denying responsibility, counterattacking (called "cross issuing"), or changing the subject when there is a complaint
- ▶ Belligerence, contempt, or intimidation. These tend to be the most serious styles adopted by troubled couples. These aggressively destructive patterns can take the form of "the best defense is a good offense."

➤ Stonewalling. Simply ignoring the spouse and the spouse's complaint.

The rabbi can help the couple develop more constructive ways of listening by asking the listener to give feedback to the speaker about the essence of what he heard. It is not sufficient for the listener to say, "I understand", because it is not clear *what* he understood and the speaker needs to know that he was understood correctly.

This is the purpose of what we call *active listening*. Actively rephrasing what has been heard and allowing the speaker to correct any misinterpretation, answer questions, and clarify what was intended is the crux of good communication. Asking a speaker to clarify an unclear point, staying focused on the message being communicated by the speaker, offering feedback at various points during the conversation, such as "What I hear you saying is…" and briefly summarizing what the listener understands from the speaker, are active listening techniques. Allowing the speaker to complete his or her thoughts, validating the position of the speaker (i.e., trying to understand how he thinks and feels, even if the listener does not view it in the same way), and paying attention to nonverbal behavior are also methods to enhance listening skills.

At first, couples will find this difficult to do, especially during times of conflict. It is, however, an important method for the rabbi to teach while the couple is seeing him for counseling. As they become more proficient in these communication skills, they will be able to apply them even during stressful times.

Some of the destructive patterns of speaking that the rabbi might observe include:

➤ The use of sarcasm
➤ Insulting or name-calling
➤ Lecturing or moralizing

➤ Blaming or criticizing

➤ Ordering or threatening

Using the word "you" in an accusatory manner is verbal finger pointing and often accompanies a blaming posture. The rabbi can help a couple learn to use "I" statements instead of "you" statements, which is one way for the speaker to take responsibility only for what s/he is thinking and feeling. The rabbi might ask the spouse who is using accusatory "you" statements, "Can you tell your wife/husband what it means to you when s/he does X?" Or, "I wonder if you can share with your wife/husband what it feels like when s/he says that?" This way, the discussion takes on a powerful sharing of feelings and clarifies the impact that a particular behavior has on the other, rather than simply engaging in blameful accusations.

Universalizing or overgeneralizing, such as saying "you *always*" or "you *never*" is also a destructive style of communication that is rarely appreciated by others. Since these statements are rarely accurate, they tend to be hurtful. The counseling rabbi might ask, "Are there times when this does not occur?" or "Is it true that he *never* takes out the garbage?" or "Is she *always* on the phone?"

Some partners tend to present a laundry list of complaints, all at once and in a cascade of blame. This is called "*kitchen sinking*". The problem is that too many accusations at one time are difficult to respond to. This is likely to occur when a person has suppressed many issues over time. When the dam breaks and the bottled up issues are evoked, it can be overwhelming for both spouses. The rabbi can be helpful here by encouraging the couple to focus on one issue at a time. The rabbi might say for example, "It seems that there are several important issues that have been brought up here today." He might then list them and ask, "Which of these would you like to discuss first?"

During counseling, a rabbi needs to manage the discussions so that hurtful communications are kept to a minimum. When one spouse is speaking, the message should be brief, succinct, and specific, rather than long-winded, meandering, and vague. Clarity can be achieved by using XYZ statements, such as: "When you do X, I feel Y, because...".

It is important during a counseling session for the rabbi to occasionally prompt partners to check out if they are being understood the way they intended. This invites feedback from the listener and allows for clarification before misunderstandings are allowed to develop.

These are some of the more common ways that a couple can be helped to improve their listening and speaking skills. If the rabbi is knowledgeable about these and various other communication skills, he can go a long way toward improving this aspect of a marital relationship, within the context of his counseling sessions.

Blame

One of the most common problems in a marital relationship is that of blaming the other things that seem wrong. This can become a real obstacle to successful interpersonal relations.

The following is an illustrative case from the annals of a royal couple whose names are Melech and Malka.

> One day, Melech and Malka came into the office after having a major argument the night before. Their castle had lately been suffering from hard times and Melech and Malka had to resort to clearing their own dinner table. At the end of last night's dinner, Melech got up to clear the dishes, and was in a bit of a rush. So on the way to the kitchen, the top plate slipped off, fell to the floor, and shattered into pieces. Malka, very upset about losing this heirloom from her royal family of origin, be-

gan to shout, "If Your Majesty was not so busy with the affairs of the kingdom, that treasure would never have shattered!" (Translation: "If my husband was not so preoccupied with his work all the time, he'd be more attuned to his responsibilities as a husband and this mishap would not have occurred!") Melech quickly retorted: "If the queen were more involved with her responsibilities, this would never have happened!" (Translation: "If my wife would perform her wifely duties, I would not have to be clearing the table.")

When a couple engages in mutual criticism, they tend to attach meaning to the other's offenses — "S/he did it on purpose, out of spite, or to get me angry." This, of course, may not be the case at all. Second-guessing or "mind reading" the other's motives is a dangerous proposition. In the case of our royal couple, Malka's theory was that her husband dropped the plate because his mind was preoccupied with his work, which resulted in his carelessness. Whether or not she is correct, the strategy of ascribing blame in this way is detrimental to their relationship.

The ultimate goal for the rabbi is to encourage each spouse to examine an issue from the other person's point of view. This entails helping each to learn to pull back and engage in a dialogue, taking into account the others' perspective, feelings, and sensitivities. As mentioned before, restating the other's position and why the partner believes or feels that way, as well as giving the other a chance to check on the accuracy of how s/he is being understood, enhance the couple's empathy and communication.

Why does this method work, especially when emotions are running high? Consider the metaphor of the quarterback in a football game. When a quarterback is thrown the ball, the first thing he does is take ten steps back. Why? — because if he stays too close to the heat, to the action, he will surely be tackled by one of his opponents. Distancing himself from the heat of the play affords him a margin of safety in which to think clearly and act effectively. By taking ten steps back, the quarterback can see the entire playing field from a wider angle. Now he can think ever so astutely, "We planned this play, but I see it won't work. What are my alternatives?" By distancing himself a bit, he has gained the ability to weigh his options. When one is feeling angry, before he jumps in and follows his impulses, he can ask himself, "Is there another possible interpretation here?" If he doesn't "quarterback", pull back and reflect before he acts, he will run a higher risk of entering a blaming mode with his partner. Blaming, assuming, or second-guessing one's partner can all spell trouble for a marriage. Pulling back long enough to think of other possibilities for a spouse saying something offensive or hurtful is an essential technique for developing empathy. Couples have found this to be a very effective tool in avoiding a blaming position.

Another approach is for the rabbi to help each partner focus on what s/he needs to change in order to make the relationship better, and not only what his spouse should be doing. Usually, people devote too much time thinking about what their spouse needs to change and not enough about what they themselves could do to make things better. The rabbi can teach them that they cannot change each other; they can only change themselves. Therefore their efforts would be better spent working on what each of them can do to improve his/her own attitude and behavior. This way each spouse, being unable to effect changes in the other, can, nevertheless, bring about changes in the relationship by effecting personal change.

When one takes responsibility for making a change of his own volition, that change becomes a "gift" to his partner, as opposed to some half-hearted altering of a behavior simply to get his partner to stop nagging him. Those kinds of changes are usually more short-lived and come with some degree of resentment toward the spouse. Likewise, when a spouse concentrates on fulfilling his own responsibility, he is more likely to apply himself to those changes he has undertaken to make. Then he will be less consumed with changing his partner's behaviors — which can only lead to frustration and anger — and be more involved in personal change — that can positively affect his relationship.

REFRAMING THE ISSUES

The technique of reframing or relabeling is another way to elicit the spouses' empathy for each other. In their book, *Marriage and Family Therapy*, Paolino and McCrady explain that reframing "consists of changing the frame of reference against which a given event is considered or judged, thus changing the meaning and value judgment of the event, without any change in the (facts of the) event itself." Learning to reframe the other's actions can help a couple begin to view each other in a different, healthier and more positive perspective.

For example, one husband was able to reframe his understanding of his wife's reluctance to travel or vacation as "her way of attempting to be in charge of the family's security." He was then able to continue negotiating with his wife about his desire to take more vacations together and get out of the house to have more fun, and his new understanding of her helped him to reduce his resentment and eliminate his former view that his wife just wanted to make his life miserable and boring. The wife, who had previously complained bitterly that her husband was never satisfied with anything they did together, was able to understand that his persistence was "his way of taking charge of excitement in the family in order to maintain growth in their relationship." This reframed understanding enabled her to better negotiate with her husband and agree to some compromises.

Seeing things in a positive way can offer people new insights and help them think and feel differently about their situation and about each other. This can lead to a better understanding of one another, and ultimately aid in the process of replacing blame with greater empathy. It is important to keep in mind, however, that the impact of a reframed issue is always a function of whether or not it rings true to the couple. If it does, then it can bring about a powerful change in perspective and a positive shift in the relationship.

THE RABBI AS MEDIATOR

Couples not only present their arguments and differences of opinion to the rabbi, but they regularly call upon the rabbi to play some role in mediating these differences. To some extent, the rabbi can help a couple arrive at compromises in order to resolve a conflict, sometimes resorting to his "spiritual authority" to make an impact.

In these conflicts, many couples, particularly young newlyweds, have difficulty making the transition from being single to being a couple. One of the basic goals of marriage is to create a partnership, a relationship entity which, when successful, is far greater than the sum of its parts. It enables each partner to reach his or her goals in ways beyond the ability of each individual alone, prior to their marriage. In order to help the couple create this partnership, the rabbi needs to help each partner move from behaving as if he lives on his own island to behaving as if they share an island.

The art of effective negotiation is a skill over and above that of good communication, and is central to healthy marital interaction. Sometimes the best thing a rabbi can do in counseling couples is no more than to help them hear each other's expressed needs more clearly and allow room for both sets of needs to find some gratification.

In working with a couple toward the goal of reaching compromises, the rabbi needs to be aware of a major pitfall that plagues many rabbis in this function, i.e., neglecting to work on the process by which the couple attempts to deal with their issues together. The rabbi can help a couple reach one compromise after another, but this endeavor rarely turns out to be much more than patchwork on the real problem — the dysfunctional process the couple uses to resolve their conflicts.

Some couples are notorious for calling upon the rabbi to mediate their crises one argument at a time. It is not long before the rabbi and the couple wonder why they are unable to learn how to reach an agreement on their own from one resolved crisis to the next. This pattern of counseling by piecemeal mediation is often a disservice to the couple, since they become overly dependent upon the rabbi, rather than self-sufficient.

In helping couples move from an expectation that the rabbi will focus on the content areas of their problems to an appreciation for the need to improve their process of negotiation together, it is helpful to share with couples the following metaphor. In doing so, they can better understand the difference between *content* and *process*.

For many years, in amateur photography, it was common to first develop pictures as slides. One could then print pictures from them or insert them into a carousel projector and enlarge the images on a screen or a wall. If the photographer was adept, the images would not only be well-framed, but also sharp and clear. However, if there was a bit of dirt on the projector lens, then every image on the screen would look flawed.

In relationships, the different slides are like the content of our lives. We may be talking about money, intimacy, parenting, in-laws, vacations, etc. If there is dirt on our lens, i.e. our process of dealing with each other is ineffective, the outcome of these discussions will be less than satisfactory.

Working to improve the couple's process in negotiating is not only a necessary ingredient for a successful marriage, but also one of the mainstays of effective marital counseling. If the couple can learn an effective process in dealing with each other, they will build the skills to meet their many challenges together in marriage.

FAMILY BOUNDARIES

One area of marital life that is important to explore is the couple's relationships with their families of origin and with their own children. This is a common cause of spousal conflict. Each couple needs to define its own boundaries, i.e., place an imaginary bubble around their marriage or around their entire nuclear family. This defines how they will relate to their children and their families of origin, and even others in their community. They are free to create a rigid or an open boundary, according to their own personalities, needs, and desires.

Do guests have to call first or can they just walk in and help themselves to a snack from the refrigerator? Some couples fashion a home that is a bit of each — sort of a semi-permeable separation. They may decide that on certain issues they are willing to be open, but on others they want more privacy. When a couple makes clear what is private and what is open, a breach of a designated private area would be considered a betrayal of loyalty.

The importance of developing clearly communicated rules is particularly critical. Here, the rabbi can play a central role in helping the couple become aware of the implicit rules they have so far established, identify which of these are not working for them, define what changes are needed, and guide them through a discussion of how to make those changes.

Sometimes the rabbi will be called upon to intervene between the couple and their families of origin in order to help the couple deal with the many pressures and demands placed upon them. Many a couple has been thrown into conflict when faced with the task of choosing a name for their newborn. They may not see eye-to-eye about whom to name the baby after, but once caught in the crossfire of their parents' or other relatives' demands (and subjected to their use of guilt as a weapon), this task becomes a minefield. This situation has literally catapulted many couples from what should have been a time of happiness in their lives to a time filled with anger and tension. The obvious problem is the unfair pressure applied by the families of origin, but the less obvious (yet more salient) problem is that the couple's failure to define their boundaries weakened their marital bond. The rabbi can help the couple strengthen the bond between them and the boundary between them and the outside world while taking charge of their own decision-making process. They may not be able to fulfill everyone else's expectations of them, but they will take control of their lives in the way they prefer, for the sake of their happiness and *shalom bayit*.

REFERRALS TO A PROFESSIONAL

As has been noted throughout this volume, it is most important for a community rabbi to establish working relationships with professionals who have expertise in various areas of counseling. Such a network of professionals upon which the rabbi can call will provide him with a solid referral base to meet a plethora of needs. In addition, he can also avail himself of their expertise as consultants. This collaboration, even prior to making a referral, can be helpful to his understanding of the couple's relationship dynamics and the advisability of his doing the counseling himself or referring the couple to a professional.

One word of caution about referring for marital therapy is in order. A rabbi may establish a working relationship with a therapist whose expertise is in individual therapy, and this will be an effective resource for individuals who would benefit from professional consultation. However, couples should be referred for marital therapy to professionals who have been specifically trained and are skilled in working with couples. Skills in working with individuals do not automatically translate to the particulars of joint counseling techniques needed for a bona fide relationship problem.

In addition to the choice of therapist, it is important for the rabbi to make a clear distinction between cases which can effectively be helped by rabbinic counseling vs. those that will require a more intensive process with a trained professional. Once he decides that the latter direction is in order, the rabbi should facilitate the referral as soon as possible and help the couple understand and accept the need for professional help. He should then assist them in making a smooth transition from his office to the therapist's.

The rabbi can play a vital role in encouraging and preparing the couple to maximize their efforts with the professional, which will often affect the outcome of that referral and the ensuing counseling. Depending on his ongoing role and relationship with the couple, the rabbi may or may not need to actively collaborate with the therapist on behalf of the couple. There have been cases where the rabbi's continued involvement has played a pivotal role in the couple's compliance in therapy. If the collaboration with the therapist can become a two-way street, then the therapist will be able to call upon the rabbi to intervene in special situations.

IN SUMMARY

Although a couple's first efforts should be to try to help themselves when faced with challenges, their lack of objectivity or skill may lead them to request assistance from a rabbi. The rabbi can help a couple:

- ► Identify their problems together
- ► Allow for an open sharing of perspectives, opinions, and feelings
- ► Help them to convert a situation, which often starts out with the spouses blaming each other, into one of enhanced mutual understanding and empathy.
- ► Teach them ways to make their communication and negotiation process more effective
- ► Establish clearer family boundaries
- ► Help them disentangle their parents and children from the marital problem so they can work on solutions without undue external pressure
- ► Focus on the couple's process of interacting with each other so they will have clear guidelines for dealing with issues in the future.

At the end of the Talmudic tractate *Uktzin*, Rabbi Shimon Ben Halafta says that Hashem could find no stronger vessel that could hold the blessings for the Children of Israel than Shalom (Peace). By helping couples achieve *shalom bayit* and enhancing their relationships through love and understanding, rabbis are fulfilling a vital part of their mission of *tikun ha-olam*, "perfecting the world".

BIBLIOGRAPHY

Haley, J. 1980. *Leaving Home*. New York: McGraw-Hill.

Carter, B. and McGoldrick, M. *The Family Life Cycle*. New York: Gardner Press.

Paolino, Thomas J. and McCrady, Barbara S., eds. 1978. *Marriage and Marital Therapy: Psychoanalytic, Behavioral and Systems Theory Perspectives*. New York: Bruner/Mazel, p.386.

Talmud Bavli, Tractate *Uktzin* 3:12.

DOMESTIC ABUSE: WHAT EVERY RABBI NEEDS TO KNOW

Abraham J. Twerski, M.D.
Lisa Goodman Twerski, M.S.W.

I WAS PRACTICING psychiatry for thirteen years before I made a "diagnosis" of spouse abuse, or rather before the diagnosis of spouse abuse was forced upon me. Small wonder. In all my psychiatric training there was not a single lecture on spouse abuse.

If this lack of awareness can occur in psychiatry, how much more likely is it to occur among rabbis, most of whom believe that Jewish husbands represent the ideal. Non-Jewish mothers are known to tell their daughters, "If you want a husband that doesn't drink, gamble, carouse, or beat you, find yourself a Jewish boy." Reliable statistics indicate that spouse abuse in the overall population is far more widespread than anyone thought. *Fifty percent of hospital emergency room admissions for women are due to battering.* Even if the incidence of spouse abuse is less among Jews than among non-Jews, it still indicates a serious problem.

It's important to explain how the first "diagnosis" was forced upon me. A man called to make an appointment for his wife with the Premenstrual Syndrome Clinic, because he was sure that was her problem. In the interview, she reported severe beatings by her husband during the seventeen years of their marriage. "When did this begin?" I asked. She said, "Two months after we were married, I attended my best friend's wedding with a black eye." Naively, I asked, "Why did you stay in the marriage?' She answered, "I thought it was my fault, that I was doing something wrong."

This is not an uncommon feeling among abused wives. Another important feature in this case was that the *husband* called to make the appointment for his wife. There was something wrong with *her*, not with *him*. The *denial* on the part of the abuser is a critical component of the problem.

Enlightened, I began to scan the psychiatric literature for more information, to no avail. I learned about spouse abuse from information provided by the media. Although the latter has brought the problem to the fore, there is still a great deal of ignorance. One rabbi, after learning about spouse abuse, said that he was certain that it did not occur among his congregants. Nevertheless, he announced from the pulpit that he had an open door and a listening ear. That week four women from his congregation revealed their plight to him.

Rabbis are in a pivotal position to be of help in spouse abuse cases. Men and women may consult the rabbi about problems in the home. A well-informed rabbi will be cognizant of the possibility of spouse abuse, and know how to look for it. Rarely does a spouse report abuse until it is in a very advanced state, and sometimes not even then.

WHAT CONSTITUTES DOMESTIC ABUSE?

Most of us still envision an abused woman as bloodied and battered, a victim of physical violence. This is a misperception. Physical violence often, but not always, accompanies domestic abuse; but it is merely the punctuation in the life story of the person who lives in an atmosphere of indescribable fear. The fact is, a person can be abused and controlled without ever being hit. Many women report that the damage done by verbal abuse is even greater.

Domestic abuse has been defined as a pattern of coercive control that one partner in a relationship exercises over the other in order to dominate or gain and maintain power and control. Although spouse abuse can go in either direction, in the overwhelming majority of situations the victim is the wife.

For many centuries and in many cultures, men have been the dominant sex. Halachah (Jewish law) gives the appearance that men have that right. The husband, rather than the wife, is seen as the head of the household. Men who are power-hungry may use this to their advantage. The more publicized cases of this are where men exploit Halachah to hold their wives hostage by refusing to give a *get* (Jewish legal divorce), which is the ultimate abuse of power and control.

Most often we discuss the husband as the aggressor because:

- ➤ This is most often the case in battering.
- ➤ The widely held opinion that the husband is the "head of the household" may make him feel powerful.
- ➤ The more common role of the husband as the main provider enables him to withhold money.
- ➤ In the event of a separation, the care of the children is usually assigned to the mother.
- ➤ A common belief is that it is the wife's responsibility to keep the marriage together (some believe, no matter what), and the termination of a marriage is often viewed as a failure on her part, rather than the husband's.
- ➤ Inasmuch as Halachah requires that the husband either initiate or accept the *get*, a vengeful husband may refuse

and make his wife into an *agunah* (a woman forbidden to remarry).

For all of the above reasons, wives may feel disenfranchised and do everything to preserve their marriage, including not complaining about abuse. Because of the wife's weak position in all of this, it is imperative that she be given great consideration. On the Torah verse, "Do not aggrieve a widow or an orphan," Rashi tells us that this applies to any person who is in a disadvantaged position. Hence, it should be kept in mind that the wife may be the abuser and the husband the victim.

Withholding money is a form of abuse, as is restricting a spouse's contact with his/her family and friends, belittling his/her family, name-calling or speaking to him/her disparagingly. The Torah requires showing respect for others and one's spouse is no exception. Spouse abuse is essentially a *control* issue. For whatever reasons, one wishes to wield control over the other.

A significant number of battered wives report that their first beating occurred with their first pregnancy. The reason for this is that the pregnancy gives the husband an increased feeling of control and power, because it is now more difficult for the wife to leave the marriage. The husband's sense of absolute control may increase with the advent of each child.

What makes a husband abusive? Although this appears to be a reasonable question, it is in fact a dangerous one. Imagine what it would be like if the fire department, responding to a house on fire, concentrated on finding what caused it instead of putting out the fire. The time to look for causes is after the fire has been put out. Abuse must be stopped. One may then look for explanations. Until the abuse has stopped, theorizing that the husband is abusive because he was abused as a child, or because he has a domineering boss at work, or because he has deep-seated emotional problems, or because he drinks, or for any other reason is counterproductive.

Most often, it is the abused wife who is searching for an explanation as to why her husband behaves the way he does. She thinks that if she can find the reason for the abuse, then when that reason is corrected or eliminated, the abuse will stop. This allows her to continue accepting the abuse. In fact, this allows the abuse to get worse. The wife must understand that the only time the abuse will stop is when her husband wants to change, and that will occur only when he no longer gains anything from being in control.

Many women believe that they can change their husbands. They should be made aware that their attempts will be futile.

They may think that they are causing the abuse because, "I'm not considerate," "I push his buttons," "I'm inadequate as a wife," "He's right, I'm too attached to my mother," or some other reason. The self-blame leads the wife to believe, "If I change, he'll behave differently." Or, she may resign herself to this kind of relationship, rationalizing, "I've got to accept this for the children's sake," or "I took him for better or for worse." The wife needs to be enlightened that whatever she does or does not do, she is not the cause of the abuse.

THE COVER-UP/WHY DOESN'T SHE COME FORWARD?

As noted above, abused wives often feel that they deserve the mistreatment because they are somehow at fault. This is aggravated by being told by trusted advisors to, "Be nicer to him," "Prepare his favorite dish," "Be more romantically forthcoming," and the like.

The wife may feel it is futile to complain because she will not be believed. After all, the community thinks the husband is a *tzaddik* and the pillar of the congregation. "The rabbi will never believe his behavior at home," she reasons.

In cultures where marriages are arranged by *shidduch* (matchmaking), the wife may feel that revealing the abuse would jeopardize the children's chances for a good match. She may hide her misery behind a happy façade that she presents to the public.

In the Jewish community, spouse abuse is considered a *shonda* (disgrace and shame). Battered women who call the police may tell them, "Please don't come with your lights flashing, and come to the back door. I don't want the neighbors to know." Incidentally, when the police do come, the wife often sends them off, refusing to press charges. In some states, police are permitted to initiate charges, even against the wife's wishes.

Finally, she may simply be too afraid. If there has been physical violence or threats, she may fear what will happen if she tells someone. This must be taken into consideration and confidentiality must be scrupulously observed. Should she consider leaving the marriage, she may be legitimately worried that her husband will become dangerously vengeful. The most dangerous time for a battered woman is the first two years after she leaves, when the risk of serious violence is much greater. "Orders of protection" have not stopped abusers from killing their wives.

Another important point to keep in mind is that even in the most abusive relationships there are good times and even tender moments. These relationships are so confusing and indeed bewildering to women precisely because they are not completely bad. This also keeps the hope alive that things will get better.

These good periods have been conceptualized in different ways. The behaviors that follow abusive episodes, which may include apologies, cards, gift giving, and trips are often not expressions of real regret for the abuse, but a way of keeping the abused wife exactly where she is and where he wants her to be — in the relationship. False apologies are simply another tactic to maintain the status quo and can be differentiated from true regret when the same behaviors keep recurring in the common escalating cycle of abuse–apology–abuse. When apologies are sincere and represent real *teshuvah*, the abuse does not continue.

INVESTIGATING ABUSE

It is not common for the wife to complain to the rabbi about abuse. Rather, she is apt to complain about some vague problem in the marriage. Or, the couple may come together seeking marital counseling. When the rabbi has reason to suspect abuse, it is important that he say, "It is my practice to see each spouse separately." It is a cardinal rule that in cases of abuse, one does not see the couple together. An abused wife may be terrified to describe her husband's abusive behavior in his presence. Women who have had to go to a hospital emergency room for treatment of injuries sustained from a violent husband have denied that they were beaten, for fear that the hospital would report this to the authorities, which would aggravate the husband's abusiveness.

When the rabbi interviews the wife, he should let her present the problem. If she does not mention any abusive behavior, he should not ask, "Has your husband behaved violently toward you?" This invariably evokes a negative response. Rather, he should say, "I understand what you are saying. But tell me, has Bernard ever been unkind to you in any way?" The wife may respond, "Oh, no! Bernard is a wonderful husband. It's just that, well, he is so much into himself."

The rabbi may then say, "Even wonderful husbands may sometimes lose control. Has he ever shouted at you or said unpleasant things like, 'You don't know what you're talking about?'" This is more likely to be admitted. "Well, you know, sometimes he has a short fuse, especially when he's had a rough day at the office." The wife might give a little more information, while making excuses for the husband's behavior.

Once the wife senses that the rabbi is sympathetic and is not likely to think of her as crazy for concocting stories about this wonderful man, she may be more willing to open up. The rabbi can ask, "Does he insist on knowing your whereabouts all the time?" This is a sign of a husband's excessive need for control. "Do you sign checks and do you have a credit card?" She may say, "My husband gives me all the money I need for the week." While this may be acceptable to her, it could in fact be a form of control. Furthermore, keeping a wife on an allowance is demeaning and degrading; it is treating her like a child.

The rabbi may ask, "What happens when you and your husband disagree on something?" "How does he handle things when he doesn't get his way?" "Does he ever prevent you from doing things you want to do?"

The rabbi can ask whether her husband restricts her contact with her family and friends. "Has he ever threatened to hurt you?" "Has he ever called you names, degraded your family, or insulted you?" "Does he criticize you for little things?" "Does he insist on making all the decisions in the family?" "Does he blame you for things that are not your fault?" These are signs of emotional abuse, regardless of the circumstances, but they are much more serious if they are done in front of the children or other people.

The rabbi may ask, "Has he ever thrown anything at you or been physical with you?" She may say, "Well, he's never hit me, but once he did push me." It is a safe assumption that where there has "once" been a push, there has been more violence.

If the rabbi has reason to believe that there has been physical or emotional abuse, he should say, "In a situation such as this, you should have expert counseling from someone familiar with these problems. I want you to call X and make an appointment with her. The referral should be to someone credentialed in the management of abuse. A good way to find a competent counselor is to contact a local women's shelter and get some recommendations from them. It is wise for the rabbi to get to know one or more of the counselors to ease referral and communication.

The rabbi should *not* call the husband and give him a sermon on how to behave toward his wife. This can only aggravate and intensify the abuse.

The wife may say, "But what should I tell my husband?" The answer is, "If your husband does not believe that he has a problem, there is no need to tell him anything. You should be receiving counseling to see what you can best do in this situation."

Where abuse exists, the wife may be very fearful of going for counseling. "I'm afraid of what he may do if he finds out." This fear is understandable, but there is really no option. Counselors with expertise in abuse can help the wife avoid aggravating the situation. Continuing to absorb the abuse will condemn the wife to a life of misery.

If the couple comes together, the rabbi may say, "At this point, couple's therapy is inappropriate. I think that you and your wife each have your own things to work on. I believe you should each consult a therapist separately, and at a later time, joint counseling may be appropriate." The rabbi should then refer the husband to a therapist qualified in abuse problems. Coming from the rabbi, this may carry some weight.

If either spouse follows through with the recommendation for counseling, the rabbi should call the counselor and tell him/her that he will be available if the counselor thinks he can be of help.

PRESERVATION OF THE MARRIAGE

Contrary to popular thinking, discovery of abuse does not necessarily lead to termination of the marriage. It is important for the rabbi to understand why the wife may not see leaving as an option and why many women choose to remain in an abusive relationship.

The wife may still love her husband. She may think:

➤ "He is wonderful in some ways and the children love him."

➤ "I don't want to give up. I think I can make him change."

➤ "His family is powerful. They have an 'in' with the judges. If I leave, he'll get custody of the kids."

➤ "I'm afraid that if I do anything, it might make it worse."

➤ "How will I support myself and the kids?"

➤ "I'm terrified of being alone."

➤ "I want my children to have a father. They need a role model."

➤ "I owe it to him. He stuck by me through hard times."

➤ "He needs me. I'm afraid that if I leave, he might kill himself. I could never live with that guilt."

The wife needs help in strengthening herself so she can make the best decision. Counseling from a competent abuse counselor can help her make the best choice.

CAN AN ABUSER CHANGE?

Yes, but only if he sincerely wants to. Just saying "I want to change" and even agreeing to see a counselor is not enough. He must recognize that his behavior is inexcusable and intolerable.

In fact, the results of programs for abusers are not very encouraging. In the absence of physical violence, the results are somewhat better. The thought, "He is seeing a counselor, so I hope everything will be okay now," is misleading.

If there is no threat of physical violence, counseling for both spouses can usually be done without separating them. The wife then has a chance to evaluate whether there are, in fact, substantive positive changes, and the counselor can help her with this. If there has been physical violence or there is a threat thereof, separation may be necessary. The counselor can help the wife decide when a trial at reunion is safe.

An abusive husband feels very threatened by separation. It deprives him of the object of his muscle flexing. He may appeal to the rabbi to intercede for a reunion, promising that he will mend his ways and never again be in any way abusive. Experience has demonstrated that these promises are completely unreliable. The rabbi should tell the husband that the only one who can make the recommendation for the proper time for reunion is the wife's counselor.

PREVENTION

The rabbi is in an ideal position to help prevent abuse. It would be well for all rabbis to refuse to perform a marriage ceremony unless the couple agrees to premarriage counseling. Many young men and women do not have the slightest concept of how to relate to a spouse. They may try to model their behavior according to what they saw in their parents' marriage, which often leaves much to be desired.

The rabbi may have an even earlier opportunity to intervene constructively if he meets with the young man, woman, or both during their courtship. While there are no firm predictors of abuse, there are some risk factors that constitute a cause for concern:

- ➤ The person was physically or emotionally abused as a child
- ➤ The person's father was an abuser
- ➤ The person loses his temper more frequently and more easily than others
- ➤ The person behaves violently toward others
- ➤ The person breaks things when angry
- ➤ The person drinks to excess or experiences a personality change after drinking

Here are some warning signs that may be detected early in marriage or during courtship:

- ➤ Does he try to isolate her from family and friends?
- ➤ Does he expect her to spend all her free time with him exclusively?
- ➤ Does he want to know her whereabouts all the time and becomes angry when she is not available?
- ➤ Is he very impatient? For example, does he get angry in a restaurant if the service is not what he wants, then perhaps blames her for wanting to eat there?
- ➤ Does he become angry if she does not follow his advice?
- ➤ Does he take responsibility for his own actions or is he always blaming others?
- ➤ Does he tend to put her down and consequently is she putting herself down in order to please him?
- ➤ Does he appear to have two sides to his personality?
- ➤ Is he ever cruel, then smothering with excessive kindness?
- ➤ Is she afraid of making him angry and so takes great caution not to do so?
- ➤ Does he have unrealistic expectations of her?

A man may have one or more of these traits or warning signs and not turn out to be an abuser, but these are factors that increase the risk of potentially abusive and controlling behavior.

If these traits disturb a woman, but she thinks "I can change him," she is asking for problems. If she wants to have a husband with these traits, that is her right, but it is unrealistic to expect change. "What you see is what you get."

SHALOM BAYIT

Early detection of abuse may prevent its progression, and proper treatment of both spouses may greatly improve the quality of the relationship. A rabbi who is sensitive to abuse problems is in an ideal position to detect abuse at a stage when it is more easily remediable. If the wife is properly counseled and is strengthened to resist abuse rather than to cower before it, the progression of abuse can be halted and the relationship preserved.

Shalom bayit (peace in the home) is one of the foundations of Judaism, and restoring harmony between husband and wife is indeed a great mitzvah. But there can be a spurious peace that is not at all *shalom bayit,* when, for instance, the wife is intimidated into subservience and acceptance of tyranny.

If abuse is ignored, it is not only the wife that suffers. Great emotional pain is inflicted on the children. The abuser may act at night when he thinks the children are asleep and will not be affected. This is not true. Children of an abusive marriage suffer deep emotional wounds. Furthermore, an abusive husband is more apt to abuse the children as well.

Ignoring spousal abuse, therefore, is not only detrimental to the lives of the couple, but unfair to the children as well. Let me just quote a sampling of remarks from children:

"I lie in bed feeling scared. I can hear them fighting in the next room, and it's getting louder and louder. I'm just waiting until I hear the smack of his hand and Mom's cry. I hear it again and again. I put the pillow over my head. I want to run away."

"If my sister Jenny and I didn't fight so much, then Dad wouldn't fight with Mom because Mom tells us to be quiet, so it must be we who set him off. It's our fault."

"I tried to stop my Dad from kicking my Mom by kicking him. I didn't really want to hurt him. I love my Dad, but I just want him to stop hurting Mom."

"Mommy knows Daddy is being a stinker. Why doesn't she stand up to him? Is she waiting for him to beat me up again before she does anything?"

Spouse abuse renders children emotional cripples, an injury that may never be healed.

Rabbis have been taught that *teshuvah* eliminates the wrongdoings of the past. However, expressions of remorse and promises to change do not constitute *teshuvah*.

Teshuvah for an abuser means wholeheartedly accepting competent professional help and wholeheartedly working on changing his/her behavior.

The key questions now become: (1) How do we make this happen? And even more importantly, (2) How can we know when it has happened, i.e. when there has been real change?

As rabbis, we have answers to many questions or we are expected to. This situation is different. If there is a possibility for change, the rabbi is not the one who will know. Hence, it is not within the rabbi's ken to tell the wife when her marriage is safe from abuse and when she may return to her husband. The therapist with expertise in this area may have some ideas, and it is the victim who will ultimately know which of these ideas, if any, might work and be safe. This is not a comfortable situation for the rabbi. He is seen as an authority and the wife has trust in his opinion.

At all times, it is important for the victim to participate in any decision involving the relationship. Here is an example:

A social worker who had conducted a training session about abuse for rabbis received a call from a local therapist, saying that the session had been very effective. A few days after the training session, a rabbi received a call from the woman supervising the *mikveh*, that there was a woman there who was hysterical because her husband had forced her to go to the *mikveh* even though it was one day before she was supposed to go. The rabbi asked to speak to the woman and suggested that she not go home that night, but stay at a friend's home and go home the following night after *mikveh*. The woman said that was too scary and that she couldn't do it.

The rabbi did not remember to ask the woman what she thought might work, and told her to call a knowledgeable therapist. The therapist helped the woman come up with a plan that she was comfortable with, which included going home and telling her husband that the rabbi had said that she was not permitted to go to the *mikveh* until the following night.

This illustrates the importance of including the victim in the decision making process. The victim is the one who knows the abuser and knows what is most safe and what has the best chance of working. Though a rabbi is generally looked upon as an authority who can provide answers, in the case of domestic abuse, he must yield the actual decision making to the very person who has come to consult him.

Similarly, when the question arises as to whether the husband has changed, the only person who can answer that is the victim. The abuser may behave as the most gentle and refined person to everybody except his wife. Consequently, no other person is capable of rendering a decision about whether he has, in fact, changed. The rabbi, therefore, cannot tell the wife, "I believe that he has changed." He simply does not have the data upon which to base such a statement.

Is there anything that a rabbi should say to the husband? *This is an area where one must exert utmost caution to avoid putting the victim at serious risk.*

The importance of *shalom bayit* notwithstanding, it should not supercede the health and welfare of the individual. For an abuser to change is difficult. It is easier to put the couple back together, and one may be tempted to take the easier route. But let us remember, *"al ta'amod al dam re'echa"* ("do not stand aside when your neighbor is in danger").

CONFLICTING ACCOUNTS

If confronted, an abusive husband may vehemently deny his wife's accusations. In the absence of objective evidence, it is her word against his. It is significant to note that the *Shulchan Aruch* states that in cases of conflicting accounts, *the wife should be believed* (*Even Ha'ezer* 156:4).

Of course, it is possible that in pursuit of a divorce, the wife may fabricate charges of abuse. Unless there are ulterior motives for the divorce, this is unlikely. However, the rabbi must consider this possibility before coming to any conclusions. A competent abuse counselor may be able to detect whether or not the account of abuse is a fabrication.

PARENTS OF ABUSE VICTIMS

The rabbi has an important role in educating the abused woman's parents. Wives who have returned home because of maltreatment by their husbands are at times urged by the parents to go back to their husbands. "Michael is really a good boy. He called us and told us how sorry he was for the way he acted to you. He is a good provider and the children love him. Besides, what would you do if you left him? We are not in any position to support you and the children."

Parents must be made aware that if the husband is an abuser, they are sending their daughter back for more abuse. They may not be in a position to support her monetarily, but they should support her emotionally while she receives counseling on how to adjust to her situation. If she wishes to stay with them temporarily while she receives counseling, she should not be forced to return to her husband right away. She should be allowed to explore all the possibilities with a competent professional.

SEXUAL ABUSE

Only in recent years has the issue of "marital rape" been considered by legislatures. In the not so distant past, forcing sexual relations upon one's wife was not considered rape. This misguided concept stripped the woman of her dignity and rendered her an object at the mercy of her husband. *Several thousand years ago, Halachah prohibited forced sex.*

When inquiring about abusive behavior, a rabbi should not hesitate to investigate sexual abuse. This information is rarely volunteered by the wife. Forcing sexual relations or sexual acts that are repellant to the wife is sexual abuse. While there are no firm guidelines as to what is the appropriate frequency for sexual relations, inordinate demands for sex may be a form of sexual addiction and abuse.

THE TORAH ATTITUDE

Controlling husbands and some poorly informed rabbis may say that the Torah authorizes the husband to exercise control over his wife. This is blatantly false. The Torah position *forbids abuse of any kind: emotional, verbal, physical, and sexual.* Halachah requires that a husband treat his wife with utmost respect and sensitivity to her feelings. In no way may he ever compromise her dignity. The Torah attitude is stated clearly in the Talmud (*Yevamot* 62b): "A husband should love his wife as himself and respect her *even more* than he respects himself."

Indicative of a still prevailing attitude is that some Judaica stores that display many of my books, keep *The Shame Borne in Silence* under the counter. One such store does not carry this book at all because, "the rabbi told us we are not permitted to carry it." It is this attitude that allows men to assume that they have a right to be in total control of their wives, and justifies abusive behavior.

At one rabbinical convention, the rabbi in charge of the program rejected an organization's request for a time slot to address spouse abuse, on the grounds that it is not a problem in the Jewish community. One year later, the rabbi called to apologize. His daughter had returned home with her two children, no longer able to tolerate her husband's beatings.

COMMUNITY RESOURCES

The rabbi should familiarize himself with the resources in the community that serve an abused spouse, and he can play an important role in urging the community to provide help. Some communities have "safe havens" for women who are in danger of being beaten. Some have hotlines, and most communities have agencies that provide competent counseling.

Emergency funds may be necessary for a woman who must leave her home. Safehavens can provide only temporary protection, however, and the rabbi may be helpful in arranging alternate living quarters. Legal help is often necessary. A battered wife may obtain a restraining Order of Protection from the court. However, it should be noted that some women who had an Order of Protection were killed by their violent husbands. Again, a professional is best suited to help a woman figure out the best option.

THE AGUNAH PROBLEM

One of the worst manifestations of vicious control is a husband's refusal to give a *get*, thereby preventing his wife from getting on with her life and finding happiness in a subsequent marriage. Halachic authorities have agonized over finding a solution to this vexing problem. Should the wife remarry without a proper *get*, the child of a subsequent marriage would be a *mamzer*, unable, according to Halachah, to marry into a Jewish family. The rabbi should be of assistance in whatever way possible to liberate the woman from these chains of bondage.

EDUCATING THE COMMUNITY

Rabbis who are enlightened about spouse abuse can contribute a great deal to the education of the community. Some wives feel that they are trapped in a marriage because the community will essentially ostracize them if they leave the marriage. Many people are still in disbelief that spouse abuse exists among Jews, and are likely to incriminate the wife if she leaves the marriage.

Spouse abuse does not mean that the marriage must be terminated. With appropriate support, counseling, and intervention, the marriage may be viable. However, if parental and community attitudes are such that the wife feels trapped and without options, there is less likelihood that the marriage can be salvaged. In such situations the abuse may escalate to grave proportions.

One woman consulted her rabbi seven months into her marriage. Upon hearing her account, the rabbi said, "You must get out of this marriage." The woman said, "I am pregnant," and the rabbi said, "Then it is too late." Several years later, pregnant with her fourth child, the woman had to flee for her life in the middle of the night.

Assaulting a person is a criminal act, and this is no less a crime if the victim is one's wife. If it is indeed established that the husband is guilty of this crime, the rabbi is in a position to bring social pressures to bear. A known abuser should not be given the privileges and honors accorded to respectable members of the congregation as long as the wife feels this is safe and comfortable for her. She may not want this public action taken because of the stigma or reprisals she might suffer.

In sermons and in the congregation's newsletter, the rabbi should address the problem of spouse abuse. As long as it remains shrouded and denied, women will continue to suffer in helplessness and silence.

BIBLIOGRAPHY

Ackerman, R. 1986. *Growing in the Shadow.* Pompano Beach: Health Communications.

Al-Anon Faces Alcoholism. 1977. Al-Anon Family Group Headquarters, New York.

Alcoholics Anonymous. 1976. A.A. World Services, New York.

Beattie, M. 1987. *Codependent No More.* Center City: Hazelden.

Berg, S. 1993. *Jewish Alcoholism & Drug Addiction — An Annotated Bibliography.* Westport: Greenwood Press.

Daley, D. 1991. *Kicking Addictive Habits Once & for All.* Lexington: Heath & Co.

Gorski, T. & Miller, M. 1986. *Staying Sober.* Independence: Herald House/Independence Press.

Julien, R. 1992. *A Primer of Drug Action.* New York: W.H. Freeman & Co.

Kurtz, E. & Ketcham, K. 1992. *The Spirituality of Imperfection.* New York: Bantam Books.

Narcotics Anonymous. World Service Conference (Available from Hazelden 1-800-328-9000).

Sandmaier, M. 1980. *The Invisible Alcoholics — Women and Alcohol Abuse.* New York: McGraw-Hill.

Twerski, A. 1997. *Addictive Thinking.* Center City: Hazelden.

Twerski, A. 1995. *Self-Improvement? — I'm Jewish!* Brooklyn: Mesorah Publications.

ॐ 17 ॐ
RESOLVING CONFLICTS:
THE RABBI AS MEDIATOR

Robert A. Baruch Bush, J.D.

WHY DO CONGREGANTS in conflict seek the help of their rabbi as a third party, and what is it that the rabbi can do to best serve them? The traditional role of a rabbi has been to settle disputes with a *psak*, a halachic decision. Contemporary rabbis, however, are more often than not called into dispute situations *not* as halachic authorities, but rather as mediators between two or more individuals.

The role of mediator is very different from that of *posek*. As a *posek*, the rabbi is asked to clarify for his congregants their religious responsibilities in relation to their dispute, drawing on his expertise as a halachic authority. However, congregants do not always come to their rabbi seeking such a ruling. In fact, individuals in conflict tend to come to their rabbi looking for the kind of assistance and support that is congruent with what mediators offer to parties in dispute.

Congregants with a dispute will at times approach their rabbi because they genuinely wish to know what the Halachah requires of them; and whatever the rabbi says the Halachah demands by way of a resolution, they are both ready and willing to accept. Even if the matter is not framed as a *din torah* (a dispute judged by a rabbinical court in accordance with the Halachah), the rabbi's role in this situation is to provide the authoritative Torah guidance that the congregants are seeking. However, it is much more often the case that congregants with a conflict come to the rabbi, *not* to obtain an authoritative halachic opinion that both are prepared to accept, but rather to gain support for each of their positions, and thus to gain a powerful ally.

Under these circumstances, if the rabbi declares his opinion, even one that is halachically-based, then he has automatically "taken sides" in the matter. Paradoxically, rather than helping the parties resolve their dispute, he has become enmeshed in it. Additionally, since congregations are often composed of close-knit networks, the rabbi's perceived "siding" with one of the parties may alienate an entire segment of the congregation. For one whose designated role is to lead the entire congregation, such alienation can create a truly serious problem.

For these reasons, it is precisely by adopting the role of mediator — rather than halachic authority, judge, or arbitrator — that the rabbi can generally be of greatest assistance in settling conflicts. The community rabbi must be able to effectively mediate conflicts without taking a directive-giving, authoritative, advice-giving role. Therefore, this chapter introduces an approach to conflict resolution known as *transformative mediation,* an approach developed by myself and a team of expert colleagues over the past decade that is now used successfully in many diverse contexts (Bush and Folger, 2004).

You may reasonably ask: "What kind of help do congregants in conflict need and want from their rabbi that does not involve a rabbinic directive about what they should do in their situation?" To answer this question, the following presents a perspective drawn from the study of conflict in general, the work done by the author and his colleagues, with continued reference to the rabbinic context.

TRANSFORMATIVE MEDIATION:
A THEORY OF CONFLICT AND INTERVENTION

When parties first contact a mediator, the reasons for their interest in mediation generally fall into the following categories: saving money, saving time, and avoiding some formal complaint process — such as court. Reducing hostility and bitterness, as well as preserving or restoring a working relationship for the future, are also important. One party may be more interested in saving time and the other in restoring the relationship. Also, with few exceptions, all parties hope to achieve a fair resolution of some kind, whether or not it is formalized in writing. At a more general level, parties are looking for "closure", for an outcome that allows them to move beyond the conflict and get on with their lives.

All the above examples of people's expectations reflect a common and deeper set of concerns that motivate parties to try mediation. That is, they reflect the parties' desire to find a different mode of dealing with their conflict — different from the one they have experienced in their private negotiations — and one they believe can be found in a more formal process. They want to feel more in control of themselves and the process. They do not want to be victimized or to victimize the other party in the process of settling their dispute; rather they want to come out of the process feeling better about themselves and the other party than they did going in.

In part, this interpretation of party expectations is the product of experience and observation in many hundreds of cases of people in conflict, be they families, businesses, communities, or other contexts. There is a strong pattern in the way people characterize what is most salient to them about their conflicts, i.e., what bothers them most and, therefore, what they most want help in addressing. One good, concrete way to describe this pattern is to give an example of a specific case — a case that also shows what intra-congregational conflict looks like. In fact, the example presented here is based on an actual case reported by a rabbinic student, whose assignment was to interview congregational rabbis about conflicts that arose in their communities.

Imagine Jacob Stein and Aaron Gold, two members of the *Ohav Tzedek* synagogue — an established congregation with some families that have belonged for generations, but with many new families — new to the synagogue and also to orthodox observance. Stein and Gold represent these two groups, both figuratively and literally. Stein, nearly sixty and past-president of the synagogue's board, is the head of a family whose religious life is rich and stable, based on generations of observance of Jewish tradition. Gold, a successful lawyer in his early forties, is a *ba'al teshuvah* whose family "discovered" Orthodox Judaism some years back and acted to solidify their new Jewish life by moving close to *Ohav Tzedek* and participating fully — leading to Aaron's recent election as president of the board.

Over the past year or so, tension has arisen because of different reactions to the changes taking place in the surrounding neighborhood, which has been declining both in "quality of life" and property values. Gold and many of the new families believe that it is time to sell the building and move to a new neighborhood, in order to attract more families and preserve the viability of the congregation. Stein and most of the older families are willing to enlarge the present building, but are deeply opposed to moving — both because of their attachment to the building and because moving would be a financial and practical hardship for many of them. Their differences over the issue have deepened into an open conflict, with hard feelings and harsh exchanges. It appears that the congregation may be headed for a split, although everyone says they want to avoid this.

Aaron Gold and Jacob Stein are the lightning rods. Here is what they say bothers them the most about this conflict.

Jacob: Well, what's really hard is to suddenly feel so frustrated and helpless. You know, the heart of this matter is the shul, even though there are personal things as well. Like to have Aaron Gold tell me that I was ignoring the good of the congregation and that I had lost touch with the present kehillah ... that I'm just not up to a leadership role anymore! That made me so angry; but it also made me doubt myself. I was shaken. I mean, should I continue pushing for what I think is best for the congregation? Do I really know anymore what that is? Maybe I have lost touch, after all. And anyway, what can I do against the relentless pressure Aaron is keeping up to move? He's making me feel helpless and uncertain, and I don't like it.

Plus, I am finding myself full of anger for Aaron all the time now. Why, he's been almost like a son to me since he's joined us — learning with me, coming for Shabbat. Look how hard he's worked to bring himself and his family along in Jewish life, and to strengthen the shul and attract others to join! It was like a new breath of life for these old bones. But you know what? I find I can't see him like that anymore. All I see now is him closing his mind and his heart to me and the other older members. He sits with his real estate planners and shuts us out, not showing up anymore for our weekly learning sessions, avoiding me on Shabbat. And then he and his followers announce that, besides their moving plans, they want to raise the shul's mechitzah (physical divider between the men and the women), right away — they don't think the one we have is high enough! Apparently our Judaism isn't kosher enough for them, even though they said they'd learned a lot from us! It's just too much! The helplessness and the hostility — that's what's so hard. And the more that this goes on, the worse it gets.

Aaron: What's been the hardest? Well, first of all, when Jacob showed up at the board meeting and declared in no uncertain terms, "The shul will never move," that really threw me. Do you know how many sleepless nights and Sundays I've poured into this thing, espe-

*cially since I was elected president and members came to me demand-
ing a plan to move the shul? Sure, there are times when we have to
consult the "founding families"—and Jacob could be a big help in
calming everyone's fears and getting their input. But he's not president anymore, and a congregation can't have two leaders. I thought
he'd understand that better than anyone. But no, he's marching in
and announcing in front of everyone that I'm disregarding the elders
and tearing the shul apart! I was stunned. I didn't know how to respond to his attack.*

*Wasn't I proposing the move precisely in order to save our syna-
gogue from dying? Wouldn't I be the last one to ignore the older
members, after all I owed them? I thought so, but now I'm not sure.
Maybe I don't know the kehillah as well as he did. Maybe there's
something else at stake I just don't understand. Maybe I was exag-
gerating about the neighborhood's decline because I came from such
different surroundings. It all suddenly seems like a huge responsibility and I'm feeling confused.*

*The other hard part is the hostility I'm now feeling toward Jacob
and his wife, Miriam. She was always telling him to stay involved
in the board after stepping down, so that he could "make sure Aaron
knows what he's doing." I thought I was pretty good at overlooking
things and "judging on the side of merit," but I started to see Jacob
and Miriam as jealous old fools. I thought, The real reason he's down
here at the meetings making trouble is that he just doesn't want the
shul—and me—to grow and succeed without him. He's determined to
keep the past alive, even if it means that the shul stagnates and dies.*

*That's also why he opposes raising the mechitzah, I think, even
though he's the one who encouraged me to grow in my Judaism.
Grow—but not beyond him! I feel ashamed for thinking these things
about Jacob and Miriam, who've been like parents to us. But I can't
help it. The worst thing about this conflict is that it's brought out the
worst in me—all of my insecurities, all of my mean-spiritedness, all
of my pettiness. At one point, I thought of quitting just to end this
nastiness.*

Jacob's and Aaron's "voices" above echo what a mediator regularly hears when parties talk about their personal experience of the conflict (though Jacob and Aaron may be more articulate than many). What most people find to be the most difficult thing about conflict is not that it frustrates their getting what they want, whether trivial or important, but that it leads and even forces them to behave in ways that they find uncomfortable and repellent. It alienates them from their sense of their own strength and their connectedness to others, and thus it disrupts and undermines how they treat people. In short, conflict precipitates a crisis in human interaction that parties find profoundly disturbing, and this is a large part of the reason why they turn to a mediator for help.

This view of why parties seek mediation is supported not only by me and my associates' experience, but also by insights from the fields of communication (McCorckle and Mills, 1992), cognitive psychology (Beck, 1999), neurophysiology (Goleman, 1995), and social psychology (Lind and Tyler, 1988). According to "transformative" theory (Bush and Folger, 2004; Folger and Bush, 2001), conflict as a social phenomenon is not only, or primarily, about rights, interests, or power. Although it includes all of those things, conflict is also, and most importantly, about peoples' interaction with one another as human beings.

Certainly there are problems to be resolved in any conflict. In the above case, they are: What is the best plan for saving the congregation and what level of observance should be followed in the shul? Certainly, the opposing parties do want to solve these problems. However, the reality is that they want to do so in a way that preserves their personal feelings of competence and autonomy, while avoiding taking advantage of the other. They want to feel that they have behaved well in handling this crisis, which means making changes in the volatile interactions that are going on between them, rather than simply coming up with the right answer to their conflict. To summarize, in order to be useful to parties, conflict intervention cannot only be about problem solving and the satisfaction of needs and interests; it must directly address the quality of the parties' interactions too.

According to transformative theory, conflict affects a person's experience of both self and other. First, conflict generates a sense of one's own weakness and incapacity. The person feels weaker, compared to his pre-conflict state. He feels he has lost control over the situation. In addition he feels confusion, doubt, uncertainty, and indecisiveness. This sense of weakness is a very natural human response to conflict; almost no one is immune to it, regardless of his or her initial position of power. At the very same time, conflict generates a state of self-absorption: each party becomes more focused on and protective of himself, as well as more suspicious, hostile, closed, and impervious to the other's perspective (Beck, 1999; Goleman, 1995).

However, there is more to the picture. The experiences of weakness and self-absorption do not occur independently. Rather, they reinforce each other in a feedback loop: the weaker I feel myself becoming, the more hostile and closed I act toward you; the more hostile I am toward you, the more you react to me in kind, making me feel weaker, more hostile, and closed, and so on. This vicious circle of disempowerment and demonization is what scholars mean when they talk about "conflict escalation" (Rubin et al., 1994). The transformative theory views it as more of an "interactional degeneration". Before the conflict, there is some decent human interaction going on, whatever the context — between family members, coworkers, neighbors etc. Then the conflict arises and, propelled by the vicious circle of disempowerment and demonization, what started as a decent interaction spirals down into one that is negative, destructive, and alienating. When nations get caught up in this spiral, the outcome may be war. For families or congregations, the result is disintegration, with the home or shul becoming an adversarial battleground.

What are the disputing parties looking for when they seek the help of someone who can serve as mediator—including their congregational rabbi? What disturbs parties most about conflict is the interactional degeneration, and therefore what they most want—even more than help in resolving specific issues—is help in reversing the downward spiral and restoring a more humane quality to their interaction.

The transformative model does this. It goes beyond the dimension of helping parties reach agreement on disputed issues, to help them end the vicious circle of disempowerment, disrespect and demonization, as well as alienation from both themselves and others. Without ending or changing that cycle, the parties cannot move beyond the negative interaction that has entrapped them and cannot escape its crippling effects.

Here is the completion of our answer to the first question posed above: Why is the mediation process sought and used? As transformative theory predicts, and research documents, parties who come to mediators are looking for and valuing more than simply reaching agreements on specific issues. They are looking for a way to change and transform their destructive conflict interaction into a more positive one, to the greatest degree possible. The transformative model of mediation is intended to help parties do this.

TRANSFORMATIVE MEDIATION:
CHANGING THE QUALITY OF CONFLICT INTERACTION

What, then, is the nature of transformative mediation and, especially, the rabbi's mediative role? Transformative mediation can best be understood as a process of "changing the quality of conflict interaction." In the transformative mediation process, parties can recapture their sense of competence and connection, reverse the negative conflict cycle, reestablish a constructive interaction, and move forward on a positive footing, with the mediator's help.

Consider again the "voices" of Jacob and Aaron, the parties to our fictional congregational dispute. After participating in a mediation session with their rabbi (who used the transformative approach), they describe some important aspects of how the process worked and how it affected them in their conflict.

Jacob: You know, it's strange, but I have to say that, in a way, the mediation helped me to come back to myself, to being the Jew I want to be, acting the way I want to act — even though I was still disagreeing with Aaron about the shul. For one thing, the rabbi's invitations for me to talk and his attentiveness created a space for me to do just that — talk it out. Even if I wasn't always making sense or wasn't very clear, the rabbi would listen, and he would repeat and go over what I said. When he did that, it let me see and hear what I was saying. It was almost like talking to myself. And doing that helped me realize what I was thinking and understand it better for myself. Then I could say it more clearly to Aaron. So I began to get clearer, calmer, and less frustrated, right there in the rabbi's study during the conversation. That was very important.

When that happened, it began to be a different situation, because then I was experiencing the whole thing differently, more calmly, more confidently. So, I could see the situation differently in some ways. And I could listen differently to Aaron. I could see him again without feeling that cloud of anger. That in itself — that I could see him that way again — was really a tremendous relief and it made an enormous difference in our ability to keep talking to each other...to go back to talking to each other about our disagreements in a constructive way.

Aaron: Like I said before, the really bitter part of the conflict was that it brought out the worst in me — my doubts in my judgment and understanding. Even worse was my need and my willingness to blame and demonize Jacob, the very person who gave me the acceptance and guidance I so needed when we came to Ohav Tzedek. In the mediation with the rabbi, I don't know how, but I began to reconnect with, how should I say it, the angels of my better nature. It's not just that I became more confident and clear about what I was thinking and saying. I also began to see Jacob again for who he really is (even if I still disagree with him): a loving, thoughtful mentor who is devoted to this congregation — and to me and my family.

I realized that, whatever happens with the shul, Jacob has been like a father to me — and keeping that connection is so important, I don't know how I could have lived with myself if I destroyed it. You can't stay connected to someone you don't trust, and it was so easy to lose that trust. It was happening so fast, and I couldn't seem to do anything about it. The rabbi's mediation allowed me to realize that's what was happening and choose not to let it happen, not to let it continue — whether or not we agreed about what was the best course for the shul. Once we turned that corner back to our sense of connection to each other, I knew that we'd eventually figure out how to do the right thing, whatever it was.

In sum, as Jacob and Aaron describe it, the nature of the mediation process in their case was one of interactional change (or transformation). That is, each of them changed the way he experienced and interacted with both self and other in the midst of their continuing conflict. To put it differently, mediation supported them in a process of changing the quality of their conflict interaction, and most importantly, reversing its negative and destructive spiral.

How can mediation by a rabbi help congregants in conflict do the same? From what resource is that transformation generated, and what is the rabbi's role in doing so? The critical resource is the parties' own basic humanity: their essential strength and their essential decency and compassion as human beings. The transformative theory of conflict recognizes that conflict tends to escalate as interaction degenerates, because of the susceptibility of human beings to experience weakness and self-absorption in the face of sudden challenge. But the theory also posits, based on what many call a "relational" theory of human nature, that human beings also have inherent capacities for strength and responsiveness, and an inherent moral resiliency that allows these capacities to overcome the tendencies to weakness and self-absorption (Bush and Folger, 2004; Della Noce, 1999). When these capacities are activated, the conflict spiral can reverse and interaction can regenerate—even, at times, without the presence of a mediator as intervener.

Conflict is not static. It is an emergent, dynamic phenomenon, in which parties can and do move and shift in remarkable ways. They move from weakness to strength, becoming (in more specific terms) calmer, clearer, more confident, more articulate, and more decisive. They shift from self-absorption to responsiveness, becoming more attentive, open, trusting, and more responsive toward the other party (Beck, 1999; Goleman, 1995). In transformative conflict theory, these dynamic shifts are called "empowerment" and "recognition" (Bush and Folger, 2004; Bush, 1996).

There is also a reinforcing feedback effect on this side of the picture. The stronger I become, the more open I am to you. The more open I am to you, the stronger you feel and the more open you become to me, and then the stronger I feel. (Indeed, the more open I become to you, the stronger I feel, simply because I'm being more open. That is, openness both requires and creates a sense of strength, of magnanimity). So, there is also a circle effect between strength and responsiveness, once they begin to emerge. Instead of a *vicious* circle of unresolvable conflict it is a *virtuous* circle of conflict transformation.

Why "conflict transformation"? Because as the parties make empowerment and recognition shifts, and as those shifts gradually reinforce one another in a virtuous circle, the interaction as a whole begins to turn the corner and regenerate. It changes back from a negative, destructive, alienating, and demonizing interaction to one that becomes positive, constructive, connecting, and humanizing, even while conflict and disagreement are still continuing.

The keys to this transformation of conflict interaction are the empowerment and recognition shifts that the parties themselves make. No matter how small and seemingly insignificant, as these shifts continue and accumulate, they can transform the entire interaction. Is it hard for those shifts to occur? It most certainly is, especially for parties who have been overcome by the sense of weakness and self-absorption that conflict first brings. It is difficult, but eminently possible. In the transformative model, it is these shifts in the dimensions of empowerment and recognition that are among the beneficial factors that mediators bring to the table (Antes et al., 2001; Bush, 1996).

This overall picture leads us to a definition of mediation and the rabbi's mediative role in the transformative model: the process by which a third party works with the other two parties to help them change the quality of their conflict interaction from negative and destructive to positive and constructive, as they explore and discuss issues and possibilities for resolution. The transformative model does not ignore the significance of resolving specific issues. It assumes that if the rabbi-mediator can help the parties change the quality of their interaction then, as a result, they themselves will find acceptable ways of resolving those specific issues.

Rabbis are not asked to bring their expert knowledge and wisdom to bear or give advice about how to solve the problems and difficulties the parties face. Rather, as mediators, rabbis can support the parties' own work, create a space for that work to go on, and — most importantly — stay out of the parties' way. As transformative mediators, rabbis will allow and trust the parties to find their own way through the conflict, and even more important, find themselves and each other, discovering and revealing strength and compassion within themselves.

TRANSLATING THEORY INTO PRACTICE: HOW DOES THE TRANSFORMATIVE MEDIATOR WORK?

How does a rabbi translate the theory of conflict transformation into specific mediation practices? In this section, we discuss the practical skills of mediation, with examples framed from the fictional conflict between Jacob Stein and Aaron Gold.

The Prerequisite Skill: Overcoming Skepticism about the Model

Paradoxically, the most important and "primary skill" of the rabbi as transformative mediator is to keep firmly in mind the "why and what" of the work he is doing as mediator: supporting the parties as they discuss the issues between them, and especially supporting their shifts from weakness to strength and self-absorption to responsiveness — empowerment and recognition shifts. Understanding and embracing this mission and being confident in its value to the parties is essential for the rabbi-mediator.

In training young rabbis in mediation skills, this "primary skill" seems to present the greatest challenge. Perhaps because they are trained in rabbinics, they have great difficulty in accepting that they can serve usefully — and ethically — as mediators, without offering advice to the parties. They remain skeptical on at least two grounds. First, they see it as central to their rabbinical role to give halachic and ethical guidance to their congregants, particularly when the situation presents questions of how a person should behave toward his fellow — as conflicts almost always do. Second, they simply cannot believe that contentious disputes will ever be settled without a substantial measure of authoritative advice-giving and moral suasion — and they assume that reaching a settlement is what the parties most need and want. In short, they question whether the transformative mediation theory is either practical or appropriate for use by congregational rabbis handling conflicts like that between Stein and Gold. Nevertheless, if mediation is to be useful as a pastoral skill for congregational rabbis, such doubts must be worked through and overcome.

First, the would-be rabbi-mediator must come to terms with the reality, that the risks involved in mediator advice-giving, especially for a congregational rabbi, are both substantial and unavoidable. There is simply no way for a rabbi-mediator to offer advice to congregants in conflict without effectively taking sides and making himself a party to the conflict — in the eyes of one or both parties, if not in reality. Unless specifically asked for an halachic ruling by persons who are clearly ready to accept whatever ruling is made, the rabbi-mediator who declares his opinions will very likely alienate at least one of the parties in the conflict, and possibly many others with whom they are allied. That certainly seems likely in the Stein/Gold case.

Second, the rabbi-mediator must genuinely understand and accept that reaching a settlement is *not* what disputing congregants most need and want, unless it is a settlement accompanied by an interactional change. Clearly, what bothers both Stein and Gold is not simply what will happen to the shul *building*, but what *is* happening in the interaction between them (and their friends) as fellow Jews and human beings. Even if the rabbi comes up with a very wise solution to the expansion/moving argument, the solution will mean little to Jacob and Aaron unless they "come back to themselves and each other," as they put it. That process of reconnection cannot be short-circuited by moralizing or advice-giving. But it can and will emerge organically from a process that supports empowerment and recognition shifts on both sides. Realizing that this is what is really at stake for Gold and Stein is essential in order for the rabbi-mediator to do the specific things needed to help them.

Essential Skill: Learning the Vocabulary of Empowerment and Recognition

In order to notice opportunities for supporting empowerment and recognition, the mediating rabbi needs to stay "in the moment" of the conversation and pay close attention to the parties' own conversational cues in the interactions between them, namely, what they do and what they say. He understands that when the mediation first begins, parties may not be able to talk about the issues or listen to each other effectively and productively, and they may be confused about what they want. As a result, the mediator will first focus on listening and observing for indications of weakness and self-absorption — because these are the points of opportunity for interactional transformation.

The rabbi-mediator must know how to recognize these opportunities; in other words, he must know what he is listening and looking for. In effect, he is learning to listen to the exchanges between the parties in a whole new way, on a new level, and in a new language. Therefore, he must master the vocabulary of empowerment and recognition, starting with signifiers of either weakness or self-absorption (Moen et al., 2001). For example: If Jacob turns to the rabbi after Aaron's arguments for moving the shul and asks, "What should I do?" it shows that Jacob sees the mediator as the decision-maker and feels dependent. If, in trying to express his objections, he says, "I'm really confused," this expresses lack of clarity and probably uncertainty. If he throws up his hands and exclaims, "I've had enough of this!" his comment expresses strong emotion and shows a sense of helplessness or frustration. If Aaron responds by asking, "What do you expect from someone like that?" it indicates a negative view of Jacob, and hence self-absorption. If he defends himself from criticism by insisting, "That's not what I meant" or "You don't understand what it's been like for me," these are requests to be understood.

A rabbi listening with a transformative ear will not ignore or dismiss statements of this nature as the parties merely "venting" their frustration or emotions. The statements will be seen and heard as important markers indicating opportunities for shifts in the conflict interaction. In this new language, every expression that conveys the message, "I feel weak," in whatever fashion, is an opportunity for an empowerment shift towards greater strength. Every expression that conveys the message, "I am trapped in my own perspective and cut off from the other," in whatever variation, is an opportunity for a recognition shift towards increased responsiveness.

Once able to work in the language of conflict transformation, the rabbi-mediator also needs to be able to enact supportive responses that assist Aaron and Jacob in making empowerment and recognition shifts, and to do this without pushing, directing, or having any agenda for them.

Essential Skill: Supportive Responses

With the understanding that one of the "hallmarks" of transformative mediation is that "small steps count," the rabbi-mediator will notice changes in the parties, indicating that empowerment and recognition shifts are occurring and that strength and responsiveness are emerging. The rabbi's role is to respond in a way that will assist the parties to make these changes on their own, by doing the following:

Close listening, combined with observation of what the parties are saying through their body language, is a basic skill that is used continuously throughout the mediation. Nuances in the language used by the parties as they move through the discussion are crucial indicators of shifts, and body language is as important as the actual words spoken. Close listening is done with no other goal in mind except to hear what is being said or trying to be said (O'Reilly, 1998). It is being fully present to the person speaking. Good, attentive listening makes possible the effective use of other key skills, such as reflection, summary, and "checking in". Without close and attentive listening, effective transformative mediation will be impossible.

Reflection is another primary supportive response. In reflecting a party's statement, the mediator simply says what he hears the party saying, using words close to the party's own language, even (or especially) when the language is offensive, loud, negative, or strongly expressed. The mediator does not soften the party's language or remove its "sting". For example, if Aaron angrily says, "Jacob, I can't stand the way you keep trying to run things, when it's me who's the president!" the rabbi-mediator does not "reframe" Aaron's anger into a polite request for behavior change by saying, "So you are asking Jacob not to interfere with you doing your job." Rather, he simply reflects the statement accurately, with the anger: "So Aaron, you're saying Jacob is still trying to run things, even though you're president, and you are very angry about that." By using the exact or similar language, without intentional distortion or softening, the mediator leaves room for the participant to choose to expand on the angry or negative statement, explain it further, or rethink it and amend it to reduce the hostility or exaggeration. All of these options can and do happen. So Aaron may respond to the rabbi's reflection by clarifying: "It's true, I do get angry, but really it's more that I'm frustrated because I can't get things done." In this brief exchange, Aaron has clarified and become more articulate about what's bothering him.

Reflection is particularly helpful in assisting a party to think through something about which he is uncertain or unclear. In all these ways, reflection allows a party to "listen and talk to himself," and by doing so to gain clarity and confidence about what he is saying. It also may give the other party an opportunity to hear something he may not have heard or understood when it was first being said. The overall effect of reflection is to "amplify" the conversation for both parties, to make what is being said more audible so the parties can understand themselves and each other better.

Here is another example of how reflection might work in practice in the Gold/Stein case:

> Jacob says, "This shul is ours. Our grandparents, mine and my friends', built it before we were born. We grew up in it. We repaired it with our own hands. This is not a building, it's our lives, and no one is going to shut it down!"
>
> The rabbi's reflection could be: "So, you feel strongly that the shul is yours. Your families built it and you grew up in it with them. When it needed repair, you fixed it with your own hands. So to you this shul is not just a building, it's 'your lives' as you put it, and you are not going to let anyone close it."
>
> Now Jacob may respond to the rabbi's reflection by adding: "Yes, our lives. We married here; we raised our children here. When the roof decayed and there were no funds to hire someone, we climbed up and fixed it. When vandals broke the windows and painted graffiti on the walls, we repaired them and cleaned up — and our children helped each time. I don't mean to say the shul is *only* ours — the newcomers have done

a lot. But you can't forget what it means to us and you can't replace it."

Even in this brief example, it is evident that the rabbi's reflection helped Jacob hear and think about what he said, consider whether he wanted to elaborate or modify it in any way, and decide what to say next. The result was an elaboration that was clearer and stronger – an empowerment shift. The reflection also allowed Aaron to listen in, hear and consider what Jacob was saying without immediate pressure to respond, and decide what he thought about it. In short, reflection supports empowerment for both parties, in a small but significant way.

Practicing this sort of reflection may sound simple and easy: just listen and say what you heard the parties say. In fact, it is not easy at all. Really hearing what is being said — hearing and reflecting it all, without editing, or judging its validity, or likely impact — is actually very difficult. First, the rabbi does not want to harden a party's position or be seen as agreeing with that position; nor does he want to implicitly dismiss the consideration of other, contradictory views. Additionally, he may be concerned that the listening party will object to the other party "getting so much attention" in a climate where all the subjects being discussed are personal and emotional. To avoid these pitfalls, the reflection must have a properly tentative tone and demeanor, indicating that the rabbi is simply trying "to get" what is being said, in order to assist party decision-making and communication without introducing any standards for judging the comment. Also, the rabbi must not allow himself to become distracted from what is being said. The calmness and ability to focus that is required for this work is far from easy.

Once the parties start talking directly with each other, *summary* may be the preferred response, rather than reflection. In fact, in mediation using the transformative model, the parties often begin talking directly to each other early on and for extended lengths of time. The rabbi's participation in the discussion may be quite minimal for those periods, but he will continue to focus on listening. When the rabbi does enter the conversation, it is important that he know the difference between *reflection* and *summary*. In a *reflection*, the rabbi speaks to one of the parties, engages that party directly and allows the other to "listen in" from a safe distance. In a *summary*, the rabbi speaks to and with both parties, reflecting back and reviewing larger blocks, or "chunks," of their conversation and interaction. For purposes of illustration, consider the following continuation of the conversations started above about the shul.

Suppose that Jacob continues his response to the mediator's reflection by speaking directly to Aaron, saying, "You just can't replace it. So we're not moving our shul. No way! No matter what you say."

Now Aaron jumps into the conversation and says, "I can't believe your attitude! If it weren't for me and the people I've brought into the shul, you'd have to close down right now! You wouldn't even have a minyan for Shabbat most weeks. You haven't complained about the new life we put into the place, and our work to refurbish it. And now it's *your* shul? For what, for a museum?" The exchange then continues:

Jacob: "*You didn't think it was a museum when you first came. You said it felt like you were 'coming home.' You loved the learning, you loved the minyan, you loved the whole ta'am (flavor) of the shul — just the way it was and is. You put in new life? And who kept it alive all these years for you to find when you finally realized you needed it? I thought you loved the shul like we do. That's what you thought? That you were coming to a museum?*"

Aaron: "*No, I'm not saying that. When I came, it was like coming home. But what's the point of having a home with no one living*"

in it? The shul can be a wonderful home for lots of new families, a
new generation, people like me who never had such a home. Isn't that
the point, to pass on your Judaism? Our shul should be someplace
where it can attract new people, build for the future. This neighbor-
hood is dying. The shul isn't the building, it's the kehillah. Do you
want to hang onto the building and let the kehillah die?"

Jacob: "What a way to put it! Look, the shul may be old, but
when your parents get old and sick, you don't leave them behind
for the suburbs because it's nicer there. You stay and take care of
them. Same with a shul, you don't cut and run — even if the neigh-
bors change. A shul is not a piece of concrete — it's alive, it's holy.
Judaism means honoring our past — or else there won't be anything
to pass on to the future. No one is moving this shul. You want to go
someplace else? Start your own shul!"

Assuming the conversation seemed to slow or "lull" at this
point, the rabbi-mediator might offer this *summary*:

It's clear you both have strong feelings about the shul, but you
also have some very strong differences about it. First of all,
you have different views about the importance of what each of
you has put into the shul. Aaron, you're saying that you and
the new families have brought in new life, strengthened the
minyan, and refurbished the place. But Jacob, you're saying
that you and the older families are the ones who kept the shul
alive over the years and who created the *ta'am*, to use your
word, that Aaron and the others found so meaningful when
they came.

And then, besides what you've each put into the shul, you
also seem to have pretty different views of how you see the
shul today and what it represents to you in your Judaism. Jacob, you're saying that the shul building itself is like a living
being, a parent, whom you can't abandon. And you see honoring the past, including the shul building, as the very essence of
Judaism. While Aaron, you see the shul as the *kehillah*, not the

building, and a *kehillah* can relocate to a better neighborhood if it needs to. Also, for you what is most important in Judaism is reaching out to newcomers who grew up without the tradition, in order to pass it on to them. So there are some serious differences between you on these points.

This example illustrates both the value and the difficulty of using summary. Summarizing is often used when there have been long periods of direct exchange and the parties come to a natural break. It is also helpful when the parties don't know "where to go next" or seem stuck. Since a good stretch of ground will have been covered during the conversation, the summary provides a review of what they have been talking about and what each has been saying. It helps the parties remember what they were discussing and to make more informed choices about where they want to go next. All of this can support empowerment shifts. However, for this very reason, offering a good summary can be challenging: the rabbi must be able to recall and describe the whole stretch of ground covered, and this is the skill that needs to be developed.

Moreover, like *reflection*, a *summary* is inclusive. The rabbi-mediator does not select from what has been said, does not "soften" what was said, and does not drop any issues, particularly intangible ones. The *summary* is not a lecture by the rabbi and has no agenda or direction built into it. It is an especially powerful tool for supporting empowerment and recognition when it highlights the differences between the parties and, thus, the choices they face. But for all these reasons, it is challenging. It requires the rabbi to resist emphasizing superficial "common ground" and to highlight instead the deeper "fault lines" in the parties' conversations (as in this summary of Jacob and Aaron's exchange) because realizing the nature and depth of their differences and then making choices about how to address those differences will empower both parties.

Without any other skills, the rabbi could effectively mediate in a supportive way using only *listening, reflection,* and *summary. Checking in,* however, is an important and effective addition to the other essential skills and is frequently coupled with reflection and summary. *Checking in* might have followed at the end of the above summary, with the rabbi asking Aaron and Jacob, "So, given these differences, where do you want to go from here?" It is often used as an intervention when it seems the parties have come to a choice point in the mediation, and it provides them with the opportunity to make a clear decision. One such choice point arises when it seems that the parties have nothing more to say to each other. So, if Aaron and Jacob were silent after the rabbi's summary, he might ask: "Do you want to continue talking about the differences in the way you see things? Do you think the conversation has gone as far as it can? Do you want to call it a day or take a break?" In effect, the conversation has come to a fork in the road, and it is helpful for the mediator to point it out and ask the parties which direction they want to take. Doing so allows the parties to make their own choice and in this way it supports empowerment.

Questions are obviously used for checking in. Questions are also used in many other supportive ways, provided that they do not steer a party in any direction. The risk is that questions can put the rabbi above the parties, leading the discussion and having the parties respond to him, rather than allowing the parties to conduct their own conversation about the matters that are important to them. In transformative mediation, questions are used to open doors or invite further discussion. "Is there more you want to say about that?" is one such question, and there are many others. However, the rabbi does not use questions for his own purposes, such as to gather information or to understand what the parties are talking about. The reason for this is simple: questions that support deliberation between the parties help them get stronger; but questions that direct or control the parties' thinking keep them from getting stronger.

There are other responses that can support empowerment and recognition shifts. *Silence* can be a rabbi's intentional response, in at least two different situations. First, when parties are directly engaging, the rabbi's silently "backing out" and nonintervention can support party decision-making and communication. Second, after a period of intense conversation, when the parties fall silent, allowing time for that silence is also an appropriate response. When something powerful has been said or has happened during the parties' interaction, it is helpful to simply let the parties decide how they want to respond, even if there is a long period of silence. The rabbi does not need to step in just because there is silence. Moreover, eye contact, facial expressions, and gestures are also part of the rabbi's communication. Just by looking at the other party when one party seems to be finished speaking, the rabbi may unwittingly send the message that he is asking the second party to speak, and this may put pressure on a party who is not yet ready to respond. In other words, since silence and nonverbal messages can be used in a way that can direct the flow of the parties' communication, as well as in a way that can simply be supportive, the rabbi needs to consider the effect of silence as carefully as any verbal communication.

All of the above mediator's responses — *reflection, summary, checking in, questions,* and intentional silence — are used over and over again throughout the mediation. They are also used steadfastly, resisting the temptation to substitute other responses that are inconsistent with transformative theory. The rabbi should not "try out" transformative moves and then abandon the approach when the "going gets tough." This approach to mediation requires the rabbi to trust a process which allows the parties to deal with their differences, even when they are expressed in the midst of chaos, confusion, and high conflict. The rabbi must be able to summarize the confusion and the differences, as well as any negative views of each other that parties might express. The courage to do so comes from trusting the parties and their ability to make empowerment and recognition shifts, as well as the best decisions for themselves.

This approach also requires a certain degree of tentativeness in the use of responses. An "in-charge" rabbinic posture will interfere with the parties' empowerment and undermine the potential for shifts. Instead, the transformative rabbinic mediator needs to realize that his reflections or summaries may not be entirely accurate, and that they should therefore be presented in ways that allow and encourage correction by the parties. Similarly, questions should be asked in ways that allow parties to refrain from answering them if they so choose. The message in both words and the rabbi's "style" should be that this is the parties' process, not the rabbi's.

The preceding paragraphs describe the essential "hows" of transformative mediation. These are the primary skills needed to practice it effectively. The rabbi's personality and conversational style have an impact on how responses are used, but consistency in the use of the responses discussed here will make him an effective mediator. A rabbi should not act differently depending on what "kind" of case is involved. No new skills or special techniques are used in mediating family disputes, as compared with business or congregational conflicts. Indeed, the examples given above from the Stein/Gold case could equally have been drawn from a typical marital or business conflict. In all kinds of cases, the rabbi-mediator can be effective in helping his congregants if he uses the basic responses described and illustrated here.

Essential Skill: Avoiding Directive Responses

Using the essential skills of *reflection, summary, checking in,* and so on, the rabbi-mediator "follows" or "accompanies" the parties; he does not have a set agenda of steps to cover (Della Noce, 2001; Pope, 2001). The parties begin where they choose to begin, and in the course of the discussion, they talk about anything of importance to them. The mediator will not rule out any subject as inappropriate or unhelpful. The mediator will not tell the parties how to have their conversation, or when to continue or end it.

Directive impulses arise when a rabbi has his own view of what the parties should accomplish, such as reducing conflict or avoiding unfairness (Grillo, 1990). Such impulses will almost certainly get in the way of his continuing ability to "follow" the parties. For example, interrupting an argument about past events by turning the focus to the future, or by asking a question about another subject, substitutes the rabbi's judgment for the parties' as to the proper focus for discussion. To change the illustrative context, for the moment, to the family conflict arena: Why a husband walked out of a family event some months back, with no explanation to his wife, may be a crucial subject for discussion when the parties first appear for a mediation about their child's educational situation — even if it appears "irrelevant". The rabbi who tries to "focus" the discussion and refuses to allow discussion of the walk-out, is disrespectful of the parties and is not following them or helping them have the discussion they choose. And if it transpires that only one person wants to discuss that event and the other refuses, then that itself becomes the new subject for discussion and mediation.

In short, the rabbi as transformative mediator is not the director of the discussion. He will not tell the parties how to talk to each other or direct the course of their discussion or its content in any way. The rabbi-mediator positions himself as a reflective and helpful "conversational companion", regardless of what the parties choose to talk about (Folger and Bush, 1996). He supports, but never supplants, party decision making. He assists the parties with their decisions by helping to identify choice points throughout the conversation, and by restraining himself from making any decisions for the parties about the process itself or the substantive results. He respects the parties and their choices. He trusts the parties. He has confidence in them, the confidence that they know best, that they know what is right for them and their situation. He will not attempt to substitute his judgment for theirs. He will not try to steer them in the direction of what he thinks is the best arrangement for them. He will not decide what is fair for them, or what is unfair. He respects and trusts the parties to make those decisions for themselves. The rabbi-mediator is not trying to "get" the parties to do anything, whether to talk to each other, to stop arguing, or to live up to moral or halachic obligations.

So, while intensely engaged in listening and observing and enacting supportive responses, the rabbi-mediator constantly maintains an awareness of and represses directive impulses. In a dispute between an elderly parent and her children about her desire to move in with them after her spouse has passed away, the parent may say, "I just don't know what to do. I'm afraid to be on my own." An almost automatic response would be to explain that many people feel that way when they find themselves alone in later years, and then move the discussion on to the "real business" of finding a solution. But that response actually minimizes the feeling of the parent: the intense feeling is "normalized" and it is then ignored — perhaps with a referral to a popular book on aging. This is directive because the rabbi controlled the content of the discussion by characterizing the feeling and then moving the discussion onward. A supportive response that truly utilizes the opportunity for empowerment being presented would be to simply reflect the statement, as illustrated earlier, and then allow time for the parent to respond as she chooses. She might, in fact, choose to move on to other points; she might herself conclude that her fear is "just normal, I guess"; she might ask how to get help in dealing with her loss and her fears; she might elaborate further on how she feels, how her children are behaving, and what she wants to do about it. Any of these possible responses will be empowering for this parent who is feeling weak and confused at the moment.

There are many other kinds of directive impulses that frustrate empowerment and recognition shifts and, thus, conflict transformation:

> ► Trying to keep the parties "on track" or "moving the discussion along" interferes with the natural cycle of conversation between the parties.

> ► Pointing out "common ground", such as "You both really care about the shul" or "You both have fears about financial security," does little, if anything, to bring the parties together and probably obscures the real and important differences between them. Differences should not be downplayed in the attempt to find and stress common ground.

> ► Probing for what the rabbi believes are the "real, underlying issues" is leading, directive, and disrespectful of party autonomy. Following the parties in their discussion will highlight all of the issues they choose to put on the table. Pushing them, probing, and asking questions to get them to do more will be experienced as just that. The parties will feel they are being pushed, and opportunities for empowerment and recognition will almost certainly be lost.

▶ "Hypothesizing" by the rabbi about what is important to one of the parties, or what will be an acceptable settlement, detracts from the intense focus needed to understand what is actually going on right in front of the rabbi. Hypothesizing requires the rabbi to develop a line of questioning to follow up on and test the accuracy of his hypothesis; the result is the pursuit of the rabbi's agenda, not that of the parties, and the loss of focus on changing conflict interaction.

CONCLUSION

The skills employed by the transformative rabbinic-mediator are simple to name:

▶ Listening

▶ Reflecting

▶ Summarizing

▶ Questioning — to open doors, to invite further discussion on a subject raised by the parties

▶ Checking in — on what the parties want to do at a choice point in the discussion

▶ Backing out and being intentionally silent — to allow for party exchange or silent party deliberation

These are not complex skills to describe. They are, however, difficult to employ. It is much easier to allow our directive impulses to steer us into leading and guiding the discussion, and as a result, the outcome. Although it is difficult to stay with the parties through their cycles of conversation as they develop strength and understanding, doing so is the work of the transformative mediator, and it is the help that parties in conflict value most.

When mediating his congregants' conflicts using the transformative model, in short, the rabbi fulfills his rabbinic mission by helping them both solve their material problems and enhance their human moral stature. Learning to do this, through learning proper mediation skills, is a truly worthwhile preparation for assuming a position as a congregational rabbi and communal leader.

BIBLIOGRAPHY

Antes, J.R., Folger, J.P. & Della Noce, D.J. (2001). "Transforming Conflict in the Workplace: Documented Effects of the USPS REDRESS™ Program." *Hofstra Labor & Employment Law Journal, 18,* 429–467.

Beck, A.T. (1999). *Prisoners of Hate: The Cognitive Basis of Anger, Hostility, and Violence.* New York: HarperCollins Publishers.

Bush, R.A.B. (1996). "What Do We Need a Mediator for?" Mediation's Value-Added for Negotiators." *Ohio State Journal of Dispute Resolution* 12:1–36.

Bush, R.A.B., & Folger, J.P. (2nd edition, 2004). *The Promise of Mediation: The Transformative Approach to Conflict.* San Francisco: Jossey-Bass Publishers.

Della Noce, D.J. (2001). "Mediation as a Transformative Process: Insights on Structure and Movement," in *Designing Mediation: Approaches to Training and Practice within a Transformative Framework,* J.P. Folger & R.A.B. Bush (eds.), pp. 71–95. New York: Institute for the Study of Conflict Transformation.

Della Noce, D.J. (1999). "Seeing Theory in Practice: An Analysis of Empathy in Mediation." *Negotiation Journal* 15(3), 271–301.

Folger, J.P. & Bush, R.A.B. (eds.) (2001). *Designing Mediation: Approaches to Training and Practice within a Transformative Framework.* New York: Institute for the Study of Conflict Transformation.

Folger, J.P. & Bush, R.A.B. (1996). "Transformative Mediation and Third-Party Intervention: Ten Hallmarks of a Transformative Approach to

Practice." *Mediation Quarterly* 13 (4), 263–78.

Goleman, D. (1995). *Emotional Intelligence.* London: Bloomsbury Publishing.

Grillo, T. (1991). The Mediation Alternative: Process Dangers for Women. *Yale Law Journal* 100: 1545–1610.

Lind, E.A. & Tyler, T. (1988). *The Social Psychology of Procedural Justice.* New York: Plenum Press.

McCorkle, S. & Mills, J. (1992). "Rowboat in a Hurricane: Metaphors of Interpersonal Conflict." *Communications Reports* 5: 57–66.

Moen, J.K., Hudson, D.T., Antes, J.R., Jorgensen, E.O. & Hendrikson, L.H. (2001). "Identifying Opportunities for Empowerment and Recognition in Mediation," in *Designing Mediation: Approaches to Training and Practice within a Transformative Framework,* J.P. Folger & R.A.B. Bush (eds.), pp. 112–132. New York: Institute for the Study of Conflict Transformation.

O'Reilley, M.R. (1998). *Radical Presence: Teaching as Contemplative Practice.* Portsmouth: Boynton/Cook Publishers.

Pope, S.G. (2001). "Beginning the Mediation: Party Participation Promotes Empowerment and Recognition," in *Designing Mediation: Approaches to Training and Practice within a Transformative Framework,* J.P. Folger & R.A.B. Bush (eds.), pp. 85–95. New York: Institute for the Study of Conflict Transformation.

Rubin, J.Z., Pruitt, D.G. & Kim, S.H. (1994). *Social Conflict: Escalation, Stalemate, and Settlement,* 2nd edition. New York: McGraw-Hill.

✥ 18 ✥
RABBINIC CONFIDENTIALITY*

Sylvan J. Schaffer, J.D., Ph.D.

RABBINIC COUNSELING IS an essential thread in the religious, spiritual, social, and communal fabric of Jewish life. For some Jews, rabbinic guidance is the only available source of counseling, since they do not feel that a secular counselor has the cultural and religious familiarity and necessary sensitivity to satisfy their special religious and cultural requirements. In order to protect and encourage this vital service, rabbis need to feel safe and secure in their role as counselors.

Most rabbis fulfill the counseling role without being able to set the same boundaries provided in the other counseling relationships that people have with psychiatrists, psychologists, social workers, or lawyers. Professionals in these roles are guided, and may be sanctioned, by laws that establish a privilege that protects client/patient confidentiality. Rabbis provide counseling within the context of what is called the "clergy-penitent privilege", which delineates some boundaries on their communications with congregants.

The clergy-penitent (congregant) privilege is a legal rule of evidence that keeps confidential communications between a religious leader and a person seeking his spiritual guidance from

---

* The author wishes to thank Ian and Sabrina Schaffer for their invaluable help in writing this chapter.

being disclosed in court.[1] Generally, unless a person waives his or her right to have a confession or confidential discussion protected by the clergy-penitent privilege, a rabbi is not permitted to disclose such a communication. Yet, some communications do not fall within the context of spiritual guidance, and so are not necessarily protected. In some circumstances, congregants may make confessions or confide to the rabbi communications that must be disclosed in accordance with state laws. For example, many states require disclosure of child abuse and child sexual abuse. In most of these states, not disclosing information about this is a criminal offense.

Rabbis can get into trouble counseling congregants. Sometimes, if the congregant is involved in a lawsuit, he can try to use the clergy-penitent privilege to prevent disclosure of his criminal or other activities. In some states, a congregant can bring a lawsuit against his rabbi, after seeking his guidance, if he believes he received negligent counseling.

There are several important considerations for rabbis in their roles as counselors. Rabbis should make it clear to congregants that they are acting in the capacity of a spiritual leader or advisor. If what is communicated is spiritual in nature, and if spiritual guidance is requested, typically that communication will be protected. If a confession is made to a rabbi, not to obtain spiritual guidance, it is not protected. For example, if someone confesses to a crime, but not for spiritual reasons or guidance, the communication is not protected.

The rules of privilege are based on the following considerations:

▶ The communication must originate in a confidence.
▶ The element of confidentiality must be essential to maintaining the relationship of the parties to the communication.

> ► The relationship in question is one that society deems important to maintain.

> ► Damage to the relationship if the communication were disclosed would be greater than the benefit to the litigation.

There are various court opinions about who may invoke or assert that the privilege protects them from having to testify to the contents of a conversation. Some cases say that it is the congregant, others the clergy, and still other cases say both may invoke the privilege.[2]

Generally, having a third party present when the rabbi and congregant meet, unless the third party is essential to the communication, may mean that the congregant is waiving the privilege of keeping the communication confidential. The rabbi may want to explain to the person that it is important that the communication be kept in confidence and that the third party should not be present. In addition, if the congregant discloses a confidence to the rabbi and then later discloses basically the same confidence to the police, this could defeat the clergy-penitent privilege.

No specific clergy privilege is necessary under Jewish law,[3] since the prohibitions against disclosing any information, including confidential information, apply to all Jews equally. However, just as United States laws have mandated exceptions to the privilege — such as the requirement to report child abuse and the duty to warn about certain types of physical danger[4] — Jewish law also mandates certain exceptions to confidentiality. Jewish law obligates a Jew to breach confidentiality based on the admonition, " Do not stand by while your brother's blood is spilled."[5] However, the scope of Jewish law concerning the prevention of harm is broader than in the U.S. legal system. Under Jewish law, both physical and monetary harm must be prevented.[6]

In the past, members of the clergy did not consider themselves to be at risk for malpractice suits that were generally thought to be limited to professionals, such as physicians. However, in 1980, the case of *Nally v. Grace Community Church*[7] radically changed the legal status of the clergy. In light of that and other more recent cases such as *Lightman v. Flaum and Weinberger*,[8] it has become essential for rabbis to understand, consider, and plan for this particular risk when engaging in counseling.

For a negligence lawsuit against a rabbi to succeed, it must include the following components: First, there must be a duty on the part of the defendant (the rabbi) toward the plaintiff (the person counseled). In other words, by the nature of their relationship, there must be a finding that the rabbi has a certain responsibility toward the plaintiff. Second, there must be a breach of that duty. This means that either the rabbi failed to fulfill an obligation or did something he should not have done. Third, there must be a proximate (direct) connection between the action (or omission) of the rabbi and the harm that was caused. Finally, there must be a quantifiable amount the plaintiff seeks to be paid in compensation for his or her damages.

In the *Nally* case, the parents of a congregant sued four Protestant ministers and the congregation after their son, who had been counseled by the pastors, committed suicide. The son had been hospitalized for a suicide attempt during the counseling process. One of the pastors recommended that Mr. Nally seek psychological and medical help and that he be institutionalized, however, the parents rejected these recommendations. Mr. Nally continued to have further counseling sessions with a pastor, during which he discussed committing suicide. Subsequent to a family argument, he carried it out. His parents then sued the pastor, claiming clergy malpractice had been responsible for the wrongful death of their son. Part of their claim was that there was negligence in the pastor's training and outrageous conduct on his part.

The California Supreme Court ruled that the burden of proof was on the parents to show that the pastor had a duty to prevent suicide, because the pastor was a non-therapist counselor and it would have been contrary to public policy to create such a duty. This was especially true since the California legislature had specifically excluded clergy from the licensing requirements that were imposed on professional counselors. The court added that secular courts did not have the authority or competence to determine the practice standards of religious counselors. The court also wanted to avoid imposing a duty, since it would have implicated the government in the many theological approaches of religions and sects. Such an involvement would also have involved constitutional issues, such as the government's control of religion.

In 2001, the highest court in New York issued a ruling in the case of *Lightman v. Flaum and Weinberger,* which addressed several other liability/counseling/religious issues. Mrs. Lightman, who was in the process of obtaining a divorce, sued two rabbis for breach of confidentiality because they had issued separate affirmations about their independent encounters with her. In those affirmations, they said that she had told them she no longer observed ritual purification (*mikveh*). Rabbi Flaum's affirmation asserted that Mrs. Lightman told him that she was seeing a man in a social setting and admitted that, "I was doing the wrong things." She also brought a defamation claim against Rabbi Weinberger, whose affirmation contained a statement that she was no longer inclined, "to adhere to Jewish law despite the fact that she...was an Orthodox Jew and her children... were being raised Orthodox as well ... and that she engaged in bizarre behavior."

The rabbis believed that they had a religious duty to disclose these statements in order to prevent the husband from violating Jewish law by engaging in prohibited sexual relations with his wife. Furthermore, they believed that their disclosures were relevant to the matrimonial proceeding because they were relevant to the best interests of the children.

The wife claimed in her lawsuit that her communications with the rabbis were confidential, that the rabbis violated the New York clergy-penitent privilege law,[9] and that they had intentionally inflicted severe emotional distress upon her.

These cases raise the issue of the relationship between religious and secular law. Rabbinic counselors need to consider the following questions when they engage in counseling relationships:

> ► What secular laws apply to rabbinic practice?
> ► What happens if secular law contradicts Jewish law?
> ► What are the rules of confidentiality under secular and Jewish law?
> ► Is the rabbi who provides counseling serving as a rabbi or as a counselor?
> ► In a case such as *Lightman*, to whom does the rabbi have a duty, the person he is counseling, the children, the father, Jewish law, state law, to all or none of the above?
> ► What constitutes clergy malpractice under secular and religious law?
> ► In a litigious climate, what type of risk management should rabbis consider?
> ► Can a congregation be liable for the actions of its rabbi?

First, it is important to understand the basis for clergy liability. Rabbinic liability may arise from sources in both Jewish and secular law. By secular law, we mean American civil law, which is not necessarily uniform and may vary by jurisdiction.

It is also important to distinguish all the different functions that rabbis perform. Their functions may be divided into the three following categories: pastoral, theological, and quasi-judicial. In the pastoral realm, rabbis may provide counseling and guidance for their community, especially their own congregants. In the ritual realm, they may provide rulings on religious issues, such as *kashrut* and Sabbath rules. In the quasi-judicial area, they may serve on rabbinical courts and issue rulings regarding marital and financial matters. In any of these areas, they may err and the issue of liability may arise.

Under Jewish law, rabbis may be held liable in certain circumstances when acting in the role of judge or counselor.[10] If a rabbi's decision goes directly against a well-known precedent (*d'var mishneh*), it may be reversed.[11] Although there is some debate about what constitutes a well-known precedent,[12] the concept of ruling contrary to precedent and reversal of such decisions exists. In many such cases, where irreversible damages occur pursuant to a rabbinical decision, the rabbi is not held liable for damages in order to protect professionals from non-negligent errors. There is a debate, however, about whether a rabbi is liable for misapplication of the law.[13]

If the rabbi's error was due to his opinion — that is, he weighed conflicting authorities in arriving at his decision — his liability will be based on the level of his legal competence, his authority to make such rulings, and whether he personally enforced the decision.[14] If the rabbi serves as a counselor and advisor, he is, in part, governed by the prohibition against bad advice, "Thou shalt not place a stumbling block before the blind."[15] However, bad advice may not be considered to be a cause of action, since advice and counseling consist of words, which may not constitute action under Jewish law.[16]

One similarity between Jewish law and secular law involves, as mentioned above, the issue of proximate cause. A rabbi may be liable under some circumstances, if his advice resulted in direct harm,[17] but may not be liable if the result came from an indirect cause (*grama*).[18] A third category, which seems to lie somewhere between proximate cause and *grama*, is called *garmi*, and its description is beyond the scope of this chapter.[19]

In addition to liability based on negligent actions, the courts have considered possible clergy liability for intentional damages. In *Hester v. Barnett*,[20] the plaintiff claimed that the clergyman committed defamation, alienation of affections, ministerial malpractice, invasion of privacy, and intentional infliction of emotional distress. In this case there may have been a clear intent on the part of the clergyman to help, despite the fact that the family perceived the outcome to be negative. The minister counseled the family and reported that the parents were abusive and that the children should leave the home. The family claimed that the minister defamed them by making reports to the child abuse hotline and writing letters. The court had to balance the minister's right to counsel his congregants — under the free exercise clause of the Constitution, which protects the unfettered practice of his religion — with the needs of the parents to be protected against someone interfering with their private lives.

In another case which involved divorce, the father sued the church, a bishop, and his mother-in-law for alienating his wife and children and hiding the children in the home of a church member. The defendants also attempted to proselytize the children, in violation of a court order. The court ruled that the minister's intrusive actions could serve as the basis for a finding of invasion of privacy.[21]

The *Hester* and *O'Neil* cases could be relevant to rabbis who participate in helping non-Orthodox children become Orthodox (*kiruv*). At times, this could include having the children enroll in yeshivas without their parents' consent, helping the children to move to Israel, or distancing them from their non-practicing parents. Such involvement with minor children could lead to liability suits by the parents against the rabbis, their *kiruv* organizations, and the yeshivas that the children attend. Assuming that the rabbi is found liable for some cause of action, under the legal principles of vicarious liability or employer responsibility, a synagogue or organization for which the rabbi works could also be held liable under certain circumstances. Therefore, both the rabbi and the congregation need to carry appropriate liability insurance. Rabbis and their employers should also be aware when working with minors without their parents' consent that some activities could carry criminal as well as civil penalties.

There is another situation of potentially conflicting goals for which the *Hester* case may have relevance. If a Jewish man and a non-Jewish woman seek premarital counseling from a rabbi, the goals of the couple may be contrary to the values and perceived mandate of the rabbi. While they may seek assistance in developing a stronger relationship in their planned marriage, the rabbi might feel that he is required to advise the man against a relationship that would be contrary to Jewish law. The act on the part of the rabbi is intentional, but from the rabbi's perspective, it is without a malicious intent. In addition, the rabbi needs to assess whether the consulting couple actually wants him to express his religious views or simply counsel them on their relationship. In such situations, a clear delineation of goals and expectations is especially important in order to avoid potential liability.

This type of situation highlights one of the most critical issues in rabbinic counseling — to whom does the rabbi owe his allegiance? The role of a secular therapist is more clearly defined than that of a rabbi. Professional codes of ethics, as well as state regulations, generally prohibit dual relationships and require the therapist to focus on the needs of the patient while being culturally sensitive to the patient's values. Even if a therapist makes a clinical recommendation or intervention that differs from the goals of the patient, it must be done solely to benefit the patient.

A rabbi may believe he is required to implement a religious value system that may not be directly related to the clinical questions posed by the patient. For example, a *kohen* (a Jew of the priestly tribe) may come to the rabbi for premarital counseling with his fiancée, who is a divorcee. The rabbi may view them as perfectly compatible from a clinical perspective, but may deem them incompatible under Jewish law, since a divorcee is biblically prohibited to a *kohen*.[22] It is essential that a rabbi/counselor be conscious of these potential conflicts and make sure that those he spiritually counsels are aware of and accept this dual value system.

Another potential conflict arises in situations involving suspected child abuse. A rabbi may believe that he is not permitted to reveal confidential information to government authorities, but may simultaneously wish to protect the victims. To date, most states mandate that licensed professionals report suspected abuse, but do not mandate the clergy. As a result of the recent reports about clergymen abusing children, there is a growing pressure on other clergy who learn about such abuse, even from confidential communications, to disclose what they have heard. Religious organizations are increasingly subject to liability claims in these situations, and the courts are in the process of redefining their areas of liability.

In discussing clergy malpractice and confidentiality, it is important to define who qualifies as clergy. A federal court ruled[23] that, although not codified, the Advisory Committee's definition of clergy for the Federal Rules of Evidence could be used as a starting point.[24] This definition states that a clergyman within the privilege was "a minister, priest, rabbi, or other similar functionary of a religious organization, or an individual reasonably believed to be so by the person consulting him." Courts have also included non-ordained assistants, whose functions were primarily religious.[25] In other situations, non-ordained counselors were not considered clergy, despite the fact that they functioned under church auspices, due to the fact that their job was closer to that of a social worker than a spiritual guide.[26]

Cases in which the clergy counselor engages in a physical relationship with the congregant present an interesting situation.[27] Courts have ruled that although such behavior is not condoned by the various religions, the clergyman may not be held to the standard of a professional counselor for whom it is specifically prohibited. The courts generally will not entertain the action for clergy malpractice when another tort (a wrong committed by one person against another) is available. In addition, the clergyman may not be acting within his religious role, since such behavior is not part of the religious counseling. However, the congregant could conceivably bring an action on other grounds, such as breach of contract as discussed above, because the clergyman failed to provide the type of counseling promised. Furthermore, while in the past, some courts may have been reluctant to find clergy malpractice, recent events involving sexual activity between clergy and congregants and the reaction to this from courts and prosecutors may signal a new trend toward greater accountability.

It is important to note that a rabbi who is also a psychologist, and who provides counseling, may be judged on the basis of two different standards. If he treats private patients for a fee in a private office, he will most likely be held to the same practice standard as any other psychologist. If, however, he provides religious guidance in his role as a rabbi, the spiritual counseling standard will be applied. The person seeking such guidance need not be a member of the rabbi's congregation and, in fact, need not be Jewish.

For the clergy privilege to apply, it must have religious content and must be received by the clergyman in his religious capacity.[28] In one well-known murder case,[29] a husband, who had stabbed his pregnant wife, went to speak with an Orthodox rabbi from New York. In court, the husband claimed that privilege should apply since he had consulted the rabbi for spiritual advice. The rabbi, on the other hand, testified that he had been contacted in a secular capacity, in order to help the man find an attorney and use his influence to negotiate a settlement. The court ruled that although New York recognizes the clergy-penitent privilege,[30] not every confession made to a clergyman is privileged, especially if it was not made for the purpose of religious counsel.[31]

The standard for breaching confidences is based on several factors:[32]

- ► There must be an intention to prevent harm.
- ► The person must be motivated by an urge to help and not by animosity.
- ► The least damaging form of revelation should be used.
- ► An instruction must be given not to repeat the information.
- ► The information should be limited to the minimum amount necessary to accomplish the goal. Broyde et al. also discuss exceptions to the mandated disclosure rules, such as when the rabbi may suffer harm as a result of his disclosure.[33]

In the *Lightman* case discussed above, the highest court in New York ruled in favor of the rabbis who made disclosures of confidences. The court ruled that although New York granted a privilege to the rabbis, it did not provide for any penalties if the rabbis breached a confidence. The court said, "In this appeal, we must decide whether CPLR 4505 imposes a fiduciary duty of confidentiality upon members of the clergy that subjects them to civil liability for the disclosure of confidential communications. We hold that it does not." The court said that a violation of the privilege would not subject the clergymen to a legal action. The court also indicated that it was reluctant to determine whether the rabbis' disclosure followed religious law, since such involvement had "troubling constitutional implications."

In order to protect and encourage the vital service of rabbinic counseling, rabbis need to feel safe and secure in their roles. In order to limit rabbis' exposure to liability, the following recommendations should be seriously considered:

> ► Skills necessary for the practice of religious counseling should become a component of rabbinic training. These skills would supplement the knowledge that rabbis already receive in Jewish law and philosophy.

> ► Rabbis should be trained to identify problem areas which may be beyond the scope of ordinary spiritual counseling, and which may require a referral to a mental health specialist. This training is especially important in the identification of potential dangers.

> ► Rabbis, synagogues, and religious organizations should develop protocols that deal with suicide risk, divorce, child abuse, minors, and other counseling situations.

> ► Rabbis and their employers should obtain liability insurance.

> ► Rabbis should be careful about the complexities inherent in dual relationships with those whom they counsel. When issues concerning potential conflicts of values or

roles arise, it is suggested that rabbis discuss these issues with those being counseled.

► Although rabbis are accustomed to giving advice and making rulings on Jewish law, they should also seek advice for themselves from other rabbis and, if necessary, from attorneys. In doing so, they may wish to participate in risk management programs to learn about the potential pitfalls in their work. Rabbis should keep in mind that even the best of caregivers might at times be in need of assistance.

NOTES

1. *United States v. Gordon*, 655 F2d 478 (1981, CA2 NY).

2. Donaldson, R.G., *American Law Reports*, 118 A.L.R. Fed 449, at Section 10.

3. *New York Civil Practice Law and Rules*, section 4505.

4. *Matter of Keenan v. Gigante*, 417 N.Y.S.2d 226; cert. Denied 100 S. Ct. 181.

5. Broyde, M., Reiss,Y. and Diament, N., *Confidentiality and Rabbinic Counseling*.

6. *Id.* at 297 (prohibitions).

7. *Nally v. Grace Church of the Valley* (1987, 2nd Dist.) 194 Cal App 3d 1147; cert denied 109 S Ct 1644.

8. *Lightman v. Flaum*, 736 N.Y.S.2d 300.

9. *New York Practice Rules*, Section 4505.

10. Dratch, M., "Suing Your Rabbi: Clergy Malpractice in Jewish Law," *Journal of Halacha and Contemporary Society*, Vol. XVIII, 62–76.

11. *Shulchan Aruch, Choshen Mishpat* 25.

12. *Pitchei Teshuvah* 2.

13. Dratch, footnote 16.

14. Dratch, at 65.

15. Leviticus 19:14.

16. *Teshuvot HaRashba*, 99.

17. Dratch, at 66.

18. Talmud *Bava Kama* 59b.

19. Albeck, S. Gerama and Garmi, *Encyclopedia Judaica*, VII pp. 430–431.

20. *Hester v. Barnett*, 723 SW2d 544 (1987, Mo App).

21. *O'Neil v. Shuckhardt*, 112 Idaho 472 (1987).

22. Leviticus 21:7.

23. *Re Grand Jury Investigation*, 918 F2d 374 (1990, CA3 Pa).

24. Donaldson, R.G., *American Law Reports*, 118 A.L.R. Fed 449.

25. *Re Verplank*, 329 F. Supp 433 (1971, CD Cal).

26. *Re Wood*, 430 F Supp 41 (1977, SDNY).

27. *Hester v. Barnett*, 723 SW2d 544 (1987, Mo App); *Destefano v. Grabrian*, 763 P2d 275 (1988, Colo).

28. *United States v. Gordon*, 655 F2d 478 (1981, CA2 NY).

29. *People v. Dreilich*, 506 N.Y.S.2d (N.Y.A.D. 2 Dept, 1986); *U.S. v. Dube*, 820 F2d 886, (1987, CA7 Ill).

30. *United States v. Gordon*, 655 F2d 478 (1981, CA2 NY).

31. *Matter of Keenan v. Gigante*, 417 N.Y.S.2d 226; cert. Denied 100 S. Ct. 181.

32. Broyde, et al., id.; Chofetz Chaim, *Rechilut*, 9:1–15.

33. Broyde, et al., id.

REFERRING TO A MENTAL HEALTH PROFESSIONAL

Norman Blumenthal, Ph.D.

SOME THINGS IN LIFE look easier than they really are. A referral to a mental health professional is one of them. What might seem no more complicated than handing over a phone number and address is, in actuality, a sensitive and involved process requiring a familiarity with the field and the internal battle a person goes through before admitting he has a problem and agreeing to go for psychotherapy.

Often at the forefront of this process, the rabbi needs to be familiar with the various types of professionals, treatment modalities, as well as the challenge of effecting the transition from the rabbi's office to the psychotherapist's. While it is beyond the scope of this chapter to cover all these matters, a rabbi must acquire and maintain some familiarity with these matters as well as an appreciation for the complexity of this process.

WHO ARE THE MENTAL HEALTH PROFESSIONALS?

There are several considerations that come into play when deciding to make a referral. In general, there is no official licensure for a psychotherapist. It is therefore legal in many states for *anyone* to declare him/herself a psychotherapist. One must be careful to only refer to those who are properly credentialed and trained.

There is no doubt that a certain intuition and innate sensitivity is necessary for many of the psychotherapeutic interventions. There are gifted people who are almost natural healers or therapists. However, no matter how talented one is, there is no substitute for formal training and supervision provided by universities and institutes. It is no different than one who is innately musical trying to succeed as a performer without any practice or training.

Given the different types of professionals in this field, it is often confusing and difficult to navigate the referral process. In addition, states and regions differ in terms of whom they accredit and for what. One needs to be familiar with the local statutes and any changes in legislation that may have a bearing on whom is considered sufficiently trained and prepared for this work.

The following are descriptions of some professionals, as well as their general areas of expertise or exclusive practice. Once again, the reader is cautioned that these descriptions can vary from region to region or from one training setting to another.

Psychiatrists

Psychiatrists complete full medical training (earning the degree of M.D. or D.O.), followed by an internship and residency in this area of expertise. These residencies generally take four years, during which time most of the exposure and training is in the areas of diagnosis, psychopharmacology (i.e., medication), and psychotherapy. In recent years, instruction in the area of the biology of mental illness and its more medical treatments have been emphasized, in some places, over training in psychotherapy. This is partly because there are so many other types of practitioners providing psychotherapy these days, and the range and effectiveness of medication has increased greatly. Nevertheless, the vast majority of psychiatrists still receive supervision and training in psychotherapy. Besides being credentialed as physicians, psychiatrists can be board certified in psychiatry and have a subspecialty in areas such as childhood and adolescence, forensics, consultation and liaison (interfacing with general medical disorders), and geriatric medicine.

Generally speaking, psychiatrists prescribe psychotropic medication. In some locales, nurse practitioners can also prescribe medication, and there is a movement to allow psychologists limited prescription privileges akin to dentistry and optometry. These efforts have been met with strong resistance from the medical profession, but have nonetheless succeeded in several settings.

Psychologists

Psychologists generally complete a Doctorate (Ph.D. or Psy.D.) in a graduate school setting, followed by a one- or two-year internship and, in some states, a year of supervised post-doctoral experience. In addition to both instruction in psychotherapy and clinical experience in placements at the graduate level, psychologists are trained in testing (used for educational purposes), diagnosis, and forensics. Many psychologists engage in post-doctoral training, as well, in areas such as psychoanalysis, family and marital therapy, and cognitive behavioral therapy.

Social Workers

Social workers generally do two years of graduate training to receive a Masters degree. Often, the first year is focused on case management and community work, while the second year involves lectures and placement with a clinical emphasis including psychotherapy. Following their graduation, they can receive further accreditation for supervised clinical experience (e.g., A.C.S.W., L.C.S.W.) Social workers often choose to complete post-graduate training in areas of specialty such as family therapy. Some social workers complete a Doctorate as well (D.S.W.).

Counselors

A relatively new type of professional that is achieving increased recognition is that of the counselor. The focus of a counselor's training is the application of treatment strategies to address wellness and growth, as well as pathology and problems. A related field is that of marriage and family therapists, with specific and extensive training in those areas.

The above descriptions are not exhaustive nor fully descriptive, given the differences between various training programs and locales. It is important to note that even within these various professional modalities there are areas of sub-specialization. These include, but are not limited to, forensics, child/adolescent, family/marital, trauma, addictions treatment, and eating disorders. To adequately address the needs of such distinct areas of specialization, the mental health professional generally needs additional training, certification, and/or supervised clinical experience.

TREATMENT MODALITIES

Mental health is a relatively young profession, characterized by rapid growth and expansion. As a result, there are an ever-growing plethora of theories and interventions, many of which have a host of advocates and detractors. Using very broad strokes, the following are the most common types of treatment and approaches.

Psychotherapy

Since Freud first wrote about a talking treatment, there have developed numerous approaches to therapy, some seemingly diametrically opposed. While there are those who promote one or a cluster of similar treatments, many therapists "beg and borrow" using that which most suits the situation. Sometimes the therapy reflects the therapist's own life experiences and outlooks. It has often been suggested that more important than the type of therapy practice is the practitioner and his or her particular skill.

Psychoanalysis and Psychodynamic Psychotherapy

With its origins in Freud, psychoanalysis is an intensive long-term treatment in which the patient attends several sessions a week. During the course of this treatment, the patient — through recollections, dreams, and his relationship with the analyst — brings unconscious issues to awareness and relives childhood issues that are subsequently subject to interpretation and change. While psychoanalysis remains a relatively rare treatment reserved for those so inclined and able to afford it, many more modern techniques have their roots in the theories and practices of this treatment. The more current "psychoanalytically oriented" treatments are shorter, more likely involve once a week sessions, and focus more on current relationships and concerns. The basic tenet of these techniques is that with the increased awareness of unconscious drives and outlooks achieved in the safety of the clinician's office, the patient can grow emotionally and overcome personal obstacles in his or her life.

Behavior Therapy

Standing in sharp contrast to psychoanalysis and its sequelae are the behavioral interventions. More empirical in theory, these techniques involve altering one's environment to effect change, particularly through systems involving rewards and punishments. Used more often with children and the more psychiatrically ill, the behavior therapist does not involve himself in the thoughts or emotions of his patient, but rather in those responses that shape or alter behavior. Some techniques involve associating more soothing responses with that which had elicited fear and agitation. These techniques are increasingly used for anxiety or panic disorders, including obsessive-compulsive disorder.

Cognitive Behavioral Therapy

An increasingly accepted approach that in many respects combines psychoanalysis and behavior theory is cognitive behavioral therapy. Simply put, the premise is that erroneous or ill-conceived thoughts or "cognitions" undermine one's well-being and need to be reassessed and changed. These techniques originated in the treatment of depression, with the assumption that negative and pessimistic thoughts contribute to a morose outlook.

Family/Marital Therapy

Some clinicians specialize in the treatment of families or marital couples. More often than not, the whole family or both members of the couple are together in the room for the therapy, while conflict and interpersonal tensions are addressed and resolved. There are numerous schools of family therapy, each with their own institutes for post-graduate training. Their theories include those that look at the family or couple as a "system", with carefully tuned patterns of interaction. Others emphasize communication, family histories, sexual dysfunction and remedies, as well as various roles each family member plays.

Group Psychotherapy

An effective and fully legitimized form of mental health treatment is group psychotherapy. This can be a very efficient way of providing services to those who cannot afford individual psychotherapy or where community charitable organizations are unable to pay the expense of individual psychotherapy. Groups can be "homogenous" or "heterogeneous", depending on whether there is a narrow focus to the group or broader goals. Children with social difficulties can often benefit from social skills training groups. Patients often describe the realization that others have had similar problems as the most effective part of this treatment. There are post-doctoral training programs in group psychotherapy.

Medication

Medications aimed at reducing psychotic symptoms, depression, anxiety, or hyperactivity are an integral part of the treatment of mental illness. There have been huge strides made in the development of effective medications that cause relatively few side effects. While not only relieving painful and disruptive symptoms, medication is often prescribed hand in hand with psychotherapy. Less burdened by distracting and debilitating symptoms, the patient can make more optimal use of psychotherapy and may more quickly reach the point when neither treatment is needed. It is not uncommon that as psychotherapy progresses the dosages of medication are reduced, if not eliminated.

Even if medication is required on a long term or permanent basis, it is well-established that many psychiatric conditions have a significant biological or genetic basis and such a regimen is no different than medication taken by those with diabetes, hypertension, and the like, who need maintenance medication for their health and functioning. Compliance with medication requirements is a perennial problem that a rabbi can help combat, both by encouraging the patient to adhere to the whole treatment plan and by publicly addressing the need to de-stigmatize mental illness and to recognize that many types of psychiatric disturbances have a strong biological or constitutional base. Even when life circumstances and stressors are at the root of the emotional disturbance (e.g., Post Traumatic Stress Disorder), medication can reduce the severity of the response and facilitate the patient's recovery.

Medication is generally prescribed by psychiatrists, though some neurologists, pediatricians, and family physicians will dispense medication — especially if the symptoms appear contained and easily diagnosed. Sometimes the initial evaluation and prescription will be provided by the psychiatrist and followed up with renewals and routine examinations for side effects by the general practitioner. In some areas, nurse practitioners and physician assistants are permitted to prescribe or renew medication.

A rabbi, teacher, or any lay professional should never directly recommend medication. Just as one would not recommend surgery or dental implants, it is beyond the scope of the rabbi's role, training, and expertise to declare that someone needs psychotropic medication, even if it seems eminently indicated. A more palatable and safe approach is to recommend a psychiatric evaluation and defer the decision whether medication is needed to the professional trained in that area.

HOSPITALIZATION

Inpatient Psychiatric

There are times when one's functioning is so compromised that he or she needs the more intensive treatment and even confinement of a psychiatric hospital. This is especially the case when the person is a danger to himself and others. Most large or teaching hospitals have psychiatric units and often the patient will be admitted to the one where his doctor has an affiliation. If there is a psychiatric emergency at night or on weekends or holidays when the physician is unavailable, it is perfectly acceptable and indicated to call an ambulance or to imperatively transport the patient to an emergency room and ask to have him or her psychiatrically evaluated.

Generally speaking, psychiatric hospitalization is voluntary and can only be implemented with the knowing consent of the patient or guardian. Once hospitalized, the patient or parent can have the patient discharged without medical consent within days of the request. In extreme circumstances, where the patient is deemed dangerous (e.g., suicidal or violent), two physicians can hospitalize the patient against his/her will.

Due to the combination of budget constraints and the availability of more effective medical interventions, the lengths of psychiatric hospital stays have been significantly reduced. In essence, the mandate of the hospital is to stabilize the patient as quickly as possible and arrange for appropriate aftercare. For this reason, the transition from the hospital to outpatient care and follow up is extremely important and becomes a consideration from the very onset of hospitalization.

Leaving a loved one, particularly a child, in a hospital setting is a heart-wrenching experience for which the family needs ongoing support and encouragement. The active involvement of the family and community in the care of the inpatient directly affects the success of this treatment.

As a transition to outpatient treatment or even as an initial course, there are day hospital programs that the patient can attend throughout the morning and afternoon, and then he can return home at night. School settings are available in these as well as inpatient settings provided by the local board of education.

Drug Rehabilitation

Adults and teenagers who have become addicted or markedly dependent on drugs or alcohol may need to attend an inpatient or day program. These programs tend to be more long term and are structured with an awareness of the compelling nature of such addictions. Often based on the proven track record of the so-called 12–step programs (e.g., Alcoholics Anonymous, Narcotics Anonymous), the patient may have limited or no contact with family or friends during at least the initial phase of this treatment. The interventions are often very direct and intense, with an eye to combat that which is biologically addictive.

There are comparable inpatient settings for eating disorders, gambling addictions, weight problems and the like, each tailored to the needs of that particular patient population and the dangers their behaviors pose.

THE REFERRAL PROCESS

Using broad strokes, one could divide the process of a rabbi referring to a mental health professional into two categories. One involves the congregant who curtly and with no elaboration calls for the name of a therapist or psychiatrist. Given the sensitivity required by such matters, it is probably ill-conceived to ask why, or to offer any follow up, or to even contemplate contacting the clinician. It is probably best to give two or three names, with some indication of their particular strengths and weaknesses, and leave it at that. The congregant may feel self-conscious and the rabbi should use the utmost caution not to reflect any additional concern or interest when subsequently meeting him.

Another route through which the rabbi may make a referral is when the congregant comes for rabbinic counseling or advice. While the congregant may be forthright or to the point about what brings him there, it is not uncommon for it to take longer. As a famous psychiatrist once put it: "Patients come to therapy for two reasons. One is to change and the other is to stay the same." Sometimes exhaustive questions about religious observance are really an attempted or awkward segue into more personally compelling and potentially shameful matters. These inquiries, especially if repetitive and picayune, may also reflect an obsessive-compulsive disorder expressed through overly meticulous religious observance. The rabbi's patience and skill in evaluating what is needed will be invaluable at such times.

In communities where social interaction between men and women is minimal and discouraged, female congregants may feel at a disadvantage when consulting the rabbi. Their contact may have been limited, while their husbands see the rabbi daily. Especially with regard to marital matters, it is not uncommon to hear wives complain that the rabbi is either biased or predisposed in many ways to the husband. This engenders a resistance or mistrust, impeding the counseling and referral process. The rabbi needs to assure the wife of his objectivity and receptivity to her perspective. If the *rebbetzin* or local female educator is so disposed and properly trained, she can be of invaluable assistance in this regard.

A nearly intangible but crucial decision is determining at which point such contact needs to shift from the rabbi to the therapist. While a clear and perfectly defined rule is impossible, there are a number of guidelines that can be considered. If a bona fide mental illness is detected, then referral to a psychiatrist or other mental health professional is indicated (partly dependent on the severity of the perceived malady). It will also matter how pervasive the problem is—is it limited to religious observance or has it penetrated all aspects of the congregant's life? An example may be a congregant who complains about a lack of enthusiasm and involvement in religious observance, but it soon becomes apparent that this apathy is pervading his family and social life as well. The rabbi should trust his internal barometer and consider making a referral or seeking assistance if he feels in over his head.

At this juncture, the rabbi needs to initiate the *process* of a referral. He can introduce the idea by explaining why these issues are outside the rubric of what a rabbi addresses and assure his congregant that he will participate in and oversee the transition. Research has shown that prospective patients who are oriented to the therapy process fare better than those who aren't (Hoen-Saric, 1964). It therefore behooves the rabbi to explain how therapy works and what to anticipate. The congregant can be provided with two or three names, including an explanation of why the rabbi feels each would be particularly suited to his needs. He can offer to make the initial call to be in touch with the therapist as the treatment is initiated, and even to be consulted if necessary during the course of treatment. This may be particularly indicated if the issues that the person or couple is addressing have religious overtones. For example, a couple dealing with fertility issues may need assistance with understanding both the divinely visited challenge as well as some of the halachic matters with regard to interventions, tests, and the observance of *mikveh*. In such instances, the ongoing participation of the rabbi is essential. Even when there aren't such obvious religious connections, the rabbi's continued interest and concern are helpful and ease the transition to the therapist. The rabbi may also want to see how effective the therapist is with this particular case in order to decide whether to send him more patients. Careful not to become intrusive, the rabbi could simply inquire from time to time about how things are going. If the impact of his question is one of caring, it will be well received.

A bedrock of psychotherapy is confidentiality. In order for patients to feel fully comfortable revealing potentially shameful concerns and life events, they need to know, beyond a shadow of a doubt, that the matters discussed will never leave the therapist's office. While there are extreme situations when confidentiality may be overridden (e.g., when the patient is a danger to himself or others), the rabbi must respect this aspect of the therapeutic relationship and obtain signed consent from his congregant in order to converse with the therapist about him. Even with the patient's consent, the therapist may choose to be circumspect about certain matters when discussing the case with the rabbi.

The Therapist's Own Level of Observance or Religious Affiliation

One of the many conundrums of the therapy process relates to aspects of the therapist's personal life and its bearing on his effectiveness in healing others. Is it advantageous or disadvantageous, for example, if the therapist lived through the same kind of experience as his patient? Would a war veteran be better off with a therapist who also experienced combat or would such a therapist be less effective for him? Can a therapist from another country or culture understand a patient as well as one who has been raised in the same town and milieu? Perhaps, if the therapist's upbringing is too similar, he or she may jump to conclusions without taking the time to properly inquire and learn about the patient. These judgments may need to be made on a case-by-case basis. Certainly one consideration is whether the overlapping issues are current and pressing versus ones that the therapist has already addressed and incorporated into his work and personality.

For the rabbi, probably the most compelling concern is whether he is obliged to refer to a therapist whose level of observance and religious beliefs are compatible with that of his congregation or his own. Several matters need to be considered regarding this. There are some approaches in psychology, particularly classical psychoanalysis, which have a somewhat scornful and denigrating view of religion. (Freud [1939], for example, proclaimed that, "We can only regret it if certain experiences of life, and experiences of nature, have made it impossible to accept the hypothesis of such a Supreme Being.") Nevertheless, there is today fairly compelling evidence that a religious affiliation is salutary and with these findings has come a greater respect for religion and spirituality (George, Ellison, and Larson, 2002). In addition, it has become increasingly accepted that there is no such thing as "value-free psychotherapy." Even in instances when the therapist makes a genuine effort to remain tolerant and respectful of a belief system that is not his or her own, sentiments are often inadvertently conveyed through nods, facial expressions, offhanded comments and the like. Many therapists marvel at how quickly and accurately patients size up their therapists despite the therapists' best efforts to remain neutral and personally private. (I have found this to be particularly true of children, adolescents, and adults who have been either abandoned or orphaned at a young age). Therapists often become very important to their patients, and it is, therefore, only natural that the one who is dependent in the relationship seeks to understand and carefully read his or her caretaker.

If there is a discrepancy between the religious beliefs of the patient and therapist, the rabbi needs to consider what potential influence this will have on his congregant. The famous and revered Rabbi Moshe Feinstein, in a printed response to a question, addresses this matter (*Igrot Moshe, Yoreh De'ah* 2:57). While allowing religious patients to receive medical care from the most expert physician, notwithstanding his or her religious beliefs, he states a distinct preference that a psychotherapist for an observant patient share a commitment to Torah values and Halachah. If such an arrangement is impractical or impossible, there should be an understanding or agreement that religious matters will not be broached during therapy (Fox, 1992). In a smaller community, where everyone knows one another, a congregant may be hesitant to disclose very personal matters to someone he sees regularly in shul. In contrast, larger cities harbor a wider selection of therapists with varied religious affiliations and sufficient geographical diversity so that the anonymity and religious beliefs of the patient can be preserved. Certainly, the risks are different for an adult with embedded religious beliefs than for a more impressionable teenager or young adult with burgeoning ideas and curiosity. Fitting sensitivity for the congregant's needs within the guidelines of Halachah and Torah is the mandate and challenge of the rabbi in the delicate process of referring for mental health services.

BIBLIOGRAPHY

Buckley, M.A. and Zimmerman, S. H. 2003. *Mentoring Children and Adolescents: A Guide to the Issues.* Westport: Praeger Publishers.

Fox, D. 1992. *Journal of Halacha and Contemporary Society* 23.

Freud, S. 1939. *Moses and Monotheism*, New York: Vintage Books.

George, L.K., Ellison, C.G. & Larson, D.B. 2002. "Explaining the Relationship Between Religious Involvement and Health," *Psychological Inquiry*, July, 13:190–200.

Hoen-Saric, R. 1964. "Systematic Preparation of Preparation of Patients for Psychotherapy," *Journal of Psychotherapy Research* 2: 267–281.

Levinson, D., Lerner, Y. & Lichtenberg, P. 2003. "Reduction in Inpatient Length of Stay and Changes in Mental Health Care in Israel over Four Decades: A National Case Register Study," *Israel Journal of Psychiatry and Related Sciences* 40 (4): 240–247.

Mechanic, D., McAlpine, D.D. & Olfson, M. 1988. "Changing Patterns of Psychiatric Inpatient Care in the United States, 1988–1994," *Archives of General Psychiatry* 55: 785–791.

THE RABBI AND HIS FAMILY

Yisrael N. Levitz, Ph.D

IN RECENT YEARS THERE has been a growing concern about the impact of rabbinic life on the rabbi and his family. In contrast to other families, the rabbinic family is not only socially more visible, but psychologically more vulnerable. Always in the public eye, the rabbi's family is subject to constant scrutiny, unrealistic expectations, distorted projections, and community intrusiveness. In all too many instances they suffer economic insecurity and frequent mobility as well (Silverstein, 1979).

In addition to the many pressures emanating from outside the family sphere, it is not uncommon for there to be many stresses emanating from within the family, as well. The rabbinate, like any other labor-intensive profession, requires an inordinately high level of commitment that can easily engulf the rabbi's life. Like an *"eretz ochelet yoshveha"* ("a land that devours its inhabitants"), the rabbinate is more than just a profession. It is an all-encompassing lifestyle that can absorb a rabbi to the point where he has neither time for himself nor his family.

This strain commonly experienced in rabbinic families can potentially affect their stability. The overwhelming complaint of most divorced clergy wives was, in fact, that their husbands devoted excessive time and energy tending to the needs of their congregation at the expense of their own families (Hutchinson and Nichols, 1980). Some researchers (Freedman, 1985) have found that out of the 30% of rabbis sampled, their wives wished that their husbands were not rabbis.

Given the complex nature of the rabbinate and its weighty demands, rabbis face unusual challenges in successfully fulfilling their roles as husbands and fathers. In order to succeed in the family arena, as well as the community sphere, rabbis need to develop a special sensitivity to the impact of rabbinic life on the members of their families, negotiate the many demands of the rabbinate, and be mindful of their priorities.

CHILDREN OF RABBIS

Family therapists have long assumed that children are a family's best measure of internal stress. Like barometers, they most accurately reflect the pressures found in their family life. For this reason I undertook a study to determine the impact of the rabbinate on children raised in rabbinic families (*Tradition*, winter 1988, vol. 23, no. 2).

Not surprisingly, children of congregational rabbis showed many of the same stresses experienced by children of clergy in general. It is well-known, for example, that the higher expectations placed upon children of clergy create for them inordinate difficulties in growing up. Consequently, children of clergy experience feelings of isolation and inner conflict emanating from their strong desire to maintain the family image, while also being accepted by peers as individuals with an identity apart from their ancillary role.

Among clergy children, intra-familial distress is often reflected in episodes of dramatic rebellion, both as a way to attract attention from the clergy parent who is enmeshed in congregational life and as an expression of anger against a way of life often experienced as overly restrictive and coercively imposed.

Children of congregational rabbis undoubtedly have much in common with clergy children in general. Yet prior to this study there was no research designed to more clearly understand the impact of congregational life on rabbinic families, particularly as seen through the eyes of children. I wanted to learn more about the particular kinds of anxieties and stresses that might be experienced by rabbinic families, as well as learn more about their resilience. How, for example, do rabbinic families, with the many tensions of rabbinic life, maintain their balance and stability as a family, or what is known among family therapists as *homeostasis*?

Using a structured set of questions, I interviewed forty-five children of congregational rabbis. In addition to the structured interview, many of them wrote candid and extensive essays about their experiences as children of congregational rabbis. All were assured of complete confidentiality.

The study focused on three areas of concern. The first was the impact of the rabbinate on rabbinic children's sense of themselves. The second was on the dynamics of the rabbinic family itself, and finally, I wanted to better understand how the rabbinate affected the children's interpersonal relationships outside of the family.

How Rabbi's Children See Themselves

By virtue of every psychosocial definition of what determines a "role", the rabbi's child emerges as a distinct role. There exist role expectations related to behavior and attitudes, as well as a set of responsibilities associated with the title "son/daughter of a rabbi." This, of course, is not the case with the children of other professionals. There are no particular role requirements for the children of dentists, lawyers, or computer engineers that relate to their parents' chosen profession. Being the child of a rabbi is an ancillary role, not unlike that of the rabbi's wife, but one acquired by birth, not choice. Furthermore, it is a role that often goes unrecognized and undefined, yet tends to have a significant impact on the developing identity of rabbinic children. As one rabbi's daughter put it:

> I always struggled to maintain an identity of my own. I was always introduced by name, followed by "the rabbi's daughter." It was as if I couldn't be whole without having the attachment to my father's profession noted. My brothers had it worse... I used to cringe at overhearing congregants comment on the "little rabbis". Even though I really believe that many of these remarks were well intended, the reality was that my brothers and I felt as if we were stripped of the dignity of being who we were first and foremost.

Another rabbi's child bemoaned the fact that for half of the community he did not even have a name. He was simply "the rabbi's son."

Not all rabbis' children experienced the role as entirely negative, however. For the most part, rabbis' children looked upon their role as one affording them special status. Vicarious identification with a prominent father and pride associated with his achievements were, for most children, the positive aspects of the role.

Figuring prominently among the negative aspects of the role, however, was that of experiencing frequent isolation. Similar to Ewing's (1980) observation of children of Christian clergy, rabbis' children also tended to recall a strong sense of isolation during their childhood and adolescence. It is not uncommon for rabbi's children to feel like poor kids living in a rich community. They tend not to have what other children have, and lacking the developed ideology that informed their parent's decision to choose a more sacrificial lifestyle, they simply feel deprived in relation to other children their age. Their friends go on exotic vacations, ride in expensive cars, and live in expansive homes, while they do not. They often not only feel like the poorest, but also the most religious, among their friends. They are the kids who can't eat in certain restaurants or go to the same places as others do.

Nevertheless, feeling both "special" and "isolated" seems to best reflect the ambivalence of rabbis' children to their role. An example of this is the rabbi's daughter who expressed strong resentment at being so closely identified with her father's profession. She resented always being seen as the rabbi's daughter and being expected to hold to a higher standard than her peers. Yet, she recalls standing proudly in front of her yeshiva day school building at the age of eleven and proclaiming to all who would listen that her father was the man who had built the school.

Similarly, a rabbi's son recalled feeling particularly privileged to sit next to his father in the synagogue, but resented being a rabbi's son when his friends excluded him from hearing any of their off-color jokes or from participating in any group mischief. Ironically, when his father left the rabbinate in an unanticipated career change, he described the experience as a "sense of profound loss."

One young woman felt especially proud when, as a student in a new school, she was recognized as the daughter of a prominent community rabbi. She remembers feeling isolated and resentful however, when a teacher said to her, following a minor misdemeanor which she committed as part of a group, "I would not have expected this kind of behavior from the rabbi's daughter."

Parental Role Expectations

Children of rabbis do not just have to deal with the projections and expectations of the community. They often have to deal with their parents' overt or covert expectations as well. The expression, *"Es past nisht"* ("It is inappropriate") or "What will people say?" often supersedes both reason and personal feelings in determining the permissibility of a behavior.

At times, rabbinic children receive mixed messages. When a rabbi told his son, "First be yourself and then you can concern yourself with being my son," the young man felt relieved that his father was being so supportive. At a later point in time, however, his father told him that he expected him to be chosen as the valedictorian of his class, because, "How would it look if the rabbi's son didn't get it?" Then he felt confused and resentful.

Adolescence

Developmentally, the issues of identity reach their peak during the often-tumultuous period of adolescence, a time of identity crisis when psychological separation from parents, known as "individuation", takes place. Strategies for dealing with identity issues vary significantly among rabbis' children.

Observations that clergy children tend to act out normal rebellion or engage in experimental behavior in particularly dramatic ways because they want peers to accept them appears to be true of rabbis' children as well. One rabbi's son recalls his mindful and persistent use of verbal obscenities so that others would not suspect him of being the son of a rabbi. More than anything else he wanted to be "one of the boys."

At the other end of the spectrum are those few who fully identify with the role of "rabbi's child", apparently without even the most subtle signs of adolescent struggle. One such young man, the only one in this study who ultimately became a rabbi himself (though not a pulpit rabbi), remembers his adolescence as the time when he first began delivering brief *derashot* (sermonettes) to the congregation.

For a significant number of rabbis' children, however, developing a personal identity simply meant not telling anyone who didn't already know that their father was a rabbi. They tended to develop relationships outside of the congregation. "For years following my marriage," noted one rabbi's daughter, "I told no one that my father was a rabbi."

Relationship to the Community

Attitudinally, among the most negative of experiences reported by children of rabbis were those involving congregants. Relationships with members of the congregation tended to be associated with a sense of pervasive distrust, discomfort, hurt, and anger. Sitting among members of the congregation, rabbis' children would often feel offended at cynical references and caustic comments critical of their fathers. Most poignant were the instances when a congregant would appoint the rabbi's son as liaison to deliver a sharp message to his father. One rabbi's son recalls that when he was no older than eight years old, a congregant leaned over and in a harsh undertone instructed him: "Tell your father not to talk too long today."

More than half of the rabbis' children who were interviewed recalled incidents with congregants that were experienced as either intrusive or abusive. In one such instance, a congregant telephoned the rabbi's daughter after Sabbath to tell her that she noticed that morning that her hair was untidy. "Would anyone ever call a dentist's daughter and tell her that?" she asked bitterly.

In another instance, a rabbi's son described his sense of vulnerability as a child. The son of the synagogue's president would regularly beat up on him, harass him, and seek him out to tease and bully him. "My parents simply told me to avoid him. They apparently felt impotent and unable to stop him from abusing me, because he was the president's son. To this day I still feel a sense of rage at my parents' unwillingness to protect me."

The often fickle nature of a congregation's allegiance to its rabbi and the turning tides of community politics were most often noted as a painful, albeit crucial, experience for children of rabbis. Congregants were often described dichotomously as either "friends" or "enemies". "The people who enter your home, no matter how friendly or supportive, are never really friends," remarked one young respondent cynically. "They are *ba'alei batim* (congregants)."

From an early age on, most children of rabbis learn that when talking to congregants one needs to be especially cautious and vigilant. To protect against the possibility of harmful gossip from the congregational network, rabbinic families tend to enforce an especially strict code of security regarding information about the family or information passing through the family. For the rabbinic family, its visibility and vulnerability apparently require firmer boundaries and greater concealment than the average family (Glazer, 1980). Anything less could jeopardize the family's job security or community status.

For children of rabbis this means special precautions and strict censorship regarding family information. For the average adolescent there would be nothing unusual about telling his closest friend that his father has a temper or that his parents argue from time to time. For a child from a rabbinic family, however, sharing such information is generally unthinkable.

One rabbi's son learned the lessons of what is permissible to share and the extent to which censorship is required at an early age. When he was seven years old, he casually told one of his friends that it was his father's 40th birthday. For reasons still unclear to him in adulthood, this was considered restricted information and potentially damaging to his father. As he recalled the incident, he could still feel the tension, anxiety, and anger when his parents discovered that he had divulged a family secret.

The Social World of Rabbi's Children

As they grew older, the respondents tended to prefer socializing outside of the community. For many, it was unthinkable to date a member of the congregation. Not only was dating within the community avoided whenever possible, "because one could not be oneself with a congregant" or "because things done or said in private might ultimately become public" with embarrassing repercussions, but because children of rabbis wanted to be seen as real people, separate and apart from their designated role. Not uncommon was the experience of one rabbi's daughter who, in fact, had seriously dated a young man from the congregation only to terminate the relationship when he told her that her being the rabbi's daughter was for him one of her most attractive attributes. "I suddenly felt as if I were only an extension of my father's profession and stripped of my own selfhood." She never dated in the community again.

Rabbinic Family Dynamics

The most dramatic impact of congregational life on the children of rabbis was reflected in the many descriptions of family life and family relationships. A significant number of respondents (70%) reported that they perceived their fathers as being overly-involved with synagogue life and their mothers overly-involved with the children. Twenty percent of the respondents described their fathers as emotionally absent from family life. "He wasn't

even there when he was there. His mind always seemed preoccupied."

In several instances rabbis' children expressed resentment at
what they perceived to be differential treatment afforded congregational children in contrast to themselves. Many respondents reported instances when they felt deeply pained by this.
For one, it was being deprived of winning a justly earned prize
because a congregant's son was competing. For another, it was
never being called upon in class to answer questions, so that it
not appear that his father (the teacher) was giving him prefer-
ential treatment.

Psychologist Ruchama Fund Ph.D. describes a case related
to her by a colleague who was seeing a rabbi's young child in
therapy. The child told her that when he grows up, he does
not want to be religious. When the therapist questioned him
about this, he said, "Because then I would get a lot of attention
from my father. He always spends hours with the nonreligious
kids."

The issue of time and the quality of time spent with others in the congregation was a frequent complaint of the rabbis'
children.

> I would watch my father speak so very patiently to everyone.
> He would sometimes spend hours with other children, but
> didn't really seem to know that I needed him as well. I wanted
> to be loved by my father who was so accessible to everyone
> else, yet had so little time and interest in me. I had this secret
> wish to be a member of the congregation so that I could get my
> father's undivided attention.

Paradoxically, even among those who resented their father's aloofness and distance, there tended to be an idealization of the rabbinic father. As one respondent wrote of her
aloof father:

The deep identification I had with my father has been the cornerstone of my personality. I was both fascinated by and scared of my father. Sometimes he stood in my eyes as the symbol of God with strength and mercy. Sometimes he was the strict judge who inspired my fearful respect. But he was always the rabbi par excellence. Unfortunately, we were never close.

Another young woman reflected on her vicarious identification with and obsessive attraction to anyone who had even the faintest resemblance to her father. For many years she was in and out of relationships that were both hurtful and disappointing. Through the insights of psychotherapy she became aware of the fact that she was in essence seeking the affections of a father whom she adored, but who had eluded her.

THE RABBI'S WIFE

As many of those interviewed for this study described their families, it emerged that the most stressful role within the family structure was that of the rabbi's wife. She tended to be the critical link between rabbinic children and their father, often functioning as both the mediator of tensions within the family as well as liaison between the family and the community. Most of the children from rabbinic families reported a strong sense of warmth and emotional closeness with their mothers, but also noted the complexities of her role. The function of preserving the private space of her public family was often a daunting challenge.

One of the most difficult aspects of the *rebbetzin*'s role is that it is so undefined. There are no guidebooks for becoming a successful *rebbetzin*. Even if there were, guidelines and expectations would differ for every community. In a recent announcement advertising a full-time rabbinic position in a large midwestern synagogue, the congregation's search committee included the following description of what they sought in a *rebbetzin*:

> A wife who is strongly supportive of her husband's career as rabbi (even as she pursues her own career), by having a warm, welcoming, *hachnassat orchim* home that can be a model of Jewish living for the community. She should have a friendly, approachable personality, with a strong background in Judaic studies (Hebrew speaker would be an asset), capable of giving *kallah* instruction, and prepared to volunteer once a month to give a *shiur*.

This is quite a job description for what amounts to an ancillary role without monetary compensation. Not only are the expectations inordinately high, but the functions are ambiguous. How "warm" is warm, and what exactly is meant by a "friendly, approachable personality"? If, in fact, she is expected to "volunteer" to give a *shiur* once a month, is she really volunteering or is this an obligation?

Dealing with other people's ill-defined expectations is particularly difficult for the young wife when her husband first becomes a rabbi. Young women do not always plan to become *rebbetzins*. They inadvertently enter the role after marrying a young man who later decides to become a congregational rabbi. The young *rebbetzin* suddenly finds herself thrust into the public arena at about the same time in her life that she is adjusting to her new role as wife and mother. She is often totally confused about what is required of her, how to succeed at it, and where to draw the line between her public and private life.

Most rabbis' wives manage to find a comfort zone between what the congregation expects of them and their own needs, but it is not without an emotional price. It is not unusual for congregants to compare one *rebbetzin* to either the previous *rebbetzin* or the neighboring one. She finds herself wanting the approval and admiration of the congregation, her husband, and her children, only to learn that their often-conflicting needs are overwhelming.

It is not uncommon for rabbis' wives to experience a deep sense of loneliness, especially if their husbands are enmeshed in congregational life or are otherwise emotionally unavailable. Women suffer more than men from the lack of a trusted friend. They have a greater need for social connection and sharing. Yet, the *rebbetzin* cannot maintain an unguarded friendship in her community out of concern that personal information will be divulged and become public fodder. She, like her children, must walk the fine line of having friends in the community, while being vigilant and especially careful about what can be safely confided to them. Any slip of the tongue can too easily become grist for the political mill.

In addition, synagogue politics often dictate that if she were to befriend one person over others, it would evoke jealousy or resentment. There would be a price to pay. Even if her marriage is good and she is able to share her inner world with a loving husband, her need for intimacy will still not be satisfied, since her husband is so often preoccupied with congregational matters and engaged in community activities. His responsibilities simply do not allow him to sufficiently be available for her in a way that would satisfy her need for intimate friendship.

The family's concern for privacy is at times even more taxed if the rabbinic marriage becomes distressed. Whereas most individuals in contemporary society in need of professional mental health services have little difficulty finding a competent therapist, the challenge is daunting for members of the rabbinic family. A rabbi or *rebbetzin* who feels depressed, anxious, or who is experiencing marital problems, cannot readily go to a therapist who practices in their community or is a member of their congregation. Being seen entering or exiting the office of a therapist can have dire consequences for those living in a veritable fishbowl. Should word get out that the rabbi and his wife are having marital problems, it would only complicate their ability to resolve their issues. Communities have a way of getting involved, taking sides, and generally complicating matters for any distressed couple — all the more so for the rabbinic couple. This only exacerbates the loneliness and sense of isolation for both a rabbi and *rebbetzin*, who might benefit from professional help at times of personal or marital distress. In such an instance, it is advisable to find a competent therapist as soon as possible who practices a comfortable distance from the community. It is better simply to reduce the risks of disclosure rather than to ignore the personal, marital, or family problem altogether.

Certainly there are women who feel fulfilled through their multiple roles of wife, mother, and *rebbetzin*. For them, there are many avenues of self-expression and fulfillment. For those wives, however, who feel that these multiple roles are a source of constant strain, they will have to find alternatives if they want to maintain their sense of self.

Many contemporary rabbinical spouses, at times without the sanction of the congregation, choose a career path outside of the community. Congregations who expect their rabbi's spouse to play an active role in the community will invariably express their disapproval or attempt to pressure the spouse to take part in community programs and activities. At this point, the rabbi might start feeling the pressure as congregants begin commenting to him about his wife's absence at community events or her lack of participation in congregational activities.

As a family therapist, my greatest concern for the rabbinic marriage is how the rabbi and his wife negotiate her role and her function with regard to the congregation. If the rabbi begins to represent the needs of the congregation and reflect his own anxieties and disappointments, there is a good chance that he will foster a deep sense of resentment in his wife. It is critical that the decision about what the rabbi's wife's role will be is a decision that takes into account both of their needs and concerns. The needs of the congregation and its expectations should not be a deciding factor in their discussions. Congregations survive and adjust to having a less active *rebbetzin*. Rabbinic marriages, however, are in greater jeopardy if the rabbi's wife feels coerced into a role that is not of her choice or if she feels emotionally isolated and not understood by her husband.

If the rabbi is able to place the needs of his wife above those of the congregation, he will find that his congregants adjust much better than a resentful wife who feels misunderstood, lonely, and coerced. A rabbi can gain much greater personal support from a wife he supports and comforts, rather from a wife who feels she comes second to the needs of the congregation. The greatest resentment expressed by divorced wives of congregational rabbis was that they always felt they had to defer to the insatiable needs of others, while not feeling sufficiently appreciated, supported, or understood by their rabbinic husbands.

THE RABBINIC FAMILY

The rabbinic family, as a family entity, appears very much to revolve around synagogue life. Often, all of the family members are recruited to run errands, take telephone messages, serve refreshments at an open house or Sabbath tea, as well as "conduct" Junior services, read the Torah, and call members to attend the daily minyan (prayer quorum). The congregation is seemingly woven into the fabric of rabbinic family life. As one respondent put it: "The rabbinate is a family business. It is open 7 days a week, 24 hours a day."

In this vein, respondents frequently noted how the urgent needs of the congregants tended to intrude on family life. Family dinners, vacations, and Sunday outings were always subject to disruption or cancellation by that urgent phone call that required the rabbi to attend a funeral, visit a hospital, or negotiate a crisis. Most rabbinic families learn to accept that congregational needs take priority over their own.

Several factors appear to be critical to the stability of the rabbinic family and the children's degree of satisfaction. As a general rule, family life and individual self-esteem are enhanced when each family member feels valued and rooted in the family structure — identifying with its ideals, goals, struggles, triumphs, and disappointments. The rabbinic family experience offers many meaningful opportunities for family members to be part of a joint venture, where both conquests and frustrations can be shared. From interviews with rabbis' children, it seemed apparent that the degree to which a child felt valued as a contributing member of the family was directly related to the degree he/she felt a sense of family solidarity as well as an enhanced self-esteem.

Another important psychological factor that determined the level of either satisfaction or discontent was related to how family members perceived the source of stress. So long as stress was perceived as emanating from outside the family (such as from congregants, community crises, etc.), emotional solidarity remained strong. Whenever hurt and stress were perceived as emanating from within the family (from a father, for example, whose responsiveness to the congregation was viewed as a rejection of his own family), then emotional disunity, rooted in hurtful deprivation, eroded family life.

In this regard, what appeared particularly critical for most of the rabbinic children was the ability of the parent to separate his/her professional role from family life, and within the family context to consider interaction with the children as important. In those instances where rabbis were able to act as parents without the encumbrances of their rabbinic role, their children seemed better able to cope with the many conflicts and stresses that they encountered.

Relatedly, it was not surprising to find that in those rabbinic families with the greatest degree of reported stability and satisfaction, the marital relationship seemed strongest. Where children perceived their parents as being emotionally close, spending time together, and apparently being invested in their marriage, positive ripple effects were felt throughout the family. Conversely, when the rabbinic father was seen as overinvolved in the congregation and the mother as overinvolved with the children, both consequently being underinvolved with each other, negative ripple effects reverberated throughout the family. This family structure was simply less efficient in buffering its members from the stressful intrusiveness of congregational life.

SUMMARY AND CONCLUSION

Thus, several factors have emerged as critical variables for understanding the dynamics of the rabbinic family. The community, always a significant factor in rabbinic life, tends to affect the rabbi's family in several ways. The greater the turbulence, factionalism, and instability a community exhibits, the more stress, anxiety, and insecurity the rabbinic family will experience. If, however, the source of stress is perceived by the rabbi's family as emanating from the congregation and not as a veiled rejection, emotional support tends to remain strong within the family.

Disillusionment with yesterday's supporters who have become today's detractors tends to make many rabbinic family members less trustful of allegiances and more wary of relationships within the community. Never too far from consciousness is the realization that the rabbi serves at the pleasure of his congregation, and that job security, financial stability, and a sense of personal well-being are contingent upon the good will of the congregation. Rabbinic families grow up in the ever-present shadow of this reality.

Kagan and di Cori (1962) point out that only "the rabbi who is strong enough can make his own privacy in spite of the demands made upon him by the community." Driven by anxiety and insecurity, however, a significant number of rabbis become overinvolved with their congregations and underinvolved with their families. They are seemingly unable to divest themselves of their rabbinic roles in order to relate to their families as husbands and fathers. As a result, feelings of loss and isolation often remain unresolved for their children even through adulthood, and the same feelings often enough have led to divorce.

Several significant conclusions have emerged from this analysis. For the rabbi's child, the special status afforded him as an extension of his father's clerical position frequently excludes him from full acceptance among peers. Isolation frequently becomes the price paid for *noblesse oblige*. The child's self-esteem, however, can be enhanced if he feels valued as an integral part of the family in its designated work with the congregation. By praising the child for helping the rabbi at home, that function takes on greater value and can serve to compensate for his social isolation.

Despite the stresses of rabbinic life, most rabbinic families appear to be successful in raising highly functional children. It is interesting to note that the majority of the children interviewed for this study who were raised in rabbinic homes were individuals who were either professionally engaged in some form of community service or were actively volunteering their time to community projects. There is an intriguing possibility that children of rabbis who grew up with the ideal of public service, albeit accompanied by the insecurity of depending on a congregation, have chosen careers or avocations that permit them to continue in public service without the insecurity of dependence on others. In a sense, most of the children of rabbis in this study chose to become what might be called secular clergy, independent of congregations, but in the service of others nevertheless.

Another finding was that the ability of rabbinic parents to separate work from family life creates "community-proof" boundaries. Divesting themselves of the trappings of the rabbinic role appears crucial to the development of a normal family life, with all the needed support it has to offer.

Finally, the most critical factor affecting the strength of the rabbinic family is the rabbi's role as husband. Where the marital relationship is strong, the positive effects are felt throughout the family system.

In examining the impact of rabbinic life on the rabbi's family, I cannot sufficiently underscore the importance of family boundaries that protect a family from outside intrusion, while permitting it to develop supportive cohesion from within. These conclusions also reconfirm the well-known observation regarding the centrality of the marital dyad and its power to either buffer children from external stress or to become a source of stress in itself.

BIBLIOGRAPHY

Ackerman. N. 1958. *The Psychodynamics of Family Life*, New York: Basic Books.

Ewing. J. 1980. As found in *Children in Crisis*, vol. I, no.2. ATCOM Publications.

Freedman, L. 1985. "Role-Related Stress in the Rabbinate: A Report on a Nationwide Study of Conservative and Reform Rabbis," *Journal of Reform Rabbis*, winter issue.

Friedman, E. 1986. *Generation to Generation: Family Process in Church and Synagogue*, New York: Guilford Publications.

Fund, Ruchama. "Emotional Issues Facing Rabbis and Their Families," *Nefesh* Conference, December 1995.

Glazer, N. 1980. "The Rabbinate and Its Impact on the Rabbi's Family," presentation at the Harold Gordon Rabbinic Conference of the New York Board of Rabbis, New York.

Hutchinson, K. and Nichols, W. "Therapy for Divorcing Clergy: Implications from Research," *Journal of Divorce*, vol. 4, no. I, Fall 19RO.

Kagan, H. and di Cori, F. 1962. "The Rabbi, His Family, and the Community," *Journal of Religion and Health*, vol. 1, no. 4, July 1962.

Klaperman. G. "Exploring the Rabbi's Inner Security," presentation at the Harold Gordon Rabbinic Conference of the New York Board of Rabbis. New York, 1980.

Minuchin, S. 1974. *Families and Family Therapy*, Cambridge: Harvard University Press.

Moss, D. 1980. As found in *Children in Crisis*, vol.I, no.2. ATCOM Publications.

Silverstein, B. 1980. "The Rabbi's Dilemma," presentation at the Harold Gordon Rabbinic Conference of the New York Board of Rabbis, New York.

Singer, H. 1985. "Rabbis and Their Discontents," *Commentary*, May issue.

CONTRIBUTORS

CONTRIBUTORS

Aiken, Lisa, Ph.D.

Lisa Aiken served as the Chief Psychologist at Lenox Hill Hospital in New York City, as clinical assistant professor at New York Medical College and St. John's University, and a clinical associate professor at Long Island University. She did psycho-diagnostic and neuropsychological consultations at Holliswood Hospital in Queens, New York, and had a private practice with individuals and couples. Dr. Aiken has authored numerous books on a variety of Judaic and psychological topics, including her latest books *"Tuning In"* and *"Guide for the Romantically Perplexed,"* Dvora Press, 2003.

Blumenthal, Norman, Ph.D.

Norman Blumenthal is a clinical psychologist in private practice and the coordinator of Group Psychotherapy Training for Interns and Residents at the North Shore Long Island Jewish Hospital System. Dr. Blumenthal is the current Education Director of the Bella and Harry Wexner *Kollel Elyon* and *Smikha* Honors Program at the Rabbi Isaac Elchanan Theological Seminary of Yeshiva University, and coordinates programs on parental loss and grief for *Chai Lifeline*, an organization for children with cancer.

Dr. Blumenthal is founder and chairman of the Board of Education of *CAHAL*, which provides special education classes for learning disabled children attending yeshiva day schools, and is a clinical consultant to *TOVA*—a special program for disenfranchised teens.

Bush, Robert A. Baruch, J.D.

Robert A. Baruch Bush is the Rains Distinguished Professor of Alternative Dispute Resolution Law at Hofstra University School of Law and President of the Institute for the Study of Conflict Transformation, Inc. at Hofstra Law School. He is co-author, with Joseph P. Folger, of *The Promise of Mediation* (2004), and author of numerous other publications on the subject of mediation.

Corn, Benjamin W., M.D.

Ben Corn is an oncologist who serves as the chairman of the Department of Radiation Oncology at Tel Aviv Medical Center. Prior to his *aliyah*, Dr. Corn was professor and vice-chairman of the Department of Radiation Oncology at Thomas Jefferson University Hospital in Philadelphia, PA. His formal training as a cancer specialist was acquired at the University of Pennsylvania. Ben and his wife Dvora are the founders of Life's Door; a non-profit organization that provides support and growth experiences for cancer patients and their families.

Corn, Phyllis Dvora, M.Sc.

Phyllis Dvora Corn is a family therapist at the Neve Yerushalayim Family Institute, and the director of *Hatomechet*, a home hospice volunteer program based in Jerusalem. Prior to her aliyah in 1997, she practiced occupational therapy for 20 years, specializing in terminally and chronically ill adults, many in the end stage of care. She was the founder and director of Garden State Therapy Associates/ Heartland Rehabilitation, Inc., a multi-disciplinary group rehabilitation practice based in southern New Jersey which services children and adults of all ages and a wide range of diagnoses. Since coming to Israel, she has been a volunteer at the Hadassah Hospice in Mt. Scopus, Jerusalem, along with being active in various educational and good will organizations in the community. A frequent lecturer in the area of end of life issues, she and her husband Benjamin are the founders of Life's Door, a non-profit organization that provides support and growth experiences for cancer patients and their families.

Einhorn, Rosie, M.S.W.

Rosie Einhorn is a licensed psychotherapist in private practice in Jerusalem, where she specializes in working with Jewish singles. She has co-authored several books including: *Talking Tachlis — A Single's Strategy for Marriage* and *In The Beginning — How to Survive Your Engagement and Build a Great Marriage.* She is the co-founder of *Sasson V'Simcha* — The Center for Jewish Marriage, a non-profit organization dedicated to helping Jewish singles marry and providing community education on issues affecting Jewish singles.

Jackson, Daniel H., Ph.D.

Daniel Jackson completed his doctoral training at the University of Washington in sociology, with specialties in social psychology, statistics, research methodologies, and the sociology of risk. Dr. Jackson completed his rabbinic training at the Rabbi Isaac Elchanan Theological Seminary and served as adjunct assistant professor of sociology at Yeshiva College and as adjunct faculty at the Family Institute at Neve Yerushalayim in Jerusalem. He completed his residency at The Johns Hopkins Hospital in Clinical Pastoral Education and currently serves as a staff chaplain with the Life-Bridge Health System of Baltimore. Dr. Jackson sits on the ethics committees of Northwest Community Hospital of Baltimore County and Sinai Hospital of Baltimore.

Jackson, Susan Taylor, Ph.D.

Susan Taylor Jackson is a clinical psychologist and a graduate of the City University of New York. Dr. Jackson completed a pre-doctoral fellowship at Yale University School of Medicine, where she also participated in post-doctoral research with The Project on the Adult Life Course. She was a member of the core faculty at Antioch University, teaching clinical psychology in the doctoral program of Antioch's New England Graduate School and directing the Masters program in psychology at Antioch University Seattle. She offered a professional development series on "The Seasons of a Woman's Life" at the Family Institute of Neve Yerushalayim. She is currently director of the *Ezer L'Cholim* Project for Holocaust Survivors at Bikur Cholim of Boro Park in Brooklyn, New York.

Lamm, Dodi Lee, M.S.W.

Dodi Lee Lamm earned her graduate degree in social work at the Wurzweiler School of Social Work, and was trained in psychoanalytic psychotherapy at The New York Counseling and Guidance Center in New York City.

Prior to becoming a psychotherapist in private practice, Dodi Lamm served as a Rebbetzin in a number of prominent synagogues, including the Lincoln Square Synagogue in New York.

Lamm, Rabbi Maurice

Maurice Lamm—distinguished rabbi, author, and lecturer—is a professor at Yeshiva University's Rabbinical Seminary in New York, where he holds the Chair in Professional Rabbinics. Rabbi Lamm served as the senior rabbi of Beth Jacob Congregation in Beverly Hills, California, one of the largest Orthodox synagogues in the United States. He was also an assistant professor at Stern College for Women, president of the National Institute for Jewish Hospice, president of the Board of Rabbis of Southern California, and dean of Akiba Academy in New York and Rambam Academy in Los Angeles. He was awarded an honorary Doctorate by Yeshiva University, as well as the University's Lifetime Professional Achievement Award. Rabbi Lamm has published 8 books, including: *The Jewish Way in Death and Mourning, The Jewish Way in Love and Marriage, The Power of Hope,* and *Consolation.*

Levitz, Yisrael N., Ph.D., ABFamP

Dr. Yisrael Levitz, Ph.D. is a clinical psychologist, an ordained rabbi, and Professor Emeritus of Yeshiva University's Wurzweiler School of Social Work, where he held the distinguished Bennett Chair, and headed the school's psychopathology and human behavior departments. He is currently the director of the Family Institute at Neve Yerushalayim and its affiliated *Machon L'Mishpacha* Counseling Center.

Dr. Levitz is a Board Certified Diplomate in Marriage and Family Therapy, a Fellow of the Academy of Family Psychology, and the founding director of the South Shore Psychological Center in Woodmere, New York. He has lectured extensively and published on a wide range of psychological and Jewish issues.

Levy, Neal D., Ph.D.

Neal Levy is a board certified psychotherapist, who, in addition to his private practice, has been training and supervising family and marital therapists for the past 25 years. He has lectured extensively to both lay and professional audiences on a variety of topics related to the emotional health of families and children. Dr. Levy is an instructor of marital counseling in the Wexner *Kollel Elyon* Program of the Rabbi Isaac Elchanan Theological Seminary.

Michelson, Rona, D.S.W.

Rona Michelson is a marriage and family therapist who holds a B.A. in philosophy from Temple University, a B.H.L. (Bachelor of Hebrew Literature) from Gratz College, an M.A. in counseling from Ball State University, and an M.S.W. and D.S.W. from the School of Social Work at the University of Pennsylvania. She

400 ————————————— Practical Guide to Rabbinical Counseling

is a clinical member and approved supervisor of the American Association for Marriage and Family Therapy (AAMFT). As a faculty member of The Family Institute at Neve Yerushalayim, she teaches, supervises trainees, and conducts training seminars on marriage and family therapy. Dr. Michelson currently resides in Modi'in, Israel, where she maintains a private practice as a family therapist.

Pelcovitz, David, Ph.D.

David Pelcovitz is professor of education and psychology at Yeshiva University's Azrieli Graduate School of Jewish Education. He also teaches Pastoral Psychology courses in the Bella and Harry Wexner *Kollel Elyon* and *Smikha* Honors Program at the university's affiliated Rabbi Isaac Elchanan Theological Seminary (RIETS).

Dr. Pelcovitz, former director of psychology at the North Shore University Hospital in Manhasset, NY, is also a clinical professor of psychology in psychiatry at the NYU School of Medicine. He has published and lectured extensively on a variety of topics related to the psychological impact of trauma and loss, child and adolescent behavior problems, parenting, and the impact of divorce and stress on children.

Schaffer, Sylvan J., J.D., Ph.D.

Sylvan Schaffer is both an attorney at law and a clinical psychologist. He is a clinical associate professor of psychiatry at the New York University School of Medicine, assistant professor of clinical psychiatry at Yeshiva University's Albert Einstein College of Medicine, as well as adjunct faculty at Hofstra University Law School and Downstate Medical School. Dr. Schaffer was formerly the director of the Forensic Psychiatry Program at the North Shore University Hospital's department of psychiatry, and instructed a course in conflict resolution at the Bella and Harry Wexner *Smikha* Honors Program of the Rabbi Isaac Elchanan Theological Seminary.

Strous, Rael, M.D.

Dr. Rael Strous completed his psychiatry training at the Albert Einstein College of Medicine and completed a research fellowship in psychopharmacology at Harvard Medical School. He is currently the director of research and psychopharmacology at the Beer Yaakov Mental Health Center in Israel, as well as head of the hospital's Chronic Inpatient Department. In addition, he is the chief psychiatric consultant at the Family Institute Counseling Center of Neve Yerushalayim in Jerusalem, and a lecturer at the Sackler School of Medicine in Tel Aviv.

Twerski, Rabbi Abraham J., M.D.

Rabbi Abraham J. Twerski, M.D., is a noted author, lecturer, and psychiatrist who specializes in addictions and rehabilitation. He is the founding director of *Gateway*, an alcohol rehabilitation center in Pittsburg, Pennsylvania. He is a prolific writer and the popular author of close to 50 self-help books, including *Successful Relationships at Home, at Work and with Friends, The Enemy Within, The Shame Born in Silence, Ten Steps to Being Your Best*, and *The First Year of Marriage*.

Twerski, Lisa Goodman, M.S.W.

Lisa Goodman Twerski, M.S.W., is the director of training and special projects for the Shalom Task Force, an organization which addresses the issue of domestic violence in the Jewish community. She is also the co-founder of *Brairot*, an educational project for men who are abusive to their spouses. She was director of several branches of Victim Services in the greater New York area, and has worked with the Bronx Crime Victim Center, which provides short-term crisis intervention as well as long-term therapy to victims of domestic violence, incest, child sexual abuse, sexual assault, and stranger crimes. During her tenure at the Victim's

Services, she also served as the coordinator of the agency's city-wide rape crisis centers. Lisa Twerski maintains a private practice in Brooklyn, New York.

Zimmerman, Sherry, J.D.

Sherry Zimmerman is an attorney specializing in family law. She is a practicing dating coach who, along with Rosie Einhorn, has co-authored several books, including: *Talking Tachlis—A Single's Strategy for Marriage* and *In The Beginning—How to Survive Your Engagement and Build a Great Marriage.* Mrs. Zimmerman is also co-founder of *Sasson V'Simcha*—The Center for Jewish Marriage.

Professional Spiritual & Pastoral Care Resources

Professional Spiritual & Pastoral Care
A Practical Clergy and Chaplain's Handbook
Edited by Rabbi Stephen B. Roberts, BCJC
The first comprehensive resource for spiritual and pastoral care—for clergy, seminarians, chaplains, pastoral counselors and caregivers of all faith traditions. Specifically intended for professionals who work in or visit congregants in acute care hospitals, behavioral health facilities, rehabilitation centers and long-term care facilities.
6 x 9, 480 pp, HC, 978-1-59473-312-3 **$50.00***

Disaster Spiritual Care
Practical Clergy Responses to Community, Regional and National Tragedy
Edited by Rabbi Stephen B. Roberts, BCJC, and Rev. Willard W.C. Ashley, Sr., DMin, DH
The definitive guidebook for counseling not only the victims of disaster but also the clergy and caregivers who are called to service in the wake of crisis. Integrates the classic foundations of pastoral care with the unique challenges of disaster response.
6 x 9, 384 pp, HC, 978-1-59473-240-9 **$50.00***

How to Be a Perfect Stranger, 5th Edition
The Essential Religious Etiquette Handbook
Edited by Stuart M. Matlins and Arthur J. Magida
The indispensable guidebook to help the well-meaning guest when visiting other people's religious ceremonies. A straightforward guide to the rituals and celebrations of the major religions and denominations in the United States and Canada from the perspective of an interested guest of any other faith, based on information obtained from authorities of each religion. Belongs in every living room, library and office. Covers:
African American Methodist Churches • Assemblies of God • Bahá'í Faith • Baptist • Buddhist • Christian Church (Disciples of Christ) • Christian Science (Church of Christ, Scientist) • Churches of Christ • Episcopalian and Anglican • Hindu • Islam • Jehovah's Witnesses • Jewish • Lutheran • Mennonite/Amish • Methodist • Mormon (Church of Jesus Christ of Latter-day Saints) • Native American/First Nations • Orthodox Churches • Pentecostal Church of God • Presbyterian • Quaker (Religious Society of Friends) • Reformed Church in America/Canada • Roman Catholic • Seventh-day Adventist • Sikh • Unitarian Universalist • United Church of Canada • United Church of Christ

> "The things Miss Manners forgot to tell us about religion."
> —*Los Angeles Times*

6 x 9, 432 pp, Quality PB, 978-1-59473-294-2 **$19.99***

The Perfect Stranger's Guide to Funerals and Grieving Practices
A Guide to Etiquette in Other People's Religious Ceremonies
Edited by Stuart M. Matlins
6 x 9, 240 pp, Quality PB, 978-1-893361-20-1 **$16.95***

Show Me Your Way
The Complete Guide to Exploring Interfaith Spiritual Direction
by Rabbi Howard A. Addison
5½ x 8½, 208 pp, PB, 978-1-893361-41-6 **$16.95***

Jewish Pastoral Care, 2nd Edition
A Practical Handbook from Traditional & Contemporary Sources
Edited by Rabbi Dayle A. Friedman, MSW, MAJCS, BCC
6 x 9, 528 pp, Quality PB, 978-1-58023-427-6 **$30.00**

Caresharing: A Reciprocal Approach to Caregiving and Care Receiving in the Complexities of Aging, Illness or Disability
by Marty Richards
6 x 9, 256 pp, Quality PB, 978-1-59473-286-7 **$16.99**; HC, 978-1-59473-247-8 **$24.99***

*A book from SkyLight Paths, Jewish Lights' sister imprint

Pastoral Care Resources
LifeLights/™אורות החיים

LifeLights/™אורות החיים are inspirational, informational booklets about challenges to our emotional and spiritual lives and how to deal with them. Offering help for wholeness and healing, each *LifeLight* is written from a uniquely Jewish spiritual perspective by a wise and caring soul—someone who knows the inner territory of grief, doubt, confusion and longing.

In addition to providing wise words to light a difficult path, each *LifeLight* booklet provides suggestions for additional resources for reading. Many list organizations, Jewish and secular, that can provide help, along with information on how to contact them.

"Invaluable for those needing comfort and
instruction in times of difficulty and loss."
—Rabbi David Wolpe, Sinai Temple, Los Angeles, CA

"Particularly useful for hospital visits and *shiva* calls—and
they enable me to help at those times when I feel helpless."
—Rabbi Sally Priesand, Monmouth Reform Temple,
Tinton Falls, NJ

Categories/Topics:

Health & Healing

Abortion and Judaism: Rabbinic Opinion and Jewish Law
Caring for Your Aging Parents
Caring for Yourself/When Someone Is Ill
Facing and Recovering from Surgery
Facing Cancer as a Family
Finding Spiritual Strength in Pain or Illness
Jewish Response to Dementia: Honoring Broken Tablets
Living with Cancer, One Day at a Time
Recognizing a Loved One's Addiction, and Providing Help
When Madness Comes Home: Living in the Shadow of a Loved One's Mental Illness

Loss / Grief / Death & Dying

Coping with the Death of a Spouse
From Death through *Shiva*: A Guide to Jewish Grieving Practices
Jewish Hospice: To Live, to Hope, to Heal
Making Sacred Choices at the End of Life
Mourning a Miscarriage
Taking the Time You Need to Mourn Your Loss
Talking to Children about Death
When Someone You Love Is Dying
When Someone You Love Needs Long-Term Care

Categories/Topics continued:

Judaism / Living a Jewish Life

Bar and Bat Mitzvah's Meaning: Preparing Spiritually with Your Child

Choosing a Congregation That Is Right for You

Considering Judaism: Choosing a Faith, Joining a People

Do Jews Believe in the Soul's Survival?

Exploring Judaism as an Adult

Jewish Meditation: How to Begin Your Practice

There's a Place for Us: Gays and Lesbians in the Jewish Community

To Meet Your Soul Mate, You Must Meet Your Soul

Yearning for God

Family Issues

Jewish Adoption: Unique Issues, Practical Solutions

Are You Being Hurt by Someone You Love? Domestic Abuse in the Jewish Community

Grandparenting Interfaith Grandchildren

Healing Estrangement in Your Family Relationships

Interfaith Families Making Jewish Choices

Jewish Approaches to Parenting Teens

Looking Back on Divorce and Letting Go

Parenting through a Divorce

Raising a Child with Special Needs

Talking to Children about God

Spiritual Care / Personal Growth

Bringing Your Sadness to God

Doing Teshuvah: Undoing Mistakes, Repairing Relationships and Finding Inner Peace

Easing the Burden of Stress

Finding a Way to Forgive

Finding the Help You Need: Psychotherapy, Pastoral Counseling, and the Promise of Spiritual Direction

Praying in Hard Times: The Soul's Imaginings

Surviving a Crisis or a Tragedy

Now available in hundreds of congregations, health-care facilities, funeral homes, colleges and military installations, these helpful, comforting resources can be uniquely presented in *LifeLights* display racks, available from Jewish Lights. **Each *LifeLight* topic is sold in packs of twelve for $9.95.** Generous discounts are available for quantity purchases.

Visit us online at www.jewishlights.com for a complete list of titles, authors, prices and ordering information, or call us at (802) 457-4000 or toll free at (800) 962-4544.

About Jewish Lights

People of all faiths and backgrounds yearn for books that attract, engage, educate, and spiritually inspire.

Our principal goal is to stimulate thought and help all people learn about who the Jewish People are, where they come from, and what the future can be made to hold. While people of our diverse Jewish heritage are the primary audience, our books speak to people in the Christian world as well and will broaden their understanding of Judaism and the roots of their own faith.

We bring to you authors who are at the forefront of spiritual thought and experience. While each has something different to say, they all say it in a voice that you can hear.

Our books are designed to welcome you and then to engage, stimulate, and inspire. We judge our success not only by whether or not our books are beautiful and commercially successful, but by whether or not they make a difference in your life.

For your information and convenience, at the back of this book we have provided a list of other Jewish Lights books you might find interesting and useful. They cover all the categories of your life:

Bar/Bat Mitzvah	Life Cycle
Bible Study / Midrash	Meditation
Children's Books	Men's Interest
Congregation Resources	Parenting
Current Events / History	Prayer / Ritual / Sacred Practice
Ecology / Environment	Social Justice
Fiction: Mystery, Science Fiction	Spirituality
Grief / Healing	Theology / Philosophy
Holidays / Holy Days	Travel
Inspiration	Twelve Steps
Kabbalah / Mysticism / Enneagram	Women's Interest

Stuart M. Matlins, Publisher

Or phone, fax, mail or e-mail to: **JEWISH LIGHTS Publishing**
Sunset Farm Offices, Route 4 • P.O. Box 237 • Woodstock, Vermont 05091
Tel: (802) 457-4000 • Fax: (802) 457-4004 • www.jewishlights.com
Credit card orders: **(800) 962-4544** (8:30AM–5:30PM EST Monday–Friday)
Generous discounts on quantity orders. SATISFACTION GUARANTEED. Prices subject to change.

For more information about each book, visit our website at www.jewishlights.com